DARK OF THE MOON

Poems of Fantasy and the Macabre
edited by August Derleth

DARK OF THE MOON

Poems
of Fantasy and
the Macabre

EDITED BY
AUGUST DERLETH

BOOKS FOR LIBRARIES PRESS
FREEPORT, NEW YORK

Permissions To Original Edition

The Little Green Orchard, The Ghost, The Listeners, by Walter de la Mare,
copyright 1912, by Walter de la Mare, for *The Listeners and Other Poems;
The Witch of Coös,* by Robert Frost, copyright 1923, by Robert Frost, for
New Hampshire; The True Lover, by A. E. Housman: by permission of
Henry Holt & Company.

The Hashish-Eater, Nightmare, by Clark Ashton Smith, copyright 1922, by
Clark Ashton Smith, for *Ebony and Crystal.*

A Dracula of the Hills, The Paper in the Gate-Legged Table, by Amy Lowell,
copyright 1926, by Houghton-Mifflin Company, for *East Wind.*

A Knight of La Mancha, On Reading Arthur Machen, by Frank Belknap Long,
copyright 1925, by Frank Belknap Long, Jr., for *A Man from Genoa and
Other Poems.*

The Harp of Alfred, by Robert E. Howard, copyright 1928; *Sonnets of the Mid-
night Hours,* by Donald Wandrei, copyright 1928, 1929, 1930; *Nyctalops,
Fantasie d'Antan,* by Clark Ashton Smith; *Moon Mockery,* by Robert E.
Howard, copyright 1929; *The Horror on Dagoth Wold,* by Frank Belknap
Long; *The Ancient Track,* by H. P. Lovecraft, copyright 1930; *Fungi from
Yuggoth,* by H. P. Lovecraft, copyright 1930, 1931; *The Abominable Snow
Men,* by Frank Belknap Long, copyright 1931; *Echidna,* by Mary Elizabeth
Counselman; *Arkham,* by Robert E. Howard, copyright 1932; *Nostalgia,* by
Mary Elizabeth Counselman, copyright 1933; *In the Shadows,* by Leah Bodine
Drake; *In Thessaly,* by Clark Ashton Smith; *Sonnet of the Unsleeping Dead,*
by Anthony Boucher, copyright 1935; *Psychopompos,* by H. P. Lovecraft;
Which Will Scarcely Be Understood, Futility, by Robert E. Howard, copy-
right 1937; *The Singer in the Mist, The Last Hour, Lines Written in the
Realization That I Must Die,* by Robert E. Howard; *Outlanders,* by Clark
Ashton Smith, copyright 1938; by The Popular Fiction Publishing Company,
for *Weird Tales.*

Recompense, The Ghost Kings, by Robert E. Howard, copyright 1938; *The King
and the Oak,* by Robert E. Howard, copyright 1939; *The Owls,* by Timeus
Gaylord, copyright 1941; *Wood Wife, Changeling,* by Leah Bodine Drake;
The Dreamer in the Desert, by Francis Flagg, copyright 1942; *The Snake,*
by Francis Flagg, copyright 1943; *The Path Through the Marsh,* by Leah
Bodine Drake, copyright 1944; *Forgetful Hours,* by Yetza Gillespie; *Tree
Woman,* by Dorothy Quick, copyright 1945; *The Haunted Stairs,* by Yetza
Gillespie, copyright 1946, by *Weird Tales.*

STANDARD BOOK NUMBER:
8369-6056-4

LIBRARY OF CONGRESS CATALOG CARD NUMBER:
73-80374

PRINTED IN THE U.S.A.

Contents

INTRODUCTION

Poetry of the macabre and fantastic abounds in the lore and legendry of every people. Such poetry exists chiefly in the form of the ballad, which, according to the succinct definition of the Oxford Dictionary is a "poem in short stanzas narrating a popular story," and, according to Dr. Johnson, is "trifling verse". Those ballads which have come down to us are in the main highly romantic, being chiefly tales of unrequited or faithless love, and ghostly vengeance, with origins in the lore of the people themselves, having been put down at last for posterity by chroniclers of a later time. Many of the ballads most widely-known today first appeared in Percy's *Reliques,* Scott's *Minstrelsy,* and lesser books.

The majority of ballads, of course, were not macabre. Of those that were, the anonymous *William and Marjorie* is typical. For some time, the pattern of the border ballads was followed by poets who chose to write in the form, even though the poets improved and altered the classic forms with every decade. Robert Burns, James Hogg, and Sir Walter Scott remained reasonably consistent, and, later, William Bell Scott, Charles Kingsley, William Allingham, and others preferred the old forms, and the contemporary, Byron Herbert Reece, is in the best tradition.

But the ballad is not the only form in which poetry of the supernatural survives. The weird and the uncanny have a natural attraction for the poet, though it is demonstrably true that poets of our own time turn increasingly less often to mysticism and enchantment for their subjects than did their forbears in verse. Nevertheless, there are many fine poems on supernatural subjects available to readers who have a predilection for such verse.

Apart from Margaret Widdemer's *The Haunted Hour* (1920), which was an anthology of spectral poems, there has been no collection of verse in the genre; indeed, I know of none which has been available in this century. In compiling the present collection, I have made no attempt to be comprehensive, yet I have tried to abide by certain limitations. I have omitted poems because of familiarity—such as *The Rime of the Ancient Mariner;* or because of length—notably Edwin Arlington Robinson's fine *Cavender's House.* In general, I have presented the too-familiar only in shorter length—Samuel Taylor Coleridge, John Keats, and Edgar Allan Poe, for instance, have but token representation; while J. Sheridan LeFanu and Fitz-James O'Brien are represented by longer, if less successful, poems. I have likewise tended to avoid translations, but I did include Johann Wolfgang von Goethe's *The Erl King* and José Asunción Silva's *Lazarus.* Despite its length, I also included all of James Thomson's *The City of Dreadful Night,* since it seems to me one of the most vivid and memorable of all poems of the macabre.

Others limitations account for lesser omissions. Copyright restrictions prevented the inclusion of any of the modern ballads of John Masefield, for instance, or any representative verse at all by William Butler Yeats, Vachel Lindsay, Alfred Noyes, and Rachel Field, all of whom have written memorable poetry of the fantastic and the supernatural, though Rachel Field is in the direct tradition of Amy Lowell, who is represented, and Miss Field's work, however adequate in her volume, *Points East,* cannot compare with that of Amy Lowell.

From the pages of *Weird Tales* and similar magazines I have chosen to reprint poems by H. P. Lovecraft, Robert E. Howard, Clark Ashton Smith, Donald Wandrei, Leah Bodine Drake, and others, which, though largely uncollected, deserve some modest recognition. The poets now writing for such markets represent the largest body of poets writing verse of the macabre and fantastic today.

Dark of the Moon was not designed as a volume to be read at one sitting, but rather as a representative collection of the best poetry of the macabre and fantastic in English. Nor was it put together so much for the general reader as for the *aficionado,* and it is to him that I commend these poems.

—AUGUST DERLETH

Sauk City, Wisconsin
31 October 1946

THE TWA CORBIES

As I was walking all alane,
I heard twa corbies making a mane:
The eane unto t' other say,
"Whar sall we gang and dine today?"

"In behint yon auld fail dyke,
I wot there lies a new-slain knight;
And naebody kens that he lies there
But his hawk, his hound, and his lady fair.

"His hound is to the hunting gane,
His hawk to fetch the wild-fowl hame,
His lady's ta'en another mate,
So we may make our dinner sweet.

"Ye'll set on his white hause-bane,
And I'll pike out his bonny blue een;
Wi' ae lock o' his gowden hair
We'll theek our nest when it grows bare.

"Mony a one for him makes mane,
But nane sall ken whar he is gane,
O'er his white banes, when they are bare,
The wind sall blaw for evermair."

A LYKE-WAKE DIRGE

This ae nighte, this ae nighte
   —Every nighte and alle,
Fire and fleet and candle-lighte,
   And Christe receive thy soule.

When thou from hence away art past,
  —*Every nighte and alle,*
To Whinny-muir thou com'st at last;
  And Christe receive thy saule.

If ever thou gavest hosen and shoon,
  —*Every nighte and alle,*
Sit thee down and put them on;
  And Christe receive thy saule.

If hosen and shoon thou ne'er gav'st nane
  —*Every nighte and alle,*
The whinnes sall prick thee to the bare bane;
  And Christe receive thy saule.

From Whinny-muir when thou may'st pass,
  —*Every nighte and alle,*
To Brig o' Dread thou com'st at last;
  And Christe receive thy saule.

From Brig o' Dread when thou may'st pass,
  —*Every nighte and alle,*
To Purgatory fire thou com'st at last;
  And Christe receive thy saule.

If ever thou gavest meat or drink,
  —*Every nighte and alle,*
The fire sall never make thee shrink;
  And Christe receive thy saule.

If meat or drink thou ne'er gav'st nane,
  —*Every nighte and alle,*
The fire will burn thee to the bare bane;
  And Christe receive thy saule.

This ae nighte, this ae nighte,
—*Every nighte and alle,*
Fire and fleet and candle-lighte,
And Christe receive thy saule.

WILLIAM AND MARJORIE

Lady Marjorie, Lady Marjorie,
Sat sewing her silken seam,
And by her came a pale, pale ghost,
Wi' mony a sigh and mane.

"Are ye my father, the king?" she says,
"Or are ye my brither John?
Or are ye my true love, sweet William,
From England newly come?"

"I'm not your father, the king," he says,
"No, no, nor your brither John;
But I'm your true love, sweet William,
From England that's newly come."

"Have ye brought me any scarlets sae red,
Or any silks sae fine;
Or have ye brought me any precious things,
That merchants have for sale?"

"I have not brought you any scarlets sae red,
No, no, nor the silks sae fine;
But I have brought you my winding-sheet
O'er many's the rock and hill.

"O Lady Marjorie, Lady Marjorie,
   For faith and charitie,
Will ye give to me my faith and troth,
   That I gave once to thee?"

"O your faith and troth I'll not give thee,
   No, no, that will not I,
Until I get ae kiss of your ruby lips,
   And in my arms you come lie."

"My lips they are sae bitter," he says,
   "My breath it is sae strang,
If you get ae kiss of my ruby lips,
   Your days will not be lang.

"The cocks they are crawing, Marjorie," he says,—
   "The cocks they are crawing again;
It's time the dead should part the quick,—
   Marjorie, I must be gane."

She followed him high, she followed him low,
   Till she came to yon churchyard green;
O there the grave did open up,
   And young William he lay down.

"What three things are these, sweet William," she says,
   "That stand here at your head?"
"It's three maidens, Marjorie," he says,
   "That I promised once to wed."

"What three things are these, sweet William," she says,
   "That stand here at your side?"
"It is three babes, Marjorie," he says,
   "That these three maidens had."

"What three things are these, sweet William," she says,
  "That stand here at your feet?"
"It is three hell-hounds, Marjorie," he says,
  "That's waiting my soul to keep."

She took up her white, white hand,
  And she struck him in the breast,
Saying,—"Have there again your faith and troth
  And I wish your soul gude rest."

THE WEE WEE MAN

As I was walking all alone,
  Atween a water and a wa',
And there I spied a wee wee man,
  He was the least that ere I saw.

His legs were scarce a shatmont's length,
  And thick and thimber was his thigh;
Between his brows there was a span,
  And between his shoulders there was three,

He took up a mickle stane,
  And he flang't as far as I could see;
Though I had been a Wallace wight,
  I couldna liften't to my knee

"O wee wee man, but thou be strang!
  Oh, tell me where thy dwelling be?"
"My dwelling's down at yon bonnie bower,
  O will ye go with me and see?"

On we lap, and awa' we rade,
   Till we came to yon bonny green;
We lighted down for to bait our horse,
   And out there cam a lady fine;

Four and twenty at her back,
   And they were a' clad out in green;
Though the King of Scotland had been there,
   The warst o' them might hae been his queen.

On we lap, and awa' we rade,
   Till we came to you bonny ha';
Where the roof was o' the beaten gowd,
   And the floor was o' the crystal a'.

When we cam to the stair foot,
   Ladies were dancing, jimp and sma';
But in the twinkling of an eye,
   My wee wee man was clean awa.

THE WIFE OF USHER'S WELL

There lived a wife at Usher's Well,
   And a wealthy wife was she,
She had three stout and stalwart sons,
   And sent them o'er the sea.

They hadna been a week from her,
   A week but barely ane,
When word came to the carline wife,
   That her three sons were gane.

They hadna been a week from her,
   A week but barely three,
When word came to the carline wife,
   That her sons she'd never see.

"I wish the wind may never cease,
   Nor flashes in the flood,
Till my three sons come hame to me,
   In earthly flesh and blood."—

It fell about the Martinmas,
   When nights are lang and mirk,
The carline wife's three sons came hame,
   And their hats were o' the birk.

It neither grew in syke nor ditch,
   Nor yet in ony sheugh;
But at the gates o' Paradise,
   That birk grew fair eneugh.

"Blow up the fire, my maidens!
   Bring water from the well!
For a' my house shall feast this night,
   Since my three sons are well."—

And she has made to them a bed,
   She's made it large and wide;
And she's ta'en her mantle her about,
   Sat down at the bed-side.

Up then crew the red red cock
   And up and crew the gray;
The eldest to the youngest said,
   " 'Tis time we were away."

The cock he hadna craw'd but once,
    And clapp'd his wing at a',
Whan the youngest to the eldest said,
    "Brother, we must awa.

"The cock doth craw, the day doth daw,
    The channerin' worm doth chide;
Gin we be mist out o' our place,
    A sair pain we maun bide.

"Fare ye weel, my mother dear!
    Fareweel to barn and byre!
And fare ye well, the bonny lass,
    That kindles my mother's fire."

WILLIAM BLAKE (1757-1827)

FAIR ELEANOR

The bell struck one, and shook the silent tower;
The graves give up their dead: fair Eleanor
Walked by the castle gate, and lookèd in;
A hollow groan ran through the dreary vaults.

She shrieked aloud, and sunk upon the steps,
On the cold stone her pale cheek. Sickly smells
Of death issue as from a sepulchre,
And all is silent but the sighing vaults.

Chill death withdraws his hand, and she revives;
Amazed she find herself upon her feet,
And, like a ghost, through narrow passages
Walking, feeling the cold walls with her hands.

At length, no fancy but reality
Distracts her. A rushing sound, and the feet
Of one that fled, approaches.—Ellen stood,
Like a dumb statue, froze to stone with fear.

The wretch approaches, crying, "The deed is done!
Take this, and send it by whom thou wilt send;
It is my life—send it to Eleanor—:
He's dead, and howling after me for blood!

"Take this," he cried: and thrust into her arms
A wet napkin, wrapt about; then rushed
Past, howling. She received into her arms
Pale death, and followed on the wings of fear.

They passed swift through the outer gate; the wretch
Howling, leaped o'er the wall into the moat,
Stifling in mud. Fair Ellen passed the bridge,
And heard a gloomy voice cry, "Is it done?"

As the deer wounded, Ellen flew over
The pathless plain; as the arrows that fly
By night, destruction flies, and strikes in darkness.
She fled from fear, till at her house arrived.

Her maids await her; on her bed she falls,
That bed of joy where erst her lord hath pressed.
"Ah woman's fear!" she cried, "Ah cursed duke!
Ah my dear lord! Ah wretched Eleanor!

"My lord was like a flower upon the brows
Of lusty May! Ah life as frail as flower!
O ghastly Death! withdraw thy cruel hand!
Seek'st thou that flower to deck thy horrid temples?

"My lord was like a star in highest heaven
Drawn down to earth by spells and wickedness;
My lord was like the opening eyes of day,
When western winds creep softly o'er the flowers.

"But he is darkened; like the summer's noon
Clouded; fall'n like the stately tree, cut down;
The breath of heaven dwelt among his leaves,
O Eleanor, weak woman, filled with woe!"

Thus having spoke, she raisèd her head,
And saw the bloody napkin by her side,
Which in her arms she brought; and now, tenfold
More terrified, saw it unfold itself.

Her eyes were fixed; the bloody cloth unfolds,
Disclosing to her sight the murdered head
Of her dear lord, all ghastly pale, clotted
With gory blood; it groaned, and thus it spake:

"O Eleanor, behold thy husband's head,
Who sleeping on the stones of yonder tower,
Was reft of life by the accursed duke:
A hired villain turned my sleep to death.

"O Eleanor, beware the cursed duke;
O give him not thy hand, now I am dead.
He seeks thy love; who, coward, in the night,
Hired a villain to bereave my life."

She sat with dead cold limbs, stiffened to stone;
She took the gory head up in her arms;
She kissed the pale lips; she had no tears to shed;
She hugged it to her breast, and groaned her last.

ROBERT BURNS (1759-1796)

ADDRESS TO THE DEIL

O Prince! O Chief of many thronèd pow'rs!
That led th' embattl'd seraphim to war.
Milton

I

O Thou! whatever title suit thee—
Auld Hornie, Satan, Nick, or Clootie—
Wha in yon cavern grim an' sootie,
   Clos'd under hatches,
Spairges about the brunstane cootie,
   To scaud poor wretches!

II

Hear me, Auld Hangie, for a wee,
An' let poor damnèd bodies be;
I'm sure sma' pleasure it can gie,
   Ev'n to a deil,
To skelp an' scaud poor dogs like me
   An' hear us squeel.

III

Great is thy pow'r an' great thy fame;
Far kend an' noted is thy name;
An' tho' yon lowin heugh's thy hame,
   Thou travels far;
An faith! thou's neither lag, nor lame,
   Nor blate, nor scaur.

IV

Whyles, ranging like a roarin lion,
For prey, a' holes corners trying;
Whyles, on the strong-wing'd tempest flyin,
      Tirlin the kirks;
Whyles, in the human bosom pryin,
        Unseen thou lurks.

V

I've heard my rev'rend graunie say,
In lanely glens ye like to stray;
Or, where auld ruin'd castles grey
      Nod to the moon,
Ye fright the nightly wand'rer's way
      Wi' eldritch croon.

VI

When twilight did my graunie summon,
To say her pray'rs, douce, honest woman!
Aft yont the dyke she's heard you bummin,
      Wi' eerie drone;
Or, rustlin, thro' the boortrees comin,
      Wi' heavy groan.

VII

Ae dreary, windy, winter night,
The star shot down wi' sklentin light,
Wi' you mysel, I gat a fright:
      Ayont the lough,
Ye, like a rash-buss, stood in sight,
      Wi' waving sugh.

VIII

The cudgel in my nieve did shake,
Each bristl'd hair stood like a stake;
When wi' an eldritch, stoor "quaick, quaick,"
　　　　Amang the springs,
Awa ye squatter'd like a drake,
　　　　On whistling wings.

IX

Let warlocks grim, an' wither'd hags,
Tell how wi' you, on ragweed nags,
They skim the muirs an' dizzy crags,
　　　　Wi' wicked speed;
And in kirk-yards renew their leagues,
　　　　Owre howkit dead.

X

Thence, countra wives, wi' toil in pain,
May plunge an' plunge the kirn in vain;
Or O! the ellow treasure's taen
　　　　By witching skill;
An' dawtit, twal-pint hawkie's gaen
　　　　As yell's the bill.

XI

Thence, mystic knots mak great abuse
On young guidmen, fond, keen an' croose;
When the best wark-lume i' the house,
　　　　By cantraip wit,
Is instant made no worth a louse,
　　　　Just at the bit.

XII

When thowes dissolve the snawy hoord,
An' float the jinglin icy boord,
Then, water-kelpies haunt the foord,
    By your direction,
An' nighted trav'llers are allur'd
      To their destruction.

XIII

And aft your moss-traversing spunkies
Decoy the wight that late an' drunk is;
The bleezin, curst, mischievous monkies
    Delude his eyes,
Till in some miry slough he sunk is,
      Ne'er mair to rise.

XIV

When masons' mystic word an' grip
In storms an' tempests raise you up,
Some cock or cat your rage maun stop,
    Or, strange to tell!
The youngest brother ye wad whip
      Aff straught to hell.

XV

Lang syne in Eden's bonie yard,
When youthfu' lovers first were pair'd,
An' all the soul of love they shar'd,
    The raptur'd hour,
Sweet on the fragrant flow'ry swaird,
      In shady bow'r:

XVI

Then you, ye auld, snick-drawing dog!
Ye cam to Paradise incog,
An' play'd on man a cursed brogue
      (Black be your fa'!),
An' gied the infant warld a shog,
      'Maist ruin'd a'.

XVII

D' ye mind that day when in a bizz
Wi' reekit duds, an' reestit gizz,
Ye did present your smoutie phiz
      'Mang better folk;
An' sklented on the man of Uzz
      Your spitefu' joke?

XVIII

An' how ye gat him i' your thrall,
An' brak him out o' house an' hal',
While scabs an' botches did him gall,
      Wi' bitter claw;
An' lows'd his ill-tongu'd wicked scaul—
      Was warst ava?

XIX

But a' your doings to rehearse,
Your wily snares an' fechtin fierce,
Sin' that day Michael did you pierce
      Down to this time,
Wad ding a Lallan tongue, or Erse,
      In prose or rhyme.

XX

An' now, Auld Cloots, I ken ye're
    thinkin,
A certain Bardie's rantin, drinkin,
Some luckless hour will send him
    linkin,
       To your black Pit;
But, faith! he'll turn a corner jinkin,
       An' cheat you yet.

XXI

But fare-you-weel, Auld Nickie-
    Ben!
O, Wad ye tak a thought an' men'!
Ye aiblins might—I dinna ken—
       Still hae a stake:
I'm wae to think upo' yon den,
       Ev'n for your sake!

TAM O' SHANTER

A Tale

Of Brownyis and of Bogillis full is this Buke
Gawin Douglas

When chapman billies leave the street,
And drouthy neebors neebors meet;
As market-days are wearing late,
An' folk begin to tak the gate;
While we sit bousing at the nappy,
An' getting fou and unco happy,
We think na on the lang Scots miles,
The mosses, waters, slaps, and styles,

That lie between us and our hame,
Whare sits our sulky, sullen dame,
Gathering her brows like gathering storm,
Nursing her wrath to keep it warm.

This truth fand honest Tam o' Shanter,
As he frae Ayr ae night did canter:
(Auld Ayr, wham ne'er a town surpasses,
For honest men and bonie lasses).

O Tam, had'st thou but been sae wise,
As taen thy ain wife Kate's advice!
She tauld thee weel thou was a skellum,
A blethering, blustering, drunken blellum;
That frae November till October,
Ae market-day thou was nae sober;
That ilka melder wi' the miller,
Thou sat as lang as thou had siller;
That ev'ry naig was ca'd a shoe on,
The smith and thee gat roaring fou on;
That at the Lord's house, even on Sunday,
Thou drank wi' Kirkton Jean till Monday.
She prophesied, that, late or soon,
Thou would be found deep drown'd in Doon,
Or catch'd wi' warlocks in the mirk
By Alloway's auld, haunted kirk.

Ah! gentle dames, it gars me greet,
To think how monie counsels sweet,
How monie lengthen'd sage advices
The husband frae the wife despises!

But to our tale: Ae market-night,
Tam had got planted unco right,

Fast by an ingle, bleezing finely,
Wi' reaming swats, that drank divinely,
And at his elbow, Souter Johnie,
His ancient, trusty, drouthy cronie:
Tam lo'ed him like a very brither;
They had been fou for weeks thegither.
The night drave on wi' sangs and clatter;
And ay the ale was growing better:
The landlady and Tam grew gracious
Wi' secret favours, sweet and precious:
The Souter tauld his queerest stories;
The landlord's laugh was ready chorus:
The storm without might rair and rustle,
Tam did na mind the storm a whistle.

Care, mad to see a man sae happy,
E'en drown'd himsel amang the nappy.
As bees flee hame wi' ladees o' treasure,
The minutes wing'd their way wi' pleasure:
Kings may be blest but Tam was glorious,
O'er a' the ills o' life victorious!

But pleasures are like poppies spread:
You seize the flow'r, its bloom is shed;
Or like the snow falls in the river,
A moment white—then melts for ever;
Or like the borealis race,
That flit ere you can point their place;
Or like the rainbow's lovely form
Evanishing amid the storm.
Nae man can tether time or tide;
The hour approaches Tam maun ride:
That hour, o' night's black arch the key-stane,
That dreary hour Tam mounts his beast in;

And sic a night he taks the road in,
As ne'er poor sinner was abroad in.

The wind blew as 't wad blawn its last;
The rattling showers rose on the blast;
The speedy gleams the darkness swallow'd;
Loud, deep, and lang the thunder bellow'd:
That night, a child might understand,
The Deil had business on his hand.

Weel mounted on his gray mare Meg,
A better never lifted leg,
Tam skelpit on thro' dub and mire,
Despising wind, and rain, and fire;
Whiles holding fast his guid blue bonnet,
Whiles crooning o'er some auld Scots sonnet.
Whiles glow'ring round wi' prudent cares,
Lest bogles catch him unawares:
Kirk-Alloway was drawing nigh,
Whare ghaists and houlets nightly cry.

By this time he was cross the ford,
Whare in the snaw the chapman smoor'd;
And past the birks and meikle stane,
Whare drunken Charlie brak's neck-bane;
And thro' the whins, and by the cairn,
Whare hunters fand the murder'd bairn;
And near the thorn, aboon the well,
Whare Mungo's mither hang'd hersel.
Before him Doon pours all his floods;
The doubling storm roars thro' the woods;
The lightnings flash from pole to pole;
Near and more near the thunders roll:
When, glimmering thro' the groaning trees,
Kirk-Alloway seem'd in a bleeze,

Thro, ilka bore the beams were glancing,
And loud resounded mirth and dancing.

Inspiring bold John Barleycorn,
What dangers thou canst make us scorn!
Wi' tippenny, we fear nae evil;
Wi' usquabae, we'll face the Devil!
The swats sae ream'd in Tammie's noddle,
Fair play, he car'd na deils a boddle
But Maggie stood, right sair astonish'd,
Till, by the heel and hand admonish'd,
She ventur'd forward on the light;
And, vow! Tam saw an unco sight!

Warlocks and witches in a dance:
Nae cotillion, brent new frae France,
But hornpipes, jigs, strathspeys, and reels,
Put life and mettle in their heels
A winnock-bunker in the east,
There sat Auld Nick, in shape o' beast;
A tousie tyke, black, grim, and large,
To gie them music was his charge:
He screw'd the pipes and gart them skirl,
Till roof and rafters a' did dirl
Coffins stood round, like open presses,
That shaw'd the dead in their last dresses;
And, by some devilish cantraip sleight,
Each in its cauld hand held a light:
By which heroic Tam was able
To note upon the haly table,
A murderer's banes, in gibbet-airns;
Twa span-lang, wee, unchristen'd bairns;
A thief new-cutted frae a rape—
Wi' his last gasp his gab did gape;

Five tomahawks wi' bluid red-rusted;
Five scymitars wi' murder crusted;
A garter which a babe had strangled;
A knife a father's throat had mangled—
Whom his ain son o' life bereft—
The grey-hairs yet stack to the heft;
Wi' mair of horrible and awefu',
Which even to name wad be unlawfu'.

As Tammie glowr'd, amaz'd, and curious,
The mirth and fun grew fast and furious;
The piper loud and louder blew,
The dancers quick and quicker flew,
They reel'd, they set, they cross'd, they cleekit,
Till ilka carlin swat and reekit,
And coost her duddies to the wark,
And linket at it in her sark!

Now Tam, O Tam! had thae been queans,
A' plump and strapping in their teens!
Their sarks, instead o' creeshie flannen,
Been snaw-white seventeen hunder linen!—
Thir breeks o' mine, my only pair,
That ance were plush, o' guid blue hair,
I was hae gi'en them off my hurdies
For ae blink o' the bonie burdies!

But wither'd beldams, auld and droll,
Rigwoodie hags wad spean a foal,
Louping and flinging on a crummock,
I wonder did na turn thy stomach!

But Tam kend what was what fu' brawlie:
There was ae winsome wench and wawlie,

That night enlisted in the core,
Lang after kend on Carrick shore
(For monie a beast to dead she shot,
An' perish'd monie a bonie boat,
And shook baith meikle corn and bear,
And kept the country-side in fear).
Her cutty sark, o' Paisley harn,
That while a lassie she had worn,
In longitude tho' sorely scanty,
It was her best, and she was vauntie. . . .
Ah! little kend thy reverend grannie,
That sark she coft for her wee Nannie,
Wi' twa pund Scots ('t was a' her riches),
Wad ever grac'd a dance of witches!

But here my Muse her wind maun cour,
Sic flights are far beyond her power:
To sing how Nannie lap and flang
(A souple pad she was and strang),
And how Tam stood like ane bewitch'd,
And thought his very een enrich'd;
Even Satan glowr'd, and fidg'd fu' fain,
And hotch'd and blew wi' might and main;
Till first ae caper, syne anither,
Tam tint his reason a'thegither,
And roars out: "Weel done, Cutty-sark!"
And in an instant all was dark:
And scarcely had he Maggie rallied,
When aut the hellish legion sallied.

As bees bizz out wi' angry fyke,
When plundering herds assail their byke;
As open pussie's mortal foes,
When, pop! she starts before their nose;

As eager runs the market-crowd,
When "Catch the thief!" resounds aloud:
So Maggie runs, the witches follow,
Wi' monie an eldritch skriech and hollo.

Ah, Tam! ah, Tam! thou'll get thy fairin!
In hell they'll roast thee like a herrin!
In vain thy Kate awaits they comin!
Kate soon will be a woefu' woman!
Now, do thy speedy utmost, Meg,
And win the key-stane of the brig;
There, at them thou thy tail may toss,
A running stream they dare na cross!
But ere the key-stane she could make,
The fient a tail she had to shake;
For Nannie, far before the rest,
Hard upon noble Maggie prest,
And flew at Tam wi' furious ettle;
But little wist she Maggie's mettle!
Ae spring brought off her master hale,
But left behind her ain grey tail:
The carlin claught her by the rump,
And left poor Maggie scarce a stump.

Now, wha this tale o' truth shall read,
Ilk man, and mother's son, take heed:
Whene'er to drink you are inclin'd,
Or cutty sarks run in your mind,
Think! ye may buy the joys o'er dear:
Remember Tam o' Shanter's mare.

DEATH AND DOCTOR HORNBOOK

A True Story

I

Some books are lies frae end to end,
And some great lies were never penn'd:
Ev'n ministers, they hae been kend,
      In holy rapture,
A rousing whid at times to vend,
       And nail 't wi' Scripture.

II

But this that I am gaun to tell,
Which lately on a night befel,
Is just as true's the Deil 's in hell
      Or Dublin city:
That e'er he nearer comes oursel
      'S a muckle pity!

III

The clachan yill had made me canty,
I was na fou, but just had plenty:
I stacher'd whyles, but yet took tent ay
      To free the ditches;
An' hillocks, stanes, an' bushes, kend ay
      Frae ghaists an' witches.

IV

The rising moon began to glow'r
The distant Cumnock Hills out-owre:
To count her horns, wi' a' my pow'r
      I set mysel;
But whether she had three or four,
      I cou'd na tell.

V

I was come round about the hill,
And todlin down on Willie's mill,
Setting my staff wi' a' my skill
      To keep me sicker;
Tho' leeward whyles, against my will,
      I took a bicker.

VI

I there wi' *Something* does forgather,
That pat me in an eerie swither;
An awfu' scythe, out-owre ae shouther,
      Clear-dangling, hang;
A three-tae'd leister on the ither
      Lay, large an' lang.

VII

Its stature seem'd lang Scotch ells twa;
The queerest shape that e'er I saw,
For fient a wame it had ava;
      And then its shanks,
They were as thin, as sharp an' sma'
      As cheeks o' branks.

VIII

'Guid-een,' quo' I; 'Friend! hae ye been mawin,
When ither folk are busy sawin?'
It seem'd to make a kind o' stan',
      But naething spak.
At length, says I: 'Friend! whare ye gaun?
      Will ye go back?'

IX

It spak right howe: 'My name is Death,
But be na fled.' Quoth I: 'Guid faith,
Ye're may be come to stap my breath;
      But tent me, billie:
I red ye weel, take care o' skaith,
        See, there 's a gully!'

X

'Gudeman,' quo' he, 'put up your whittle,
I'm no design'd to try its mettle;
But if I did, I wad be kittle
      To be mislear'd:
I wad na mind it, no that spittle
        Out-owre my beard.'

XI

'Weel, weel!' says I, 'a bargain be 't;
Come, gie's your hand, an' say we 're gree't:
We 'll ease our shanks, an' tak a seat:
      Come, gie 's your news:
This while ye hae been monie a gate,
        At monie a house.'

XII

'Ay, ay!' quo' he, an' shook his head,
'It's e'en a lang, lang time indeed
Sin' I began to nick the thread
      An' choke the breath:
Folk maun do something for their bread,
        An' sae maun Death.

XIII

'Sax thousand years are near-hand fled
Sin' I was to the butching bred,
An' monie a scheme in vain 's been laid
      To stap or scar me;
Till ane Hornbook 's ta'en up the trade,
      And faith! he'll waur me.

XIV

'Ye ken Jock Hornbook i' the clachan?
Deil mak his king's-hood in a spleuchan!—
He's grown sae weel acquaint wi' *Buchan*
      And ither chaps,
The weans haud out their fingers laughin,
      An' pouk my hips.

XV

'See, here's a scythe, an' there's a dart,
They hae pierc'd monie a gallant heart;
But Doctor Hornbook wi' his art
      An' cursed skill,
Has made them baith no worth a fart,
      Damn'd haet they'll kill!

XVI

' 'T was but yestreen, nae farther gane,
I threw a noble throw at ane;
Wi' less, I'm sure, I've hundreds slain;
      But Deil-ma-care!
It just played dirl on the bane,
      But did nae mair.

XVII

'Hornbook was by wi' ready art,
An' had sae fortify'd the part,
That when I looked to my dart,
       It was sae blunt,
Fient haet o 't wad hae pierc'd the heart
       Of a kail-runt.

XVIII

'I drew my sycthe in sic a fury,
I near-hand cowpit wi' my hurry,
But yet the bauld Apothecary
       Withstood the shock:
I might as weel hae try'd a quarry
       O'hard whin-rock.

XIX

'Ev'n them he canna get attended,
Altho' their face he ne'er had kend it,
Just shit in a kail-blade an' send it,
       As soon's he smells 't,
Baith their disease and what will mend it.
       At once he tells 't.

XX

'And then a' doctor's saws and whittles
Of a' dimensions, shapes, an' mettles,
A' kind o' boxes, mugs, and bottles,
       He's sure to hae:
Their Latin names as fast he rattles
       As A B C.

XXI

'Calces o' fossils, earth, and trees
True *sal-marinum* o' the seas;
The *farina* of beans an' pease,
        He has 't in plenty;
Aqua-fontis, what you please,
        He can content ye.

XXII

'Forbye some new, uncommon weapons,
Urinus spiritus of capons;
Or mite-horn shavings, filings, scrapings
        Distill'd *per se;*
Sol-alkali o' midge-tail-clippings,
        And monie mae.'

XXIII

'Waes me for Johnie Ged's Hole now,'
Quoth I, 'if that thae news be true!
His braw calf-ward whare gowans grew
        Sae white and bonie,
Nae doubt they'll rive it wi' the plew:
        They'll ruin Johnie!'

XXIV

The creature grain'd an eldritch laugh,
And says: 'Ye needna yoke the pleugh,
Kirkyards will soon be till'd eneugh,
        Tak ye nae fear:
They'll a' be trench'd wi' monie a sheugh
        In twa-three year.

XXV

'Whare I kill'd ane, a fair strae death
By loss o' blood or want o' breath,
This night I'm free to tak my aith,
      That Hornbook's skill
Has clad a score i' their last claith
      By drap an' pill.

XXVI

'An honest wabster to his trade,
Whase wife's twa nieves were scarce weel-bred,
Gat tippence-worth to mend her head,
      When it was sair;
The wife slade cannie to her bed,
      But ne'er spak mair.

XXVII

'A countra laird had taen the batts,
Or some curmurring in his guts,
His only son for Hornbook sets,
      An' pays him well:
The lad, for twa guid gimmer-pets,
      Was laird himsel.

XXVIII

'A bonie lass—ye kend her name—
Some ill-brewn drink had hov'd her wame;
She trusts hersel, to hide the shame,
      In Hornbook's care;
Horn sent her aff to her lang hame
      To hide it there.

XXIX

'That's just a swatch o' Hornbook's way;
Thus goes he on from day to day,
Thus does he poison, kill, an' slay,
              An 's weel paid for 't;
Yet stops me o' my lawfu' prey
              Wi' his damn'd dirt:

XXX

'But, hark! I'll tell you of a plot,
Tho' dinna ye be speakin o 't:
I'll nail the self-conceited sot,
              As dead's a herrin;
Niest time we meet, I'll wad a groat,
              He gets his fairin!'

XXXI

But just as he began to tell,
The auld kirk-hammer strak the bell
Some wee short hour ayont the twal,
              Which raised us baith:
I took the way that pleas'd mysel,
              And sae did Death.

JAMES HOGG (1770-1835)

KILMENY

Bonnie Kilmeny gaed up the glen;
But it wasna to meet Duneira's men,
Nor the rosy monk of the isle to see,
For Kilmeny was pure as pure could be.

It was only to hear the yorlin sing,
And pu' the cress-flower round the spring;
The scarlet hypp and the hind-berrye,
And the nut that hung frae the hazel tree;
For Kilmeny was pure as pure could be.
But lang may her minny look o'er the wa';
And lang may she seek i' the greenwood shaw;
Lang the lair o' Duneira blame,
And lang, lang greet or Kilmeny come hame!

When many a day had come and fled,
When grief grew calm, and hope was dead,
When mass for Kilmeny's soul had been sung,
When the bedes-man had pray'd and the dead-bell rung,
Late, late in a gloamin', when all was still,
When the fringe was red on the westlin' hill,
The wood was sere, the moon i' the wane,
The reek o' the cot hung o'er the plain,
Like a little wee cloud in the world its lane;
When the ingle lowed wi' an eiry leme—
Late, late in the gloamin' Kilmeny came hame!

"Kilmeny, Kilmeny, where have you been?
Lang hae we sought baith holt and dene;
By burn, by ford, by greenwood tree,
Yet you are halesome and fair to see.
Where gat ye that joup o' the lily sheen?
That bonnie snood o' the birk sae green?
And these roses, the fairest that ever were seen?
Kilmeny, Kilmeny, where have you been?"

Kilmeny look'd up wi' a lovely grace,
But nae smile was seen on Kilmeny's face;
As still was her looks, and as still was her ee,
As the stillness that lay on the emerant lea,

Or the mist that sleeps on a waveless sea.
For Kilmeny had been, she kenn'd not where,
And Kilmeny had seen what she could not declare,
Kilmeny had been where the cock never crew,
Where the rain never fell, and the wind never blew.
But it seemed as the harp of the sky had rung,
And the airs of heaven played round her tongue,
When she spoke of the lovely forms she had seen,
And a land where sin had never been;
A land of love and a land of light,
Withouten sun, or moon, or night;
Where the river swa'd a living stream,
And the light a pure and cloudless beam
The land of vision, it would seem,
A still, an everlasting dream.

In yon green wood there is a waik,
And in that waik there is a wene,
And in that wene there is a maike;
That neither has flesh, nor blood, nor bane;
And down in yon greenwood he walks his lane.

In that green wene Kilmeny lay,
Her bosom hap'd wi' flowerets gay;
But the air was soft, and the silence deep,
And bonnie Kilmeny fell sound asleep,
She kenned nae mair, nor open'd her ee,
Till wak'd by the hymns of a far countrye.

She woke on a couch of silk sae slim,
All striped wi' the bars of the rainbow's rim;
And lovely beings round were rife,
Who erst had travelled mortal life;
And aye they smiled and gan' to speer,
"What spirit has brought this mortal here?"

They clasped her waist, and her hands sae fair,
They kissed her cheeks, and they kemed her hair;
And round came many a blooming fere,
Saying, "Bonnie Kilmeny, ye're welcome here!
Women are freed of the littand scorn,
O blessed be the day Kilmeny was born!
Now shall the land of the spirits see,
Now shall it ken what a woman may be!

"O, bonnie Kilmeny! free frae stain,
If ever you seek the world again,
That world of sin, of sorrow, and fear,
O tell of the joys that are awaiting here;
And tell of the signs you shall shortly see;
Of the times that are now, and the times that shall be."

They lifted Kilmeny, they led her away,
And she walked in the light of a sunless day;
The sky was a dome of crystal bright,
The fountain of vision, and fountain of light;
The emerant fields were of dazzling glow,
And the flowers of everlasting blow.
Then deep in the stream her body they laid,
That her youth and her beauty never might fade;
And they smil'd on Heaven, when they saw her lie
In the stream of life that wandered by.
And she heard a song, she heard it sung,
She ken'd not where; but sae sweetly it rung,
It fell on the ear like a dream of the morn:—
"O! blest be the day Kilmeny was born!
Now shall the land of the spirits see,
Now shall it ken what a woman may be!
The sun that shines on the world sae bright,
A borrowed gleid frae the fountain of light,

And the moon that sleeks the sky sae dun,
Like a gouden bow or a beamless sun,
Shall wear away and be seen nae mair,
And the angels shall miss them travelling the air;
But lang, lang after, baith nicht and day,
When the sun and the world have fled away,
When the sinner has gane to his waesome doom,
Kilmeny shall smile in eternal bloom!"

They bore her away, she wist not how,
For she felt not arm nor rest below;
But so swift they wained her through the light,
'T was like the motion of sound or sight;
They seemed to split the gales of air,
And yet nor gale nor breeze was there.
Unnumbered groves below them grew,
They came, they passed, and backward flew,
Like floods of blossoms gliding on,
A moment seen, in a moment gone.
O! never vales to mortal view
Appeared like those o'er which they flew,
That land to human spirits given,
The lowermost vales of the storied heaven;
From whence they can view the world below,
And heaven's blue gates with sapphires glow,
More glory yet unmeet to know.

They bore her far to a mountain green,
To see what mortal never had seen;
And they seated her high on a purple sward,
And bade her heed what she saw and heard,
And not the changes the spirits wrought;
For now she lived in the land of thought.
She looked, and she saw nor sun nor skies,
But a crystal dome of a thousand dyes;

She looked, and she saw nae land aright,
But an endless whirl of glory and light:
And radiant beings went and came,
Far swifter than wind, or the linkèd flame.
She hid her e'en frae the dazzling view;
She looked again, and the scene was new.

She saw a sun in a summer sky,
And clouds of amber sailing by;
A lovely land beneath her lay,
And that land had lakes and mountains grey;
And that land had valleys and hoary piles,
And marled seas and a thousand isles.
Its fields were speckled, its forest green,
And its lakes were all of the dazzling sheen,
Like magic mirrors, where shining lay
The sun, and the sky, and the cloudlet grey,
Which heaved and trembled and gently swung;
On every shore they seemed to be hung:
For there they were seen on their downward plain
A thousand times and a thousand again;
In winding lake, and placid firth,
Little peaceful heavens in the bosom of earth.

Kilmeny sighed and seemed to grieve,
For she found her heart to that land did cleave;
She saw the corn wave on the vale;
She saw the deer run down the dale;
She saw the plaid and the broad claymore,
And the brows that the badge of freedom bore;
And she thought she had seen the land before.

She saw below her fair unfurled
One-half of all the glowing world,

Where oceans rolled, and rivers ran,
To bound the aims of sinful man.

But to sing the sights Kilmeny saw,
So far surpassing nature's law,
The singer's voice wad sink away,
And the string of his harp wad cease to play.
But she saw till the sorrows of man were by,
And all was love and harmony;—
Till the stars of heaven fell calmly away,
Like flakes of snow on a winter day.
Then Kilmeny begged again to see
The friends she had left in her ain countrye
To tell of the place where she had been,
And the glories that lay in the land unseen;
To warn the living maidens fair,
The loved of heaven, the spirits' care,
That all whose minds unmeled remain
Shall bloom in beauty when time is gane.

With distant music, soft and deep,
They lulled Kilmeny sound asleep,
And when she awakened, she lay her lane,
All hap'd with flowers, in the greenwood wene.
When seven long years had come and fled,
When grief was calm, and hope was dead,
When scarce was remembered Kilmeny's name,
Late, late in a gloamin' Kilmeny came hame.
And O, her beauty was fair to see,
But still and steadfast was her ee!
Such beauty bard may never declare,
For there was no pride nor passion there;
And the soft desire of maiden's een
In that mild face could never be seen.

Her seymar was the lily flower,
And her cheek was the moss-rose in the shower;
And her voice like the distant melodye,
That floats along the twilight sea.
But she loved to raike the lanely glen,
And keep afar frae the haunts of men,
Her holy hymns unheard to sing,
To suck the flowers, and drink the spring;
But wherever her peaceful form appeared,
The wild beasts of the hill were cheered;
The wolf played blithely round the field,
The lordly byson lowed, and kneeled;
The dun deer wooed with manner bland,
And cowered beneath her lily hand,
And when at eve the woodlands rung,
When hymns of other worlds she sung
In ecstasy of sweet devotion,
O, then the glen was all in motion!
The wild beasts of the forest came,
Broke from their bughts and faulds the tame,
And goved around, charmed and amazed;
Even the dull cattle crooned and gazed,
And murmured, and looked with anxious pain
For something the mystery to explain
The buzzard came with the throstle-cock;
The corby let her houf in the rock;
The blackbird alang wi' the eagle flew;
The hind came tripping o'er the dew;
The wolf and the kid their raike began,
And the tod and the lamb and the leveret ran;
The hawk and the hern attour them hung.
And the merle and the mavis forhooyed their young;
And all in a peaceful ring were hurled—
It was like an eve in a sinless world!

When a month and a day had come and gane,
Kilmeny sought the greenwood wene;
There laid her down on the leaves sae green,
And Kilmeny on earth was never mair seen.
But O! the words that fell frae her mooth
Were words of wonder, and words of truth!
But all the land were in fear and dread,
For they kendna whether she was living or dead.
It wasna her hame, and she couldna remain;
She left this world of sorrow and pain,
And returned to the land of thought again.

SIR WALTER SCOTT (1771-1832)

THE EVE OF ST. JOHN

The Baron of Smaylho'me rose with day,
    He spurr'd his courser on,
Without stop or stay, down the rocky way,
    That leads to Brotherstone.

He went not with the bold Buccleuch,
    His banner broad to rear;
He went not 'gainst the English yew,
    To lift the Scottish spear.

Yet his plate-jack was braced, and his helmet
        was laced,
    And his vaunt-brace of proof he wore:
At his saddle-gerthe was a good steel sperthe,
    Full ten pound weight and more.

The Baron returned in three days' space,
  And his looks were sad and sour;
And weary was his courser's pace,
  As he reach'd his rocky tower.

He came not from where Ancram Moor
  Ran red with English blood;
Where the Douglas true, and the bold Buccleuch,
  'Gainst keen Lord Evers stood.

Yet was his helmet hack'd and hew'd
  His action pierced and tore,
His axe and his dagger with blood imbrued,—
  But it was not English gore.

He lighted at the Chapellage,
  He held him close and still;
And he whistled thrice for his little foot-page,
  His name was English Will.

"Come thou hither, my little foot-page,
  Come hither to my knee;
Though thou art young and tender of age,
  I think thou art true to me.

"Come, tell me all that thou hast seen,
  And look thou tell me true!
Since I from Smaylho'me tower have been,
  What did thy lady do?"—

"My lady, each night, sought the lonely light,
  That burns on the wild Watchfold;
For, from height to height, the beacons bright
  Of the English foemen told.

"The bittern clamour'd from the moss,
  The wind blew loud and shrill;
Yet the craggy pathway she did cross,
  To the eiry Beacon Hill.

"I watch'd her steps, and silent came
  Where she sat her on a stone;—
No watchman stood by the dreary flame,
  It burned all alone.

"The second night I kept her in sight,
  Till to the fire she came,
And, by Marys might! an Armed Knight
  Stood by the lonely flame.

"And many a word that warlike lord
  Did speak to my lady there;
But the rain fell fast, and loud blew the blast,
  And I heard not what they were.

"The third night there the sky was fair,
  And the mountain-blast was still,
As again I watch'd the secret pair,
  On the lonesome Beacon Hill.

"And I heard her name the midnight hour,
  And name this holy eve;
And say, 'Come this night to thy lady's bower;
  Ask no bold Baron's leave.

" 'He lifts his spear with the bold Buccleuch;
  His lady is all alone;
The door she'll undo, to her knight so true,
  On the eve of good St. John.'—

" 'I cannot come; I must not come;
　　I dare not come to thee;
On the eve of St. John I must wander alone:
　　In thy bower I may not be.'—

" 'Now, out on thee, faint-hearted knight!
　　Thou shouldst not say me nay;
For the eve is sweet, and when lovers meet,
　　Is worth the whole summer's day.

" 'And I'll chain the blood-hound, and the warder
　　　shall not sound,
　　And rushes shall be strew'd on the stair;
So, by the black rood-stone, and by holy St. John,
　　I conjure thee, my love, to be there!'—

" 'Though the blood-hound be mute, and the rush
　　　beneath my foot,
　　And the warder his bugle should not blow,
Yet there sleepeth a priest in a chamber to the east,
　And my footstep he would know.'—

" 'O fear not the priest, who sleepeth to the east!
　　For to Dryburgh the way he has ta'en;
And there to say mass, till three days do pass,
　　For the soul of a knight that is slayne.'—

"He turn'd him around and grimly he frown'd;
　　Then he laughed right scornfully—
'He who says the mass-rite for the soul of that knight,
　　May as well say mass for me.

" 'At the lone midnight hour, when bad spirits have power,
　　In thy chamber will I be.'—

With that he was gone, and my lady left alone,
　　And no more did I see."

Then changed, I trow, was that bold Baron's brow,
　　From the dark to the blood-red high;
"Now, tell me the mien of the knight thou hast seen,
　　For, by Mary, he shall die!"—

"His arms shone full bright, in the beacon's red light:
　　His plume it was scarlet and blue;
On his shield was a hound, in a silver leash bound,
　　And his crest was a branch of the yew."—

"Thou liest, thou liest, thou little foot-page,
　　Loud dost thou lie to me!
For that knight is cold, and low laid in the mould,
　　All under the Eildon-tree."—

"Yet hear but my word, my noble lord!
　　For I heard her name his name;
And that lady bright, she called the knight
　　Sir Richard of Coldinghame."—

The bold Baron's brow then changed, I trow,
　　From high blood-red to pale—
"The grave is deep and dark—and the corpse is
　　　stiff and stark—
　　So I may not trust thy tale.

"Where fair Tweed flows round holy Melrose,
　　And Eildon slopes to the plain,
Full three nights ago, by some secret foe,
　　That gay gallant was slain.

"The varying light deceived thy sight,
   And the wild winds drown'd the name;
For the Dryburgh bells ring, and the white monks
     do sing,
   For Sir Richard of Coldinghame!"

He pass'd the court-gate, and he oped the tower-gate,
   And he mounted the narrow stair,
To the bartizan-seat, where, with maids that on
     her wait,
   He found his lady fair.

That lady sat in mournful mood
   Look'd over hill and vale;
Over Tweed's fair flood, and Mertoun's wood,
   And all down Teviotdale.

"Now hail, now hail, thou lady bright!"—
   "Now hail, thou Baron true!
What news, what news, from Ancram fight?
   What news from the bold Buccleuch?"—

"The Ancram Moor is red with gore,
   For many a Southern fell;
And Buccleuch has charged us, evermore,
   To watch our beacons well."—

The lady blush'd red, but nothing she said:
   Nor added the Baron a word:
Then she stepp'd down the stair to her chamber fair,
   And so did her moody lord.

In sleep the lady mourn'd, and the Baron toss'd and turn'd,
   And oft to himself he said,—

"The worms around him creep, and his bloody
    grave is deep . . .
It cannot give up the dead!"

It was near the ringing of matin-bell,
    The night was well-nigh done,
When a heavy sleep on that Baron fell,
    On the eve of good St. John.

The lady look'd through the chamber fair,
    By the light of a dying flame;
And she was aware of a knight stood there—
    Sir Richard of Coldinghame!

"Alas! away, away!" she cried,
    "For the holy Virgin's sake!"—
"Lady, I know who sleeps by thy side;
    But, lady, he will not awake.

"By Eildon-tree, for long nights three,
    In bloody grave have I lain;
The mass and the death-prayer are said for me,
    But, lady, they are said in vain.

"By the Baron's brand, near Tweed's fair strand,
    Most foully slain, I fell;
And my restless sprite on the beacon's height,
    For a space is doomed to dwell.

"At our trysting-place, for a certain space,
    I must wander to and fro;
But I had not had power to come to thy bower,
    Had'st thou not conjured me so."—

Love master'd fear—her brow she cross'd;
  "How, Richard, hast thou sped?
And art thou saved, or art thou lost?"—
  The vision shook his head!

"Who spilleth life, shall forfeit life;
  So bid thy lord believe:
That lawless love is guilt above,
  This awful sign receive."

He laid his left palm on an oaken beam;
  His right upon her hand;
The lady shrunk, and fainting sunk,
  For it scorch'd like a fiery brand.

The sable score, of fingers four,
  Remains on that board impress'd;
And for evermore that lady wore
  A covering on her wrist.

There is a nun in Dryburgh bower,
  Ne'er looks upon the sun;
There is a monk in Melrose tower
  He speaketh word to none.

That nun, who ne'er beholds the day,
  That monk, who speaks to none—
That nun was Smaylho'me's Lady gay,
  That monk the bold Baron.

SAMUEL TAYLOR COLERIDGE (1772-1834)

KUBLA KHAN

In Xanadu did Kubla Khan
A stately pleasure-dome decree:
Where Alph, the sacred river, ran
Through caverns measureless to man
Down to a sunless sea.
So twice five miles of fertile ground
With walls and towers were girdled round:
And there were gardens bright and sinuous rills,
Where blossomed many an incense-bearing tree;
And there were forests ancient as the hills,
Enfolding sunny spots of greenery.

But oh! that deep romantic chasm which slanted
Down the green hill athwart a cedarn cover!
A savage place! as holy and enchanted
As e'er beneath a waning moon was haunted
By woman wailing for her demon-lover!
And from this chasm, with ceaseless turmoil seething,
As if this earth in fast thick pants were breathing,
A mighty fountain momently was forced:
Amid whose swift half-intermitted burst
Huge fragments vaulted like rebounding hail,
Or chaffy grain beneath the thresher's flail:
And 'mid these dancing rocks at once and ever
It flung up momently the sacred river.
Five miles meandering with a mazy motion
Through wood and dale the sacred river ran,
Then reached the caverns measureless to man,
And sank in tumult to a lifeless ocean:
And 'mid this tumult Kubla heard from far
Ancestral voices prophesying war!

The shadow of the dome of pleasure
Floated midway on the waves;
Where was heard the mingled measure
From the fountain and the caves.
It was a miracle of rare device,
A sunny pleasure-dome with caves of ice!

A damsel with a dulcimer
In a vision once I saw:
It was an Abyssinian maid,
And on her dulcimer she played,
Singing of Mount Abora.
Could I revive within me
Her symphony and song,
To such a deep delight 'twould win me,
That with music loud and long,
I would build that dome in air,
That sunny dome! those caves of ice!
And all who heard should see them there,
And all should cry, Beware! Beware!
His flashing eyes, his floating hair!
Weave a circle round him thrice,
And close your eyes with holy dread,
For he on honey-dew hath fed,
And drunk the milk of Paradise.

PHANTOM

All look and likeness caught from earth,
All accident of kin and birth,
Had pass'd away. There was no trace
Of aught on that illumined face,
Uprais'd beneath the rifted stone
But of one spirit all her own;—
She, she herself, and only she,
Shone thro' her body visibly.

THOMAS MOORE (1779-1852)

THE LAKE OF THE DISMAL SWAMP

"They made her a grave, too cold and damp
   "For a soul so warm and true;
"And she's gone to the Lake of the Dismal Swamp,
"Where, all night long, by a fire-fly lamp,
   "She paddles her white canoe.

"And her fire-fly lamp I soon shall see,
   "And her paddle I soon shall hear;
"Long and loving our life shall be,
"And I'll hide the maid in a cypress tree,
   "When the footstep of death is near."

Away to the Dismal Swamp he speeds—
   His path was rugged and sore,
Through tangled juniper, beds of reeds,
Through many a fen, where the serpent feeds,
   And man never trod before.

And, when on the earth he sunk to sleep,
   If slumber his eyelids knew,
He lay, where the deadly vine doth weep
Its venomous tear and nightly steep
   The flesh with blistering dew!

And near him the she-wolf stirred the brake,
   And the copper-snake breathed in his ear,
Till he starting cried, from his dream awake,
"Oh! when shall I see the dusky Lake,
"And the white canoe of my dear?"

He saw the Lake, and a meteor bright
    Quick over its surface played—
"Welcome," he said, "my dear-one's light!"
And the dim shore echoed, for many a night,
    The name of the death-cold maid.

Till he hollowed a boat of the birchen bark,
    Which carried him off from shore;
Far, far he followed the meteor spark,
The wind was high and the clouds were dark,
    And the boat returned no more.

But oft, from the Indian hunter's camp
    This lover and maid so true
Are seen at the hour of midnight damp
To cross the Lake by a fire-fly lamp,
    And paddle their white canoe!

RICHARD HARRIS BARHAM (1788-1845)

THE HAND OF GLORY

On the lone bleak moor, At the midnight hour,
Beneath the Gallows Tree,
    Hand in hand The Murderers stand,
By one, by two, by three!
And the Moon that night With a grey, cold light
Each baleful object tips;
    One half of her form Is seen through the storm,
The other half's hid in Eclipse!
And the cold Wind howls, And the Thunder growls,
And the lightning is broad and bright;
    And altogether It's very bad weather,

And an unpleasant sort of a night!
  'Now mount who list, And close by the wrist,
Sever me quickly the Dead Man's fist!
Now climb who dare Where he swings in air
And pluck me five locks of the Dead Man's hair!'

There's an old woman dwells upon Tappington Moor,
She hath years on her back at the least fourscore,
And some people fancy a great many more;
  Her nose it is hook'd, Her back it is crook'd,
  Her eyes blear and red: On the top of her head
  Is a mutch, and on that A shocking bad hat
Extinguisher-shaped, the brim narrow and flat!
Then,—My Gracious!—her beard!—it would sadly perplex
A spectator at first to distinguish her sex;
Nor, I'll venture to say, without scrutiny could he
Pronounce her, off-handed, a Punch or a Judy.
Did you see her, in short, that mud-hovel within,
With her knees to her nose, and her nose to her chin,
Leering up with that queer, indescribable grin,
You'd lift up your hands in amazement, and cry,
'—Well!—I never *did* see such a regular Guy!'

  And now before That old Woman's door,
  Where nought that's good may be,
    Hand in hand The Murderers stand,
  By one, by two, by three!
Oh! 'tis a horrible sight to view,
In that horrible hovel, that horrible crew,
By the pale blue glare of that flickering flame,
Doing the deed that hath never a name!
  'Tis awful to hear Those words of fear!
The prayer mutter'd backwards, and said with a sneer!
(Matthew Hopkins himself has assured us that when

A witch says her prayers, she begins with 'Amen.')—
    'Tis awful to see   On that old Woman's knee
The dead, shrivell'd hand, as she clasps it with glee!—
    And now with care,   The five locks of hair
From the skull of the Gentleman dangling up there,
    With the grease and the fat   Of a black Tom Cat
    She hastens to mix,   And to twist into wicks,
And one on the thumb and each finger to fix.—
(For another receipt the same charm to prepare,
Consult Mr. Ainsworth and *Petit Albert.*)

    Now open lock   To the Dead Man's knock!
    Fly bolt, and bar, and band!—
    Nor move, nor swerve,   Joint, muscle, or nerve,
    At the spell of the dead man's hand!
Sleep all who sleep!—Wake all who wake!—
But be as the Dead for the Dead Man's sake!

All is silent! all is still,
Save the ceaseless moan of the bubbling rill
As it wells, from the bosom of Tappinton Hill,
    And in Tappington Hall   Great and Small,
Gentle and Simple, Squire and Groom,
Each one hath sought his separate room,
And sleep her dark mantle hath o'er them cast,
For the midnight hour hath long been past!
All is darksome in earth and sky,
Save, from yon casement, narrow and high,
    A quivering beam   On the tiny stream
Plays, like some taper's fitful gleam
By one that is watching wearily.

Within that casement, narrow and high,
In his secret lair, where none may spy,

Sits one whose brow is wrinkled with care,
And the thin grey locks of his failing hair
Have left his little bald pate all bare;
    For his full-bottom'd wig   Hangs, bushy and big,
On the top of his old-fashion'd, high-backed chair.
    Unbraced are his clothes,   Ungarter'd his hose,
His gown is bedizen'd with tulip and rose,
Flowers of remarkable size and hue,
Flowers such as Eden never knew;
—And there by many a sparkling heap
    Of the good red gold,   The tale is told
What powerful spell avails to keep
That careworn man from his needful sleep!

Haply, he deems no eye can see
As he gloats on his treasure greedily,—
    The shining store   Of glittering ore,
The fair rose-noble, the bright moidore,
And the broad Double-Joe from ayont the sea,—
But there's one that watches as well as he;
    For, wakeful and sly,   In a closet hard by,
On his truckle bed lieth a little Foot-page,
A boy who's uncommonly sharp of his age,
    Like young Master Horner,   Who erst in a corner
    Sat eating a Christmas pie:
And, while that Old Gentleman's counting his hoards,
Little Hugh peeps through a crack in the boards!

———————

    There's a voice in the air,   There's a step on the stair,
The old man starts in his cane-back'd chair;
    At the first faint sound   He gazes around,
And holds up his dip of sixteen to the pound.
    Then half arose   From beside his toes
His little pug-dog with his little pug nose,

But, ere he can vent one inquisitive sniff,
That little pug-dog stands stark and stiff,
   For low, yet clear, Now fall on the ear
—Where once pronounced for ever they dwell—
The unholy words of the Dead Man's spell!

   'Open lock To the Dead Man's knock!
  Fly bolt, and bar, and band!—
    Nor move, nor swerve, Joint, muscle, or nerve,
  At the spell of the Dead Man's hand!
Sleep all who sleep!—Wake all who wake!—
But be as the Dead for the Dead Man's sake!'

Not lock, nor bolt, nor bar avails,
Nor stout oak panel thick-studded with nails,
Heavy and harsh the hinges creak,
Though they had been oil'd in the course of the week;
The door opens wide as wide may be,
And there they stand, That murderous band,
   Lit by the light of that GLORIOUS HAND,
    By one!—by two!—by three!

They have pass'd through the porch, they have pass'd through
    the hall,
Where the Porter sat snoring against the wall;
  The very snore froze In his very snub nose,
You'd have verily deem'd he had snored his last
When the GLORIOUS HAND by the side of him pass'd!
E'en the little wee mouse, as it ran o'er the mat,
At the top of its speed to escape from the cat,
  Though half dead with affright, Paused in its flight;
And the cat that was chasing that little wee thing
Lay crouch'd as a statue in act to spring!
  And now they are there, On the head of the stair,
And the long crooked whittle is gleaming and bare!

—I really don't think any money would bribe
Me the horrible scene that ensued to describe,
   Or the wild, wild glare of that old man's eye,
   His dumb despair, and deep agony.

The kid from the pen, and the lamb from the fold,
Unmoved may the blade of the butcher behold;
They dream not—ah, happier they!—that the knife,
Though uplifted, can menace their innocent life;
It falls;—the frail thread of their being is riven,
They dread not, suspect not, the blow till 'tis given.—
But, oh! what a thing 'tis to see and to know
That the bare knife is raised in the hand of the foe,
Without hope to repel, or to ward off the blow!—
—Enough!—let's pass over as fast as we can
The fate of that grey, that unhappy old man!

   But fancy poor Hugh,   Aghast at the view,
   Powerless alike to speak or to do!
   In vain doth he try   To open the eye
That is shut, or close that which is clapt to the chink
Though he'd give all the world to be able to wink!—
   No!—for all that this world can give or refuse,
I would not be now in that little boy's shoes,
Or indeed any garment at all that is Hugh's!
—'Tis lucky for him that the chink in the wall
He has peep'd through so long, is so narrow and small!

   Wailing voices, sounds of woe
      Such as follow departing friends,
   That fatal night around Tappington go,
         Its long-drawn roofs and its gable ends:
   Ethereal Spirits, gentle and good,
      Aye weep and lament o'er a deed of blood.

'Tis early dawn—the morn is grey,
And the clouds and the tempest have pass'd away,
And all things betoken a very fine day;
But, while the lark her carol is singing,
Shrieks and screams are through Tappington ringing!
   Upstarting all, Great and small.
Each one who's found within Tappington Hall,
Gentle and Simple, Squire or Groom,
All seek at once that old Gentleman's room;
   And there, on the floor, Drench'd in its gore,
A ghastly corpse lies exposed to the view,
Carotid and jugular both cut through!
    And there, by its side, 'Mid the crimson tide,
Kneels a little Foot-page of tenderest years;
Adown his pale cheek the fast-falling tears
Are coursing each other round and big,
And he's stanching the blood with a full-bottom'd wig,
Alas! and alack for his stanching!—'tis plain,
As anatomists tell us, that never again
Shall life revisit the foully slain,
   When once they've been cut through the jugular vein.

There's a hue and a cry through the County of Kent,
And in chase of the cut-throats a Constable's sent,
But no one can tell the man which way they went:
There's a little Foot-page with that Constable goes,
And a little pug-dog with a little pug nose.

   In Rochester town, At the sign of the Crown,
Three shabby-genteel men are just sitting down
To a fat stubble-goose, with potatoes done brown;
   When a little Foot-page Rushes in, in a rage,
Upsetting the apple-sauce, onions, and sage.

That little Foot-page takes the first by the throat,
And a little pug-dog takes the next by the coat,
And a Constable seizes the one more remote;
And fair rose-nobles and broad moidores,
The Waiter pulls out of their pockets by scores,
  And the Boots and the Chambermaids run in and stare;
And the Constable says, with a dignified air,
  'You're *wanted,* Gen'lemen, one and all,
For that 'ere precious lark at Tappington Hall!'

There's a black gibbet frowns upon Tappington Moor,
Where a former black gibbet has frowned before;
  It is as black as black may be,
    And murderers there   Are dangling in air,
By one!—by two!—by three!

There's a horrid old hag in a steeple-crown'd hat,
Round her neck they have tied to a hempen cravat
A dead Man's hand, and a dead Tom Cat!
They have tied up her thumbs, they have tieds up her toes,
  They have tied up her eyes, they have tied up her limbs:
Into Tappington mill-dam souse she goes,
    With a whoop and a halloo!—'She swims!—She swims!'
      They have dragg'd her to land,   And every one's hand,
    Is grasping a faggot, a billet, or brand,
When a queer-looking horseman, drest all in black,
Snatches up that old harridan just like a sack
To the crupper behind him, puts spurs to his hack,
Makes a dash through the crowd, and is off in a crack!
  No one can tell,   Though they guess pretty well,
Which way that grim rider and old woman go,
For all see he's a sort of infernal Ducrow;
  And she scream'd so, and cried, We may fairly decide
That the old woman did not much relish her ride!

This truest of stories confirms beyond doubt
That truest of adages—'Murder will out!'
In vain may the blood-spiller 'double' and fly,
In vain even witchcraft and sorcery try:
Although for a time he may 'scape, by-and-by
He'll sure to be caught by a Hugh and a Cry!

JOHANN WOLFGANG VON GOETHE (1789-1832)

THE ERL KING

Who rideth so late through the night-wind wild?
It is the father with his child;
He has the little one well in his arm;
He holds him safe, and he folds him warm.

My son, why hidest thy face so shy?
Seest thou not, father, the Erl-king nigh?
The Erl-king, with train and crown?
It is a wreath of mist, my son.

"Come, lovely boy, come, go with me;
Such merry plays I'll play with thee;
Many a bright flower grows on the strand,
And my mother has many a gay garment at hand."

My father, my father, and dost thou not hear
What the Erl-king whispers in my ear?—
Be quiet, my darling, be quiet, my child;
Through withered leaves the wind howls wild.

"Come, lovely boy, wilt thou go with me?
My daughters fair shall wait on thee;

My daughters their nightly revels keep;
They'll sing, and they'll dance, and they'll rock thee to sleep."

My father, my father, and seest thou not
The Erl-king's daughters in yon dim spot?—
My son, my son, I see and I know
'Tis the old gray willow that shimmers so.

"I love thee; thy beauty has ravished my sense;
And, willing or not, I will carry thee hence."
O Father, the Erl-king now puts forth his arm!
O Father, the Erl-king has done me harm!

The father shudders; he hurries on;
And faster he holds his moaning son;
He reaches home with fear and dread,
And lo! in his arms the child is dead.

—Translated by Frederic H. Hedge

JOHN KEATS (1795-1845)

LA BELLE DAME SANS MERCI

O what can ail thee, knight-at-arms,
 Alone and palely loitering?
The sedge has wither'd from the lake,
 And no birds sing.

O what can ail thee, knight-at-arms,
 So haggard and so woe-begone?
The squirrel's granary is full,
 And the harvest's done.

I see a lily on thy brow
  With anguish moist and fever dew;
And on thy cheeks a fading rose
  Fast withereth too.

I met a lady in the meads,
  Full beautiful—a faëry's child,
Her hair was long, her foot was light,
  And her eyes were wild.

I made a garland for her head,
  And bracelets too, and fragrant zone;
She look'd at me as she did love,
  And made sweet moan.

I set her on my pacing steed,
  And nothing else saw all day long,
For sidelong would she bend, and sing
  A faëry's song.

She found me roots of relish sweet,
  And honey wild, and manna dew,
And sure in language strange she said,
  I love thee true!

She took me to her elfin grot,
  And there she wept and sigh'd full sore,
And there I shut her wild, wild eyes
  With kisses four.

And there she lull'd me asleep,
  And there I dream'd, ah! woe betide!
The latest dream I ever dream'd
  On the cold hill's side.

I saw pale kings and princes too,
    Pale warriors, death-pale were they all;
They cried—La Belle Dame sans Merci
    Hath thee in thrall!

I saw their starved lips in the gloam,
    With horrid warning gapèd wide,
And I awoke and found me here,
    On the cold hill's side.

And this is why I sojourn here,
    Alone and palely loitering,
Though the sedge is wither'd from the lake,
    And no birds sing.

THOMAS HOOD (1799-1845)

THE HAUNTED HOUSE

PART I

Some dreams we have are nothing else but dreams,
Unnatural, and full of contradictions;
Yet others of our most romantic schemes
Are something more than fictions.

It might be only on enchanted ground;
It might be merely by a thought's expansion;
But, in the spirit or the flesh, I found
An old deserted Mansion.

A residence for woman, child, and man,
A dwelling place,—and yet no habitation;
A House,—but under some prodigious ban
Of Excommunication.

Unhinged the iron gates half open hung,
Jarr'd by the gusty gales of many winters,
That from its crumbled pedestal had flung
One marble globe in splinters.

No dog was at the threshold, great or small;
No pigeon on the roof—no household creature—
No cat demurely dozing on the wall—
Not one domestic feature.

No human figure stirr'd, to go or come,
No face looked forth from shut or open casement;
No chimney smoked—there was no sign of Home
From parapet to basement.

With shatter'd panes the grassy court was starr'd;
The time-worn coping-stone had tumbled after!
And thro' the ragged roof the sky shone, barr'd
With naked beam and rafter.

O'er all there hung a shadow and a fear;
A sense of mystery the spirit daunted,
And said, as plain as whisper in the ear,
The place is Haunted!

The flow'r grew wild and rankly as the weed,
Roses with thistles struggled for espial,
And vagrant plants of parasitic breed,
Had overgrown the Dial.

But gay or gloomy, steadfast or infirm,
No heart was there to heed the hour's duration;
All times and tides were lost in one long term
Of stagnant desolation.

The wren had built within the Porch, she found
Its quiet loneliness so sure and thorough;
And on the lawn,—within its turfy mound,—
The rabbit made his burrow.

The rabbit wild and grey, that flitted thro'
The shrubby clumps, and frisk'd, and sat, and vanish'd
But leisurely and bold, as if he knew
His enemy was banish'd.

The wary crow,—the pheasant from the woods—
Lull'd by the still and everlasting sameness,
Close to the mansion, like domestic broods,
Fed with a "shocking tameness."

The coot was swimming in the reedy pond,
Beside the water-hen, so soon affrighted;
And in the weedy moat the heron, fond
Of solitude, alighted.

The moping heron, motionless and stiff,
That on a stone, as silently and stilly,
Stood, an apparent sentinel, as if
To guard the water-lily.

No sound was heard except, from far away,
The ringing of the witwall's shrilly laughter,
Or, now and then, the chatter of the jay,
That Echo murmur'd after.

But Echo never mock'd the human tongue;
Some weighty crime that Heaven could not pardon,
A secret curse on that old Building hung
And its deserted Garden.

The beds were all untouch'd by hand or tool;
No footstep mark'd the damp and mossy gravel,
Each walk as green as is the mantled pool,
For want of Human travel.

The vine unpruned, and the neglected peach,
Droop'd from the wall with which they used to grapple;
And on the kanker'd tree, in easy reach,
Rotted the golden apple.

But awfully the truant shunn'd the ground,
The vagrant kept aloof, and daring poacher,
In spite of gaps that thro' the fences round
Invited the encroacher.

For over all there hung a cloud of fear,
A sense of mystery the spirit daunted,
And said, as plain as whisper in the ear,
The place is Haunted!

The pear and quince lay squander'd on the grass;
The mould was purple with unheaded showers
Of bloomy plums—a Wilderness it was
Of fruits, and weeds, and flowers!

The marigold amidst the nettles blew,
The gourd embraced the rose-bush in its ramble;
The thistle and the stock together grew,
The hollyhock and bramble.

The bear-bine with the lilac interlaced,
The sturdy burdock choked its slender neighbour,
The spicy pink. All tokens were effaced
Of human care and labour.

The very yew Formality had train'd
To such a rigid pyramidal stature,
For want of trimming had almost regain'd
The raggedness of nature.

The Fountain was a-dry—neglect and time
Had marr'd the work of artisan and mason,
And efts and croaking frogs, begot of slime,
Sprawl'd in the ruin'd basin.

The Statue, fallen from its marble base,
Amidst the refuse leaves, and herbage rotten,
Lay like the Idol of some bygone race,
Its name and rites forgotten.

On ev'ry side the aspect was the same,
All ruin'd, desolate, forlorn and savage:
No hand or foot within the precinct came
To rectify or ravage.

For over all there hung a cloud of fear,
A sense of mystery the spirit daunted,
And said, as plain as whisper in the ear,
The place is Haunted!

Part II

O very gloomy is the House of Woe,
Where tears are falling while the bell is knelling,
With all the dark solemnities which show
That Death is in the dwelling.

O very, very dreary is the room
Where Love, domestic Love, no longer nestles,
But, smitten by the common stroke of doom,
The Corpse lies on the trestles!

But House of Woe, and hearse, and sable pall,
The narrow home of the departed mortal,
Ne'er look'd so gloomy as that Ghostly Hall,
With its deserted portal!

The centipede along the threshold crept,
The cobweb hung across in mazy tangle,
And in its winding sheet the maggot slept,
At every nook and angle.

The keyhole lodged the earwig and her brood,
The emmets of the steps had old possession,
And march'd in search of their diurnal food
In undisturb'd procession.

As undisturb'd as the prehensile cell
Of moth or maggot, or the spider's tissue,
For never foot upon that threshold fell,
To enter or to issue.

O'er all there hung the shadow of a fear,
A sense of mystery the spirit daunted,
And said, as plain as whisper in the ear,
The place is Haunted!

Howbeit, the door I push'd—or so I dream'd—
Which slowly, slowly gaped,—the hinges creaking
With such a rusty eloquence, it seem'd
That Time himself was speaking.

But Time was dumb within the Mansion old,
Or left his tale to the heraldic banners,
That hung from the corroded walls, and told
Of former men and manners:—

Those tatter'd flags, that with the open'd door,
Seem'd the old wave of battle to remember,
While fallen fragments danced upon the floor,
Like dead leaves in December.

The startled bats flew out,—bird after bird,
The screech-owl overhead began to flutter,
And seem'd to mock the cry that she had heard
Some dying victim utter!

A shriek that echo'd from the joisted roof,
And up the stair, and further still and further,
Till in some ringing chamber far aloof
It ceased its tale of murther!

Meanwhile the rusty armour rattled round,
The banner shudder'd, and the ragged streamer;
All things the horrid tenor of the sound
Acknowledged with a tremor.

The antlers, where the helmet hung, and belt,
Stirr'd as the tempest stirs the forest branches,
Or as the stag had trembled when he felt
The bloodhound at his haunches.

The window jingled in its crumbled frame,
And thro' its many gaps of destitution
Dolorous moans and hollow sighings came,
Like those of dissolution.

The woodlouse dropp'd, and roll'd into a ball,
Touch'd by some impulse occult or mechanic;
And nameless beetles ran along the wall
In universal panic.

The subtle spider that from overhead
Hung like a spy on human guilt and error,
Suddenly turn'd and up its slender thread
Ran with a nimble terror.

The very stains and fractures on the wall
Assuming features solemn and terrific,
Hinted some Tragedy of that old Hall,
Lock'd up in hieroglyphic.

Some tale that might, perchance, have solved the doubt,
Wherefore amongst those flags so dull and livid,
The banner of the BLOODY HAND shone out
So ominously vivid.

Some key to that inscrutable appeal,
Which made the very frame of Nature quiver;
And every thrilling nerve and fibre feel
So ague-like a shiver.

For over all there hung a cloud of fear,
A sense of mystery the spirit daunted;
And said, as plain as whisper in the ear,
The place is Haunted!

If but a rat had linger'd in the house,
To lure the thought into a social channel!
But not a rat remain'd, or tiny mouse,
To squeak behind the panel.

Huge drops roll'd down the walls, as if they wept;
And where the cricket used to chirp so shrilly,
The toad was squatting, and the lizard crept
On that damp hearth and chilly.

For years no cheerful blaze had sparkled there,
Or glanced on coat of buff or knightly metal;
The slug was crawling on the vacant chair,—
The snail upon the settle.

The floor was redolent of mould and must,
The fungus in the rotten seams had quicken'd;
While on the oaken table coats of dust
Perennially had thicken'd.

No mark of leathern jack or metal can,
No cup—no horn—no hospitable token,—
All social ties between that board and Man
Had long ago been broken.

There was so foul a rumour in the air,
The shadow of a presence so atrocious:
No human creature could have feasted there,
Even the most ferocious.

For over all there hung a cloud of fear,
A sense of mystery the spirit daunted,
And said, as plain as whisper in the ear,
The place is Haunted!

Part III

'Tis hard for human actions to account,
Whether from reason or from impulse only—
But some internal prompting bade me mount
The gloomy stairs and lonely.

Those gloomy stairs, so dark, and damp, and cold,
With odours as from bones and relics carnal,
Deprived of right, and consecrated mould,
The chapel vault or charnel.

Those dreary stairs, where with the sounding stress
Of ev'ry step so many echoes blended,
The mind, with dark misgivings, feared to guess
How many feet ascended.

The tempest with its spoils had drifted in,
Till each unwholesome stone was darkly spotted,
As thickly as the leopard's dappled skin,
With leaves that rankly rotted.

The air was thick—and in the upper gloom
The bat—or something in its shape—was winging;
And on the wall, as chilly as a tomb,
The Death's-Head moth was clinging.

That mystic moth, which, with a sense profound
Of all unholy presence, augurs truly;
And with a grim significance flits round
The taper burning bluely.

Such omens in the place there seem'd to be,
At ev'ry crooked turn, or on the landing,
The straining eyeball was prepared to see
Some Apparition standing.

For over all there hung a cloud of fear,
A sense of mystery the spirit daunted,
And said, as plain as whisper in the ear,
The place is Haunted!

Yet no portentous Shape the sight amazed;
Each object plain, and tangible, and valid;
But from their tarnish'd frames dark Figures gazed,
And Faces spectre-pallid.

Not merely with the mimic life that lies
Within the compass of Art's simulation;
Their souls were looking thro' their painted eyes
With awful speculation.

On ev'ry lip a speechless horror dwelt;
On ev'ry brow the burthen of affliction;
The old Ancestral Spirits knew and felt
The House's malediction.

Such earnest woe their features overcast,
They might have stirr'd, or sigh'd, or wept, or spoken;
But, save the hollow moaning of the blast,
The stillness was unbroken.

No other sound or stir of life was there,
Except my steps in solitary clamber,
From flight to flight, from humid stair to stair,
From chamber into chamber.

Deserted rooms of luxury and state,
That old magnificence had richly furnish'd
With pictures, cabinets of ancient date,
And carvings gilt and burnish'd.

Rich hangings, storied by the needle's art
With Scripture history, or classic fable;
But all had faded, save one ragged part,
Where Cain was slaying Abel.

The silent waste of mildew and the moth
Had marr'd the tissue with a partial ravage;
But undecaying frown'd upon the cloth
Each feature stern and savage.

The sky was pale; the cloud a thing of doubt;
Some hues were fresh, and some decay'd and duller:
But still the BLOODY HAND shone strangely out
With vehemence of colour!

The BLOODY HAND that with a lurid stain
Shone on the dusty floor, a dismal token,
Projected from the casement's painted pane,
Where all beside was broken.

The BLOODY HAND significant of crime,
That glaring on the old heraldic banner,
Had kept its crimson unimpaired by time,
In such a wondrous manner.

O'er all there hung the shadow of a fear,
A sense of mystery the spirit daunted,
And said, as plain as whisper in the ear,
The place is Haunted!

The Death Watch tick'd behind the panell'd oak,
Inexplicable tremors shook the arras,
And echoes strange and mystical awoke,
The fancy to embarrass.

Prophetic hints that fill'd the soul with dread,
But thro' one gloomy entrance pointing mostly,
The while some secret inspiration said,
That Chamber is the Ghostly!

Across the door no gossamer festoon
Swung pendulous—no web—no dusty fringes,
No silky chrysalis or white cocoon
About its nooks and hinges.

The spider shunn'd the interdicted room,
The moth, the beetle, and fly were banish'd,
And where the sunbeam fell athwart the gloom
The very midge had vanish'd.

One lonely ray that glanced upon a Bed,
As if with awful aim direct and certain,
To show the BLOODY HAND in burning red
Embroidered on the curtain.

And yet no gory stain was on the quilt—
The pillow in its place had slowly rotted;
The floor alone retain'd the trace of guilt,
Those boards obscurely spotted.

Obscurely spotted to the door, and thence
With mazy doubles to the grated casement—
Oh what a tale they told of fear intense,
Of horror and amazement!

What human creature in the dead of night
Had coursed like hunted hare that cruel distance?
Had sought the door, the window in his flight,
Striving for dear existence?

What shrieking Spirit in that bloody room
Its moral frame had violently quitted?—
Across the sunbeam, with a sudden gloom,
A ghostly Shadow flitted.

Across the sunbeam, and along the wall,
But painted on the air so very dimly,
It hardly veil'd the tapestry at all,
Or portrait frowning grimly.

O'er all there hung the shadow of a fear,
A sense of mystery the spirit daunted,
And said, as plain as whisper in the ear,
The place is Haunted!

THE DREAM OF EUGENE ARAM

'Twas in the prime of summer time,
    An evening calm and cool,
And four-and-twenty happy boys
    Came bounding out of school;
There were some that ran, and some that leapt
    Like troutlets in a pool.

Away they sped with gamesome minds
    And souls untouched by sin;
To a level mead they came, and there
    They drove the wickets in:
Pleasantly shone the setting sun
    Over the town of Lynn.

Like sportive deer they coursed about,
    And shouted as they ran,
Turning to mirth all things of earth
    As only boyhood can;
But the usher sat remote from all,
    A melancholy man!

His hat was off, his vest apart,
　To catch heaven's blessèd breeze;
For a burning thought was in his brow,
　And his bosom ill at ease,
So he leaned his head on his hands, and read
　The book between his knees.

Leaf after leaf he turned it o'er,
　Nor ever glanced aside—
For the peace of his soul he read that book
　In the golden eventide;
Much study had made him very lean,
　And pale, and leaden-eyed.

At last he shut the ponderous tome;
　With a fast and fervent grasp
He strained the dusky covers close,
　And fixed the brazen hasp:
"O God! could I so close my mind,
　And clasp it with a clasp!"

Then leaping on his feet upright,
　Some moody turns he took—
Now up the mead, then down the mead,
　And past a shady nook;
And, lo! he saw a little boy
　That pored upon a book.

"My gentle lad, what is 't you read—
　Romance or fairy fable?
Or is it some historic page,
　O kings and crowns unstable?"
The young boy gave an upward glance—
　"It is 'The Death of Abel.'"

The usher took six hasty strides,
  As smit with sudden pain—
Six hasty strides beyond the place,
  Then slowly back again;
And down he sat besides the lad,
  And talked with him of Cain;

And, long since then, of bloody men,
  Whose deeds tradition saves;
And lonely folk cut off unseen,
  And hid in sudden graves;
And horrid stabs, in groves forlorn;
  And murders done in caves;

And how the sprites of injured men
  Shriek upward from the sod;
Ay, how the ghostly hand will point
  To show the burial-clod;
And unknown facts of guilty acts
  Are seen in dreams from God.

He told how murderers walked the earth
  Beneath the curse of Cain—
With crimson clouds before their eyes,
  And flames about their brain;
For blood has left upon their souls
  Its everlasting stain!

"And well," quoth he, "I know, for truth,
  Their pangs must be extreme—
Woe, woe, unutterable woe!—
  Who spill life's sacred stream!
For why? Methought, last night I wrought
  A murder, in a dream!

"One that had never done me wrong—
   A feeble man and old;
I led him to a lonely field—
   The moon shone clear and cold;
Now here, said I, this man shall die;
   And I will have his gold!

"Two sudden blows with a ragged stick,
   And one with a heavy stone,
One hurried gash with a hasty knife—
   And then the deed was done:
There was nothing lying at my feet
   But lifeless flesh and bone!

"Nothing but lifeless flesh and bone,
   That could not do me ill;
And yet I feared him all the more
   For lying there so still:
There was a manhood in his look
   That murder could not kill!

"And lo! the universal air
   Seemed lit with ghastly flame—
Ten thousand thousand dreadful eyes
   Were looking down in blame;
I took the dead man by his hand,
   And called upon his name.

"O God; it made me quake to see
   Such sense within the slain;
But when I touched the lifeless clay,
   The blood gushed out amain!
For every clot a burning spot
   Was scorching in my brain!

"My head was like an ardent coal,
  My heart as solid ice;
My wretched, wretched soul, I knew,
  Was at the Devil's price:
A dozen times I groaned—the dead
  Had never groaned but twice.

"And now, from forth the frowning sky,
  From the heaven's topmost height,
I heard a voice—the awful voice
  Of the blood-avenging sprite;
'Thou guilty man! take up thy dead,
  And hide it from my sight!'

"I took the dreary body up,
  And cast it in a stream—
The sluggish water black as ink,
  The depth was so extreme:
My gentle boy, remember, this
  Is nothing but a dream!

"Down went the corpse with a hollow plunge,
  And vanished in the pool;
Anon I cleansed my bloody hands,
  And washed my forehead cool,
And sat among the urchins young,
  That evening, in the school.

"O Heaven! to think of their white souls,
  And mine so black and grim!
I could not share a childish prayer,
  Nor join in evening hymn;
Like a devil of the pit I seemed,
  'Mid holy cherubim!

"And peace went with them, one and all,
   And each calm pillow spread;
But Guilt was my grim chamberlain,
   That lighted me to bed,
And drew my midnight curtains round
   With fingers bloody red!

"All night I lay in agony,
   In anguish dark and deep;
My fevered eyes I dared not close,
   But stared aghast at Sleep:
For sin had rendered unto her
   The keys of hell to keep!

"All night I lay in agony,
   From weary chime to chime;
With one besetting horrid hint
   That racked me all the time—
A mighty yearning, like the first
   Fierce impulse unto crime—

"One stern tyrannic thought, that made
   All other thoughts its slave!
Stronger and stronger every pulse
   Did that temptation crave—
Still urging me to go and see
   The dead man in his grave!

"Heavily I rose up, as soon
   As light was in the sky,
And sought the black accursèd pool
   With a wild, misgiving eye:
And I saw the dead in the river-bed,
   For the faithless stream was dry.

"Merrily rose the lark, and shook
  The dew-drop from its wing;
But I never marked its morning flight,
  I never heard it sing:
For I was stooping once again
  Under the horrid thing.

"With breathless speed, like a soul in chase,
  I took him up and ran;
There was no time to dig a grave
  Before the day began—
In a lonesome wood, with heaps of leaves,
  I hid the murdered man!

"And all that day I read in school,
  But my thought was otherwhere;
As soon as the midday task was done,
  In secret I was there—
And a mighty wind had swept the leaves,
  And still the corpse was bare!

"Then down I cast me on my face,
  And first began to weep,
For I knew my secret then was one
  That earth refused to keep—
On land or sea, though he should be
  Ten thousand fathoms deep.

"So wills the fierce avenging sprite,
  Till blood for blood atones!
Ay, though he's buried in a cave,
  And trodden down with stones,
And years have rotted off his flesh—
  The world shall see his bones!

"O God! that horrid, horrid dream
  Besets me now awake!
Again—again, with dizzy brain,
  The human life I take;
And my red right hand grows raging hot,
  Like Cranmer's at the stake.

"And still no peace for the restless clay
  Will wave or mold allow;
The horrid thing pursues my soul—
  It stands before me now!"
The fearful boy looked up, and saw
  Huge drops upon his brow.

That very night, while gentle sleep
  The urchin eyelids kissed,
Two stern-faced men set out from Lynn,
  Through the cold and heavy mist;
And Eugene Aram walked between,
  With gyves upon his wrist.

POMPEY'S GHOST

'Twas twelve o'clock, not twelve at night,
  But twelve o'clock at noon;
Because the sun was shining bright
  And not the silver moon.
A proper time for friends to call,
  Or pots, or penny-post;
When lo! as Phoebe sat at work,
  She saw her Pompey's ghost!

Now when a female has a call
    From people that are dead,
Like Paris ladies, she receives
    Her visitors in bed.
But Pompey's spirit would not come
    Like spirits that are white,
Because he was a Blackamoor,
    And wouldn't show at night!

But of all unexpected things
    That happen to us here,
The most unpleasant is a rise
    In what is very dear.
So Phoebe screamed an awful scream
    To prove the seaman's text,
That after black appearances,
    White squalls will follow next.

"O Phoebe dear! Oh, Phoebe dear!
    Don't go and scream or faint;
You think because I'm black, I am
    The Devil, but I ain't!
Behind the heels of Lady Lambe
    I walked while I had breath,
But that is past, and I am now
    A-walking after death!

"No murder, though, I come to tell,
    By base and bloody crime;
So, Phoebe dear, put off your fits
    To some more fitting time.
No coroner, like a boatswain's mate,
    My body need attack,
With his round dozen to find out
    Why I have died so black.

"One Sunday, shortly after tea,
　　My skin began to burn,
As if I had in my inside
　　A heater like an urn.
Delirious in the night I grew,
　　And as I lay in bed,
They say I gathered all the wool
　　You see upon my head.

"His lordship for his doctor sent,
　　My treatment to begin;
I wish that he had called him out
　　Before he called him in!
For though to physic he was bred,
　　And passed at Surgeons' Hall,
To make his post a sinecure,
　　He never cured at all!

"The Doctor looked about my breast
　　And then about my back,
And then he shook his head and said,
　　'Your case looks very black'
At first he sent me hot cayenne,
And then gamboge to swallow.
But still my fever would not turn
　　To scarlet or to yellow!

"With madder and with tumeric,
　　He made his next attack;
But neither he nor all his drugs
　　Could stop my dying black.
At last I got so sick of life,
　　And sick of being dosed,
One Monday morning I gave up
　　My physic and the ghost!

"Oh, Phoebe dear, what pain it was
   To sever every tie!
You know black beetles feel as much
   As giants when they die.
And if there is a bridal bed,
   Or bride of little worth,
It's lying in a bed of mould,
   Along with Mother Earth.

"Alas! Some happy, happy day,
   In church I hoped to stand,
And like a muff of sable skin
   Receive your lily hand.
But sternly with that piebald match,
   My fate untimely clashes;
For now, like Pompey-double-i,
   I'm sleeping in my ashes!

"And now farewell! a last farewell!
   I'm wanted down below,
And have but time enough to add
   One word before I go—
In mourning crepe and bombazine
   Ne'er spend your precious pelf;
Don't go in black for me—for I
   Can do it for myself.

"Henceforth within my grave I rest,
   But Death, who there inherits,
Allowed my spirit leave to come,
   You seemed so near your spirits:
But do not sigh, and do not cry,
   By grief too much engrossed,
Nor for a ghost of color turn
   The color of a ghost!

"Again, farewell, my Phoebe dear!
    Once more a last adieu!
For I must make myself as scarce
    As swans of sable hue."
From black to gray, from gray to nought
    The shape began to fade—
And like an egg, though not so white,
    The ghost was newly laid!

THE GHOST

In Middle Row, some years ago,
    There lived one Mr. Brown;
And many folks considered him
    The stoutest man in town.

But Brown and stout will both wear out—
    One Friday he died hard,
And left a widow'd wife to mourn
    At twenty pence a yard.

Now widow B. in two short months
    Thought mourning quite a tax;
And wished, like Mr. Wilberforce,
    To *manumit* her blacks.

With Mr. Street she soon was sweet;
    The thing came thus about:
She asked him in at home, and then
    At church, he asked her out!

Assurance such as this the man
    In ashes could not stand;
So like a Phoenix he rose up
    Against the Hand in Hand!

One dreary night the angry sprite
 Appeared before her view;
It came a little after one,
 But she was after two!

"Oh, Mrs. B., O Mrs. B.,
 Are these your sorrow's deeds,
Already getting up a flame
 To burn our widows' weeds?

"It's not so long since I have left
 For aye the mortal scene;
My memory—like Roger's—
 Should still be bound in green!

"Yet if my face you still retrace
 I almost have a doubt—
I'm like an old Forget-Me-Not
 With all the leaves torn out!

"To think that on that finger-joint
 Another pledge should cling;
O Bess! upon my very soul
 It struck like 'Knock and Ring.'

"A ton of marble on my breast
 Can't hinder my return;
Your conduct, ma'am, has set my blood
 A-boiling in its urn!

"Remember, oh, remember how
 The marriage rite did run,—
If ever we one flesh should be
 'Tis now—when I have none!

"And you, Sir—once a bosom friend—
   Of perjured faith convict,
As ghostly toe can give no blow,
   Consider yourself kicked.

"A hollow voice is all I have,
   But this I tell you plain,
Marry come up! you marry, ma'am,
   And I'll come up again."

More he had said, but chanticleer
   The spritely shade did shock
With sudden crow—and off he went
   Like fowling piece at cock!

THOMAS LOVELL BEDDOES (1803-1849)

THE PHANTOM-WOOER

A ghost, that loved a lady fair,
Ever in the starry air
   Of midnight at her pillow stood;
And, with a sweetness skies above
The luring words of human love,
   Her soul the phantom wooed.
Sweet and sweet is their poisoned note,
The little snakes of silver throat,
In mossy skulls that nest and lie,
Ever singing "die, oh! die."

Young soul put off your flesh, and come
With me into the quiet tomb,

Our bed is lovely, dark, and sweet;
The earth will swing us, as she goes,
Beneath our coverlid of snows,
    And the warm leaden sheet.
Dear and dear is their poisoned note,
The little snakes of silver throat,
In mossy skulls that nest and lie,
Ever singing "die, oh! die."

THE GHOSTS' MOONSHINE

It is midnight, my wedded;
  Let us lie under
The tempest bright, my dreaded,
  In the warm thunder:

Tremble and weep not! What can you fear?
    My heart's best wish is thine,—
  That thou wert white, and bedded
      On the softest bier,
        In the ghosts' moonshine.
      Is that the wind? No, no;
      Only two devils, that blow
      Through the murderer's ribs to and fro,
        In the ghosts' moonshine.

    Who is there, she said afraid, yet
      Stirring and awaking
  The poor old dead? His spade it
      Is only making—
(Tremble and weep not! What do you crave?)
    Where yonder grasses twine,
  A pleasant bed, my maid, that

Children call a grave
    In the cold moonshine.
Is that the wind? No, no;
Only two devils, that blow
Through the murderer's ribs to and fro,
    In the ghosts' moonshine.

What dost thou strain above her
    Lovely throat's whiteness?
A silken chain, to cover
Her bosom's brightness?
Tremble and weep not: what dost thou fear?
    —My blood is spilt like wine,
Thou hast strangled and slain me, lover,
    Thou hast stabbed me, dear,

    In the ghosts' moonshine.
Is that the wind? No, no;
Only her goblin doth blow
Through the murderer's ribs to and fro,
    In its own moonshine.

HENRY WADSWORTH LONGFELLOW (1807-1882)

THE PHANTOM SHIP

In Mather's Magnalia Christi,
    Of the old colonial time,
May be found in prose the legend
    That is here set down in rhyme.

A ship sailed from New Haven,
    And the keen and frosty airs,
That filled her sails at parting,
    Were heavy with good men's prayers.

"O Lord! if it be thy pleasure"—
    Thus prayed the old divine—
"To bury our friends in the ocean,
    Take them, for they are thine!"

But Master Lamberton muttered,
    And under his breath said he,
"This ship is so crank and walty,
    I fear our grave she will be!"

And the ships that came from England,
    When the winter months were gone,
Brought no tidings of this vessel
    Nor of Master Lamberton

This put the people to praying
    That the Lord would let them hear
What in his greater wisdom
    He had done with friends so dear.

And at last their prayers were answered:
    It was in the month of June,
An hour before the sunset
    Of a windy afternoon,

When, steadily steering landward,
    A ship was seen below,
And they knew it was Lamberton, Master,
    Who sailed so long ago.

On she came, with a cloud of canvas,
   Right against the wind that blew
Until the eye could distinguish
   The faces of the crew.

Then fell her straining topmasts,
   Hanging tangled in the shrouds,
And her sails were loosened and lifted,
   And blown away like clouds.

And the masts, with all their rigging,
   Fell slowly, one by one,
And the hulk dilated and vanished,
   As a sea-mist in the sun!

And the people who saw this marvel
   Each said unto his friend,
That this was the mould of their vessel,
   And thus her tragic end.

And the pastor of the village
   Gave thanks to God in prayer,
That, to quiet their troubled spirits,
   He had sent this Ship of Air.

THE LEGEND OF RABBI BEN LEVI

Rabbi Ben Levi, on the Sabbath, read
A volume of the Law, in which it said,
"No man shall look upon my face and live"
And as he read, he prayed that God would give
His faithful servant grace with mortal eye
To look upon His face and yet not die.

Then fell a sudden shadow on the page,
And, lifting up his eyes, grown dim with age,
He saw the Angel of Death before him stand,
Holding a naked sword in his right hand.

Rabbi Ben Levi was a righteous man,
Yet through his veins a chill of terror ran
With trembling voice he said, "What wilt thou here?"
The Angel answered, "Lo! the time draws near
When thou must die; yet first, by God's decree,
Whate'er thou askest shall be granted thee."
Replied the Rabbi, "Let these living eyes
First look upon my place in Paradise."

Then said the Angel, "Come with me and look."
Rabbi Ben Levi closed the sacred book,
And rising, and uplifting his gray head,
"Give me thy sword," he to the Angel said,
"Lest thou shouldst fall upon me by the way."
The Angel smiled and hastened to obey,
Then led him forth to the Celestial Town,
And set him on the wall, whence, gazing down,
Rabbi Ben Levi, with his living eyes,
Might look upon his place in Paradise.

Then straight into the city of the Lord
The Rabbi leaped with the Death-Angel's sword,
And through the streets there swept a sudden breath
Of something there unknown, which men call death.
Meanwhile the Angel stayed without, and cried,
"Come back!" To which the Rabbi's voice replied,
"No! in the name of God, whom I adore,
I swear that hence I will depart no more!"

Then all the Angels cried, "O Holy One,
See what the son of Levi here hath done!
The kingdom of Heaven he takes by violence,
And in Thy name refuses to go hence!"
The Lord replied, "My Angels, be not wroth;
Did e'er the son of Levi break his oath?
Let him remain; for he with mortal eye
Shall look upon my face and yet not die."

Beyond the outer wall the Angel of Death
Heard the great voice, and said, with panting breath,
"Give back the sword, and let me go my way."
Whereat the Rabbi paused, and answered, "Nay!
Anguish enough already hath it caused
Among the sons of men." And while he paused
He heard the awful mandate of the Lord
Resounding through the air, "Give back the sword!"

The Rabbi bowed his head in silent prayer,
Then said he to the dreadful Angel, "Swear
No human eye shall look on it again;
But when thou takest away the souls of men,
Thyself unseen, and with an unseen sword,
Thou wilt perform the bidding of the Lord."
The Angel took the sword again, and swore,
And walks on earth unseen forevermore.

THE GHOSTS

Never stoop the soaring vulture
On his quarry in the desert,
On the sick or wounded bison,
But another vulture, watching
From his high aerial look-out,

Sees the downward plunge, and follows;
And a third pursues the second,
Coming from the invisible ether,
First a speck, and then a vulture,
Till the air is dark with pinions.

So disasters come not singly;
But as if they watched and waited,
Scanning one another's motions,
When the first descends, the others
Follow, follow, gathering flock-wise
Round their victim, sick and wounded,
First a shadow, then a sorrow,
Till the air is dark with anguish.

Now, o'er all the dreary North-land,
Mighty Peboan, the Winter,
Breathing on the lakes and rivers,
Into stone had changed their waters.
From his hair he shook the snow-flakes,
Till the plains were strewn with whiteness,
One uninterrupted level,
As if, stooping, the Creator
With his hand had smoothed them over.

Through the forest, wide and wailing,
Roamed the hunter on his snow-shoes;
In the village worked the women,
Pounded maize, or dressed the deer-skin;
And the young men played together
On the ice the noisy ball-play,
On the plain the dance of snow-shoes.

One dark evening, after sundown,
In her wigwam Laughing Water
Sat with old Nokomis, waiting
For the steps of Hiawatha
Homeward from the hunt returning.

On their faces gleamed the firelight,
Painting them with streaks of crimson,
In the eyes of old Nokomis
Glimmered like the watery moonlight,
In the eyes of Laughing Water
Glistened like the sun in water;
And behind them crouched their shadows
In the corners of the wigwam,
And the smoke in wreaths above them
Climbed and crowded through the smoke-flue.

Then the curtain of the doorway
From without was slowly lifted;
Brighter glowed the fire a moment.
And a moment swerved the smoke-wreath,
As two women entered softly,
Passed the doorway uninvited,
Without word of salutation,
Without sign of recognition,
Sat down in the farthest corner,
Crouching low among the shadows.

From their aspect and their garments,
Strangers seemed they in the village;
Very pale and haggard were they,
As they sat there sad and silent,
Trembling, cowering with the shadows.

Was it the wind above the smoke-flue,
Muttering down into the wigwam?
Was it the owl, the Koko-koho,
Hooting from the dismal forest?
Sure a voice said in the silence:
"These are corpses clad in garments,
These are ghosts that come to haunt you,
From the kingdom of Ponemah,
From the land of the Hereafter!"

Homeward now came Hiawatha
From his hunting in the forest,
With the snow upon his tresses,
And the red deer on his shoulders.
At the feet of Laughing Water
Down he threw his lifeless burden;
Nobler, handsomer she thought him,
Than when first he came to woo her,
First threw down the deer before her,
As a token of his wishes,
As a promise of the future.

Then he turned and saw the strangers,
Cowering, crouching with the shadows;
Said within himself, "Who are they?
What strange guests has Minnehaha?"
But he questioned not the strangers,
Only spake to bid them welcome
To his lodge, his wood, his fireside.

When the evening meal was ready,
And the deer had been divided,
Both the pallid guests, the strangers,
Springing from among the shadows,
Seized upon the choicest portions,
Seized the white fat of the roebuck,
Set apart for Laughing Water,
For the wife of Hiawatha;
Without asking, without thanking,
Eagerly devoured the morsels,
Flitted back among the shadows
In the corner of the wigwam.

Not a word spake Hiawatha,
Not a motion made Nokomis,
Not a gesture Laughing Water;
Not a change came o'er their features;

Only Minnehaha softly
Whispered, saying, "They are famished;
Let them do what best delights them;
Let them eat, for they are famished."

Many a daylight dawned and darkened,
Many a night shook off the daylight
As the pine shakes off the snow-flakes
From the midnight of its branches;
Day by day the guests unmoving
Sat there silent in the wigwam;
But by night, in storm or starlight,
Forth they went into the forest,
Bringing firewood to the wigwam,
Bringing pine-cones for the burning,
Always sad and always silent.

And whenever Hiawatha
Came from fishing or from hunting,
When the evening meal was ready,
And the food had been divided,
Gliding from their darksome corner,
Came the pallid guests, the strangers,
Seized upon the choicest portions
Set aside for Laughing Water,
And without rebuke or question
Flitted back among the shadows.

Never once had Hiawatha
By a word or look reproved them;
Never once had old Nokomis
Made a gesture of impatience;
Never once had Laughing Water
Shown resentment at the outrage.
All had they endured in silence,
That the rights of guest and stranger,
That the virtue of free-giving,

By a look might not be lessened.
By a word might not be broken.

Once at midnight Hiawatha,
Ever wakeful, ever watchful,
In the wigwam, dimly lighted
By the brands that still were burning,
By the glimmering, flickering firelight,
Heard a sighing, oft repeated,
Heard a sobbing, as of sorrow.

From his couch rose Hiawatha,
From his shaggy hides of bison,
Pushed aside the deer-skin curtain,
Saw the pallid guests, the shadows,
Sitting upright on their couches,
Weeping in the silent midnight.

And he said: "O guests! why is it
That your hearts are so afflicted,
That you sob so in the midnight?
Has perchance the old Nokomis,
Has my wife, my Minnehaha,
Wronged or grieved you by unkindness,
Failed in hospitable duties?"

Then the shadows ceased from weeping,
Ceased from sobbing and lamenting,
And they said, with gentle voices:
"We are ghosts of the departed,
Souls of those who once were with you.
From the realms of Chibiabos
Hither have we come to try you,
Hither have we come to warn you.

"Cries of grief and lamentation
Reach us in the Blessed Islands;
Cries of anguish from the living,
Calling back their friends departed,

Sadden us with useless sorrow
Therefore have we come to try you;
No one knows us, no one heeds us.
We are but a burden to you,
And we see that the departed
Have no place among the living.

"Think of this, O Hiawatha!
Speak of it to all the people,
That henceforward and forever
They no more with lamentations
Sadden the souls of the departed
In the Islands of the Blessed.

"Do not lay such heavy burdens
In the graves of those you bury,
Not such weight of furs and wampum,
Not such weight of pots and kettles,
For the spirits faint beneath them.
Only give them food to carry,
Only give them fire to light them.

"Four days is the spirit's journey
To the land of ghosts and shadows,
Four its lonely night-encampments;
Four times must their fires be lighted.
Therefore, when the dead are buried,
Let a fire, as night approaches,
Four times on the grave be kindled,
That the soul upon its journey
May not lack the cheerful firelight,
May not grope about in darkness.

"Farewell, noble Hiawatha!
We have put you to the trial,
To the proof have put your patience,
By the insult of our presence,
By the outrage of our actions.

We have found you great and noble.
Fail not in the greater trial,
Faint not in the harder struggle."
   When they ceased, a sudden darkness
Fell and filled the silent wigwam.
Hiawatha heard a rustle
As of garments trailing by him,
Heard the curtain of the doorway
Lifted by a hand he saw not,
Felt the cold breath of the night air,
For a moment saw the starlight;
But he saw the ghosts no longer,
Saw no more the wandering spirits
From the kingdom of Ponemah,
From the land of the Hereafter.

EDGAR ALLAN POE (1809-1849)

THE RAVEN

Once upon a midnight dreary, while I pondered, weak and weary,
Over many a quaint and curious volume of forgotten lore,
While I nodded, nearly napping, suddenly there came a tapping,
As of some one gently rapping, rapping at my chamber door.
" 'Tis some visitor," I muttered, "tapping at my chamber door —
   Only this and nothing more."

Ah, distinctly I remember it was in the bleak December,
And each separate dying ember wrought its ghost upon the floor.
Eagerly I wished the morrow; vainly I had sought to borrow
From my books surcease of sorrow—sorrow for the lost Lenore,
For the rare and radiant maiden whom the angels name Lenore—
   Nameless *here* for evermore.

And the silken, sad, uncertain rustling of each purple curtain
Thrilled me—filled me with fantastic terrors never felt before;
So that now, to still the beating of my heart, I stood repeating,
"'Tis some visitor entreating entrance at my chamber door—
Some late visitor entreating entrance at my chamber door—
      This it is and nothing more."

Presently my soul grew stronger: hesitating then no longer,
"Sir," said I, "or Madam, truly your forgiveness I implore;
But the fact is I was napping, and so gently you came rapping,
And so faintly you came tapping, tapping at my chamber door,
That I scarce was sure I heard you"—here I opened wide the door—
      Darkness there and nothing more.

Deep into the darkness peering, long I stood there, wondering, fearing,
Doubting, dreaming dreams no mortal ever dared to dream before;
But the silence was unbroken, and the stillness gave no token,
And the only word there spoken was the whispered word "Lenore!"
This I whispered, and an echo murmured back the word "Lenore!"
      Merely this and nothing more.

Back into the chamber turning, all my soul within me burning,
Soon again I heard a tapping, somewhat louder than before.
"Surely," said I, "surely that is something at my window lattice;
Let me see, then, what thereat is, and this mystery explore,—
Let my heart be still a moment and this mystery explore—
      'Tis the wind and nothing more."

Open here I flung the shutter, when, with many a flirt and flutter,
In there stepped a stately Raven of the saintly days of yore.
Not the least obeisance made he, not a minute stopped or stayed he,
But with mien of lord or lady perched above my chamber door—
Perched upon a bust of Pallas just above my chamber door—
      Perched and sat, and nothing more.

Then, this ebony bird beguiling my sad fancy into smiling
By the grave and stern decorum of the countenance it wore,
"Though thy crest be shorn and shaven, thou," I said, "art sure no
   craven,
Ghastly, grim, and ancient Raven, wandering from the nightly shore:
Tell me what thy lordly name is on the night's Plutonian shore!"
   Quoth the Raven, "Nevermore."

Much I marveled this ungainly fowl to hear discourse so plainly,
Though its answer little meaning, little relevancy bore;
For we cannot help agreeing that no living human being
Ever yet was blessed with seeing bird above his chamber door—
Bird or beast upon a sculptured bust above his chamber door—
   With such name as "Nevermore."

But the Raven, sitting lonely on the placid bust, spoke only
That one word, as if his soul in that one word he did outpour.
Nothing farther then he uttered, not a feather than he fluttered;
Till I scarcely more than muttered, "Other friends have flown before:
On the morrow *he* will leave me, as my hopes have flown before."
   Then the bird said, "Nevermore."

Startled at the stillness broken by reply so aptly spoken,
"Doubtless," said I, "what it utters is its only stock and store,
Caught from some unhappy master whom unmerciful Disaster
Followed fast and followed faster till his songs one burden bore,
Till the dirges of his hope that melancholy burden bore
   Of 'Never—nevermore.' "

But the Raven still beguiling my sad fancy into smiling,
Straight I wheeled a cushioned seat in front of bird and bust and door;
Then, upon the velvet sinking, I betook myself to linking
Fancy unto fancy, thinking what this ominous bird of yore,
What this grim, ungainly, ghastly, gaunt, and ominous bird of yore
   Meant in croaking "Nevermore."

This I sat engaged in guessing, but no syllable expressing
To the fowl, whose fiery eyes now burned into my bosom's core;
This and more I sat divining, with my head at ease reclining
On the cushion's velvet lining that the lamplight gloated o'er,
But whose velvet violet lining with the lamplight gloating o'er,
    She shall press, ah, nevermore!

Then, methought, the air grew denser, perfumed from an unseen censer
Swung by seraphim whose foot-falls tinkled on the tufted floor.
"Wretch," I cried, "thy God hath lent thee—by these angels he hath
    sent thee
Respite—respite and nepenthe from thy memories of Lenore!
Quaff, oh quaff this kind nepenthe, and forget this lost Lenore!"
    Quoth the Raven, "Nevermore."

"Prophet!" said I, "thing of evil! prophet still, if bird or devil!
Whether Tempter sent, or whether tempest tossed thee here ashore,
Desolate yet all undaunted, on this desert land enchanted—
On this home by Horror haunted—tell me truly, I implore:
Is there—*is* there balm in Gilead?—tell me—tell me, I implore!"
    Quoth the Raven, "Nevermore."

"Prophet!" said I, "thing of evil—prophet still, if bird or devil!
By that Heaven that bends above us, by the God we both adore,
Tell this soul with sorrow laden if, within the distant Aidenn,
It shall clasp a sainted maiden whom the angels name Lenore:
Clasp a rare and radiant maiden whom the angels name Lenore!"
    Quoth the Raven, "Nevermore."

"Be that word our sign of parting, bird or fiend!" I shrieked, upstarting:
"Get thee back into the tempest and the night's Plutonian shore!
Leave no black plume as a token of that lie thy soul hath spoken!
Leave my loneliness unbroken; quit the bust above my door!
Take thy beak from out my heart, and take thy form from off my door!"
    Quoth the Raven, "Nevermore."

And the Raven, never flitting, still is sitting, still is sitting
On the pallid bust of Pallas just above by chamber door;
And his eyes have all the seeming of a demon's that is dreaming,
And the lamp-light o'er him streaming throws his shadow on the floor;
And my soul from out that shadow that lies floating on the floor
  Shall be lifted—nevermore!

DREAM-LAND

By a route obscure and lonely,
Haunted by ill angels only,
Where an Eidolon, named NIGHT,
On a black throne reigns upright,
I have reached these lands but newly
From an ultimate dim Thule—
From a wild weird clime that lieth, sublime,
    Out of SPACE—out of TIME.

Bottomless vales and boundless floods,
And chasms, and caves and Titan woods,
With forms that no man can discover
For the tears that drip all over;
Mountains topping evermore
Into seas without a shore;
Seas that restlessly aspire,
Surging, unto skies of fire;
Lakes that endlessly outspread
Their lone waters—lone and dead,—
Their still waters—still and chilly
With the snows of the lolling lily.

By the lakes that thus outspread
Their lone waters, lone and dead,—

Their sad waters, sad and chilly
With the snows of the lolling lily,—
By the mountains—near the river
Murmuring lowly, murmuring ever,—
By the grey woods,—by the swamp
Where the toad and the newt encamp,—
By the dismal tarns and pools
   Where dwell the Ghouls,—
By each spot the most unholy—
In each nook most melancholy,—
There the traveller meets, aghast,
Sheeted Memories of the Past—
Shrouded forms that start and sigh
As they pass the wanderer by—
White-robed forms of friends long given,
In agony, to the Earth—and Heaven.

For the heart whose woes are legion
'T is a peaceful, soothing region—
For the spirit that walks in shadow
'T is—oh, 't is an Eldorado!
But the traveller, travelling through it,
May not—dare not openly view it;

Never its mysteries are exposed
To the weak human eye unclosed;
So wills its King, who hath forbid
The uplifting of the fringéd lid;
And thus the sad Soul that here passes
Beholds it but through darkened glasses.

By a route obscure and lonely,
Haunted by ill angels only,
Where an Eidolon, named NIGHT
On a black throne reigns upright,

I have wandered home but newly
From this ultimate dim Thule.

ULALUME

The skies they were ashen and sober;
　　The leaves they were crisped and sere—
　　The leaves they were withering and sere;
It was night in the lonesome October
　　Of my most immemorial year;
It was hard by the dim lake of Auber,
　　In the misty mid region of Weir—
It was down by the dank tarn of Auber,
　　In the ghoul-haunted woodland of Weir.

Here once, through an alley Titanic,
　　Of cypress, I roamed with my Soul—
　　Of cypress, with Psyche, my Soul
These were days when my heart was volcanic
　　As the scoriac rivers that roll—
　　As the lavas that restlessly roll
Their sulphurous currents down Yaanek
　　In the ultimate climes of the pole—
That groan as they roll down Mount Yaanek
　　In the realms of the boreal pole.

Our talk had been serious and sober,
　　But our thoughts they were palsied and sere—
　　Our memories were treacherous and sere—
For we knew not the month was October,
　　And we marked not the night of the year—
　　(Ah, night of all nights in the year!)
We noted not the dim lake of Auber—
　　(Though once we had journeyed down here)—

Remembered not the dank tarn of Auber,
   Nor the ghoul-haunted woodland of Weir.

And now, as the night was senescent
   And star-dials pointed to morn—
   As the star-dials hinted of morn—
At the end of our path a liquescent
   And nebulous lustre was born,
Out of which a miraculous crescent
   Arose with a duplicate horn—
Astarte's bediamonded crescent
   Distinct with its duplicate horn.

And I said—"She is warmer than Dian:
   She rolls through an ether of sighs—
   She revels in a region of sighs:
She has seen that the tears are not dry on
   These cheeks, where the worm never dies
And has come past the stars of the Lion
   To point us the path to the skies—
   To the Lethean peace of the skies—
Come up, in despite of the Lion,
   To shine on us with her bright eyes—
Come up through the lair of the Lion,
   With love in her luminous eyes."

But Psyche, uplifting her finger,
   Said—"Sadly this star I mistrust—
   Her pallor I strangely mistrust:—
Oh, hasten!—oh, let us not linger!
   Oh, fly!—let us fly!—for we must."
In terror she spoke, letting sink her
   Wings until they trailed in the dust—
In agony sobbed, letting sink her
   Plumes till they trailed in the dust—
   Till they sorrowfully trailed in the dust.

I replied—"This is nothing but dreaming:
   Let us on by this tremulous light!
   Let us bathe in this crystalline light!
Its Sibyllic splendor is beaming
   With Hope and in Beauty to-night:—
   See!—it flickers up the sky through the night!
Ah, we safely may trust to its gleaming,
   And be sure it will lead us aright—
We safely may trust to a gleaming
   That cannot but guide us aright,
Since it flickers up to Heaven through the night."

Thus I pacified Psyche and kissed her,
   And tempted her out of her gloom—
   And conquered her scruples and gloom;
And we passed to the end of the vista,
   But were stopped by the door of a tomb—
   By the door of a legended tomb;
And I said—"What is written, sweet sister,
   On the door of this legended tomb?"
   She replied—"Ulalume—Ulalume—
   'T is the vault of thy lost Ulalume!"

Then my heart it grew ashen and sober
   As the leaves that were crisped and sere—
   As the leaves that were withering and sere,
And I cried—"It was surely October
   On *this* very night of last year
   That I journeyed—I journeyed down here—
   That I brought a dread burden down here—
   On this night of all nights in the year,
   Ah, what demon has tempted me here?
Well I know, now, this dim lake of Auber—
   This misty mid region of Weir—
Well I know now, this dank tarn of Auber,
   This ghoul-haunted woodland of Weir."

ALFRED, LORD TENNYSON (1809-1892)

RIZPAH

Wailing, wailing, wailing, the wind over land and sea—
And Willy's voice in the wind, "O mother, come out to me!"
Why should he call me tonight, when he knows that I cannot go?
For the downs are as bright as day, and the full moon stares at the snow.

We should be seen, my dear; they would spy us out of the town.
The loud black nights for us, and the storm rushing over the down,
When I cannot see my own hand, but am led by the creak of the chain,
And grovel and grope for my son till I find myself drenched with the rain.

Anything fallen again? Nay—what was there left to fall?
I have taken them home, I have numbered the bones, I have hidden them all.
What am I saying—and what are *you*? Do you come as a spy?
Falls? What falls? Who knows? As the tree falls so must it lie.

Who let her in? How long has she been? You—what have you heard?
Why did you sit so quiet? You never have spoken a word.
Oh—to pray with me—yes—a lady—none of their spies—
But the night has crept into my heart, and begun to darken my eyes.

Ah—you that have lived so soft, what should *you* know of the night,
The blast and the burning shame and the bitter frost and the fright?
I have done it, while you were asleep—you were only made for the day.
I have gathered my baby together—and now you may go your way.

Nay—for it's kind of you, madam, to sit by an old dying wife.
But say nothing hard of my boy, I have only an hour of life.
I kissed my boy in the prison, before he went out to die.
"They dared me to do it," he said, and he never has told me a lie.

I whipped him for robbing an orchard once when he was but a child—
"The farmer dared me to do it," he said; he was always so wild—
And idle—and couldn't be idle—my Willy—he never could rest.
The king should have made him a soldier, he would have been one o
    his best.

But he lived with a lot of wild mates, and they never would let him b
    good;
They swore that he dare not rob the mail, and he swore that he would
And he took no life, but he took one purse, and when all was don
He flung it among his fellows—"I'll none of it," said my son.

I came into court to the judge and the lawyers. I told them my tale
God's own truth—but they killed him, they killed him for robbing the
    mail.
They hanged him in chains for a show—we had always borne a goo
    name—
To be hanged for a thief—and then put away—isn't that enough shame
Dust to dust—low down—let us hide! But they set him so high
That all the ships of the world could stare at him, passing by.
God'll pardon the hell-lack raven and horrible fowls of the air,
But not the black heart of the lawyer who killed him and hanged him
    there.

And the jailer forced me away. I had bid him my last good-by;
They had fastened the door of his cell. "O mother!" I heard him cry
I couldn't get back though I tried, he had something further to say
And now I never shall know it. The jailer forced me away.
Then since I couldn't but hear that cry of my boy that was dead,
They seized me and shut me up: they fastened me down on my bed
"Mother, O mother!"—he called in the dark to me year after year—
They beat me for that, they beat me—you know that I couldn't but hear
And then at the last they found I had grown so stupid and still
They let me abroad again—but the creatures had worked their will.

lesh of my flesh was gone, but bone of my bone was left—
stole them all from the lawyers—and you, will you call it a theft?—
y baby, the bones that had sucked me, the bones that had laughed and
  had cried—
heirs? Oh no! They are mine—not theirs—they had moved in my
  side.
o you think I was scared by the bones? I kissed 'em, I buried 'em all—
can't dig deep, I am old—in the night by the churchyard wall.
y Willy 'll rise up whole when the trumpet of judgment 'll sound,
ut I charge you never to say that I laid him in holy ground.

hey would scratch him up—they would hang him again on the curséd
  tree.
in? Oh, yes, we are sinners, I know—let all that be,
nd read me a Bible verse of the Lord's goodwill toward men—
Full of compassion and mercy, the Lord"—let me hear it again;
Full of compassion and mercy—long-suffering." Yes, oh, yes!
or the lawyer is born but to murder—the Saviour lives but to bless.
e'll never put on the black cap except for the worst of the worst,
nd the first may be last—I have heard it in church—and the last may
  be first.
uffering—O long-suffering—yes, as the Lord must know,
ear after year in the mist and the wind and the shower and the snow.

eard, have you? what? They have told you he never repented his sin.
ow do they know it? Are *they* his mother? Are *you* of his kin?
eard! Have you ever heard, when the storm on the downs began,
he wind that'll wail like a child and the sea that'll moan like a man?

ection, Election, and Reprobation—it's all very well.
ut I go tonight to my boy, and I shall not find him in hell.
or I cared so much for my boy that the Lord has looked into my care,
nd He means me I'm sure to be happy with Willy, I know not where.

And if *he* be lost—but to save *my* soul, that is all your desire—
Do you think that I care for *my* soul if my boy be gone to the fire
I have been with God in the dark—go, go, you may leave me alone—
You never have borne a child—you are just as hard as a stone.
Madam, I beg your pardon! I think that you mean to be kind,
But I cannot hear what you say for my Willy's voice in the wind—
The snow and the sky so bright—he used but to call in the dark,
And he calls to me now from the church and not from the gibbet—
    for hark!
Nay—you can hear it yourself—it is coming—shaking the walls—
Willy—the moon's in a cloud—Good-night. I am going. He call

WILLIAM BELL SCOTT (1811-1890)

A LOWLAND WITCH BALLAD

The old witch-wife beside her door
    Sat spinning with a watchful ear,
A horse's hoof upon the road
    Is what she waits for, longs to hear.

The mottled gloaming dusky grew,
    Or else we might a furrow trace,
Sowed with small bones and leaves of yew,
    Across the road from place to place.

Hark he comes! The young bridegroom,
    Singing gaily down the hill,
Rides on, rides blindly to his doom,
    His heart that witch hath sworn to kill

Up to the fosse he rode so free,
   There his steed stumbled and he fell,
He cannot pass, nor turn, nor flee;
   His song is done, he's in the spell.

She dances round him where he stands,
   Her distaff touches both his feet,
She blows upon his eyes and hands,
   He has no power his fate to cheat.

"Ye cannot visit her to-night,
   Nor ever again," the witch-wife cried;
"But thou shalt do as I think right,
   And do it swift without a guide.

"Upon the top of Tintock Hill
   This night there rests the yearly mist,
In silence go, your tongue keep still,
   And find for me the dead man's kist.

"Within the kist there is a cup,
   Thou'lt find it by the dead man's shine,
Take it thus! thus fold it up,—
   It holds for me the wisdom-wine.

"Go to the top of Tintock hill,
   Grope within that eerie mist,
Whatever happens, keep quite still
   Until ye find the dead man's kist.

"The kist will open, take the cup,
   Heed ye not the dead man's shine,
Take it thus, thus fold it up,
   Bring it to me and I am thine."

He went, he could make answer none,
 He went, he found all as she said,
Before the dawn had well begun
 She had the cup from that strange bed.

Into the hut she fled at once,
 She drank the wine;—forthwith behold!
A radiant damozel advance
 From that black door in silken fold.

The little Circe flower she held
 Towards the boy with such a smile
Made his heart leap, he was compelled
 To take it gently as a child.

She turned, he followed, passed the door,
 Which closed behind: at noon next day,
 Ambling on his mule that way,
The Abbot found the steed, no more,
 The rest was lost in glamoury.

J. Sheridan Le Fanu (1815-1873)

THE LEGEND OF THE GLAIVE

Fair-shoulder, Fionula fair,
 The wondrous child of Lir's old race,
Answered the hero of the raven hair
 Of the strong hand and princely grace,
  The great Cathair.

"Five leagues hence doth the Norseman lie
    Beneath his cromlech gray;
Three miles round no soul draws nigh
    From eve till dawn of day.
Nor friend of man, nor horse, nor hound,
Nought that hath life must cross that ground;
And in that cromlech, side by side,
The dead man and his sword abide.
And if thou lovest me as thou swearest,
And for my love thou greatly darest,
Alone tonight thou'lt seize for me
The giant glaive of the King of the Sea.
And so, for aye, his fame and thine,
And, with thy fame more humbly mine—
Like three harps sounding in the hall
              To the same high story,
              Of hero glory,
Shall ring for ever in the ears of all."

Oh! who'd have dreamed that beneath the grace
Of that rich and wondrous form and face,
In the midnight blue of her dewy eye,
As she dropt her gaze with a blush and sigh,
              Alas! could lie
              Such cruelty?
        Or who could deem
That beauty's talisman should gleam—
A spell to blast him, not to bless—
From the white brow of the sorceress?

    Her little sandalled foot before,
Flushed with the wildering light of beauty,
    He kneeled and swore—
    "Lady, this moment overpays,
    The long eclipse of future days—

'Tis my joy to dare, to die my duty,
If only from my endless night
One lingering star ascends of light
Worthy of thine auroral crown,
And of true love's forlorn renown.
    The story of my adoration,
Like a jewel from the sea
Where I am lost, returned shall be,
    A relic and a decoration;
And minstrels mingle, in the Feats of Fame,
My requiem with thy living beauty's flame."

With those words Cathair is gone,
And Fionula is alone.

The hero's hair blew back and showed
His gleaming eyes and forehead broad;
His marble face and haughty head,
In resolve already dead.

On to the altar and the knife,
Like one renunciant of his life,
Who nears the sacrificial goal
Holding in his hand his soul—
On, on he paces, mute, alone,
By moss-grown cairn and druid stone,
Broad fields of corn and sloping meadow,
And level light and lengthening shadow,
By purpling hills and yellow woods,
And blazonry of western clouds
That o'er pale green and amber sky,
Weltering in cold and crimson, lie.
    Bathed in the evening's spirit tender,
A brown bird sitting on a spray
Whistles its happy soul away,

And thrills with life the silent splendour.
The glorious moment wanes and dies,
And Night rides up the Eastern skies—
Line behind line, and hand in hand,
In sable cloaked, the aërial band,
From pole to pole, ascending far,
In every helm a blinking star;
While their voiceless march before
Like dust the white mist rises hoar.

So darkness and the dew and hush
Of night came down on slope and bush,
And every glen and blue ravine
  Was filmed with smoky haze.
And autumn's glow and russet green
    Grew blurred and waste before the gaze
        Of Cathair as he went by,
And beetling mountain, stark and high
And fringe of hedgerow 'gainst the sky,
And wild flowers 'neath his foot that lay,
Together melted into gray,
        Together in gloom were lost.

As through the Lisses three he crossed,
He knows that unseen shapes are near,
And tittered words are in his ear,
    Now here and now there,
  Faint harping and singing
  And fairy spurs ringing,
And the whirr of their coursers' shrill tremble in air,
And hovering glee and hovering pain
Their fearful burthen o'er his brain,
  Their dreadful fancies shedding;
As swiftly o'er the throbbing sward,
  Through haunted vapours treading,

He sees loom black before his tranced regard
Morrua's forest, nobly wild,
Afar in billowy verdure piled.

Far behind him crept blackness and flickering glimmer,
To the northward, slow mounting, the tempest was rising,
While luridly glaring all earth lay expecting,
Voiceless and breathless, the yell of the tyrant.

Thus he entered the high, vacant halls of the forest:
No bird in its branches, no antler beneath them,
Nor boom of the beetle, nor bay of the wild dog.
Only, Priestess of Mystery, glides a White Shadow,
On her lip her forefinger—and faithful he followed,
Well knowing his fate led him on to the combat,
Well knowing a mandate of silence upon him.
The trunks of the great trees like time-furrowed castles,
Gray glimmered through darkness impassive and awful,
Broad at base and at battlement broader the oak boles.
And a canopy dusky, snake-twisted, of branches,
Like crypts of cathedrals, low-groined and broad-pillared,
Stretched mazily this way and that in perspective.

As sweet the evening glories faded
    O'er Fionula's bower,
A lone sad voice the maid upbraided,
    Charming the twilight hour.
With parted lips and hand to ear
    She harkened to the melody
So wildly and so faintly clear,
    At the open casement dreamily.
The lonely splendour of a star
    Lay trembling in her virgin tear;
And with the music, night or far,
    There fell upon her heart a fear;

Swift round her ivory throat she drew
　　The cloak that doth in crimson fold her—
Swift round her shoulder, veined with blue,
　　And polished as a statue's shoulder;
Then snapped the jewel in her cloak,
　　Still through the casement wildly gazing,
Like one whom spirit-songs have woke
　　From earthly sleep to sights amazing
The Princess to the postern hied,
　　Upon her throat the jewel's spark;
Her hand her pearly ear beside,
　　Her great eyes gleaming through the dark.

"From close of flower, till song of lark,
　　By mist or moonshine, hill and hollow—
To follow still and still to hark—
　　To hearken still and still to follow."

Strange music of an ecstasy—
　　'Twas hardy sound, and came unsought;
She smiled, and listened to the lay
　　As listening to a sad, sweet thought.
Glares in the west a stain of blood,
　　The Wizard North its black storm raises—
And eastward o'er Morrua's wood,
　　One great white star portentous gazes.

Sitting, spinning in the hall,
　　With lamps alight, the sunset after,
The whirring task her maids speed all
　　With silvery song and girlish laughter.
But, like an apparition, she
　　Is lost—and lost—and lost for ever,
And O their loving eyes shall see
　　The splendrous Fionula—never.

Lost; but her love she'll never find—
 Sooner the foam wreath in its wake,
O'er ocean's waste, in ocean's wind,
The flying ship shall overtake.

Through the woods of Morrua and over its root-knotted flooring,
The hero speeds onward, alone, on his terrible message;
When faint and far-off, like the gathering gallop of battle,
The hoofs of the hurricane louder and louder come leaping,
There's a gasp and a silence around him a swooning of nature,
And the forest trees moan, and complain with a presage of evil.
And nearer, like great organ's wailing, high-piping through thunder,
Subsiding, then lifted again to a thousand-tongued tumult,
And crashing, and deafening and yelling in clangorous uproar
Soaring onward, down-riding, and rending the wreck of its conquest,
The tempest swoops on: all the branches before it bend, singing
Like cordage in shipwreck; before it sear leaves fly like vapour;
Before it bow down like wide armies, plumed heads of the forest,
In frenzy dark-rolling, up-tossing their scathed arms like Maenads.
Dizzy lightnings split this way and that in the blind void above him;
For a moment long passages reeling and wild with the tempest,
In the blue map and dazzle of lightning, throb vivid and vanish;
And white glare the wrinkles and knots of the oak-trees beside him,
While close overhead clap the quick mocking palms of the Storm-Fiend.

Now southward drift the din and glare,
Like navies battling in the air;
On boom the thunder and the wind,
And wreck and silence lie behind,
While whirlwind roars and lightning burns,
The hero neither tires nor turns.
'Mid the wild wail of shrilly boughs,
And pealing thunder's claps and soughs;
And by the lightning's livid tapers,
And the black pall of eddying vapours,

He follows the White Shadow's call,
That never swerved for flash or wind,
And never stops nor looks behind,
   But leads him to his funeral.

The forest opens as he goes,
And smitten trees in groups and rows
   Beneath the tempest's tune,
Stand in the mists of midnight drooping,
By moss-grown rocks fantastic stooping,
   In the blue shadows of the yellow moon.

And in the moonlight, bleached as bones,
Uprose the monumental stones,
Meeting the hero suddenly
            With a blind stare
            Dull as despair.
The formless boulder that blocked the door
Like a robed monster broad and hoar
   He twice essayed to earth to throw
With quivering sinew, bursting vein,
   With grinding teeth and scowling brow.
From his dark forehead with the strain,
Beads start and drop like thunder-rain;
And in the breathless tug and reek,
All his lithe body seems to creak.
   The mighty stone to earth is hurled,
Black gapes the violated door,
Through which he rushes to rise no more
   Into this fair, sad world.

Where high the vaults of midnight gape
In the black waste, a blacker shape—
And near against a distant dark,
He could the giant Norseman mark

A black tarn's waters sitting by;
Beneath a brazen, stormy sky,
That never moves but dead doth lie,—
And on the rock could darkly see
The mighty glaive beside his knee.
The hero's front and upreared form,
Loomed dim as headlands in a storm.
No more will flicker passion's meteors
O'er the dead shadow of his features,
Fixed in the apathy eternal
That lulls him in repose infernal.
The cornice of his knotted brows
A direful shadow downward throws
Upon his eyeballs dull and stark,
Like white stones glimmering in the dark;
And, carved in their forlorn despair,
His glooming features changeless wear
Gigantic sorrow and disdain,
The iron sneer of endless pain.
From the lips of the awful phantom woke
A voice, and thus, by the tarn, it spoke:—

"Son of Malmorra, what canst thou gather here?"

The spell was broke that struck him dumb,
And held his soul aghast and numb,
  With a wild throb,
  A laugh, and sob,
The frenzied courage came again
Of Cathair, the Prince of men.
With planted foot, with arm extended,
And his ferine gaze distended,
Back flowed the cataract of his hair
From the gleaming face of the great Cathair;

And he shouted lion-voiced,
Like one defying who rejoiced:—
"Thorgil, king of the wintry sea,
Of the nine-gapped sword and minstrel glee,
Of mountains dark and craggy valleys,
Of the golden cup and hundred galleys,
Malmorra's son, myself, have sworn
To take thy sword or ne'er return!"
The Norseman's phantom, black and dread,
Turned not, lifted not his head.
Mute, without anger or alarm,
As shadow stretches, stretched his arm;
Upon the hilt his hand he laid,
The metal dull one bell-note made—
One cold flash from the awakened blade
Flecked the waste sky with flying glare,
            Like northern lights
            That sport o' nights,
Shuddering across the empty air.
High overhead, where died the light
Through the wide caverns of the night,
The imprisoned echoes, whispering first,
Afar in moaning thunders burst.
Mortal armour nought avails—
Shearing the air, the enchanted blade
Of Thorgil a strange music made;
The brazen concave of the sky
Returns its shrilly sigh,
Above—around—along—
With the roaring shiver of a gong.
Black night around him floating, and booming of the sea
Have borne away the hero on the spirit-maelstrom free;
The shadows round him deepen in his soft and dreamless flight—
            The pause of a new birth,

A forgetting of the earth,
Its action and its thinking,
A mighty whirl and sinking,
A lapsing into Lethe, and the ocean caves of night.

A silvery song is in his ears,
A melody all sad and lone,
The voice that Fionula hears,
And follows still by brake and stone.
It is the voice of early years,
The early love long dead and gone.
His wounded head is on her knee,
Her hand his sable locks among
And still the song enchantingly
By that remembered voice is sung
And dreamily he opes his eyes.
Beneath in rosy lustre lies,
With many a shivered line of gold,
A misty lake in many a fold
Of wood, and slope, and rock, and hill,
And riven peak, and winding rill.
Long golden reeds and floating lilies tell
Their secrets and rejoicings to the breeze,
And every flowery star and bloomy bell
That glow like oriel windows 'neath the trees,
In gules and azure mottling the soft sward,
In fragrance and dim music sigh,
And sleep, and wake, but never die.
Such is the blessèd mystery
That of their weakness is the ward.
Here memory doth the hour beguile
And never too much pains or cheers,
Here all things sad are with a smile,
And all rejoicing is with tears.
Through everything there thrills a gladness,

Through everything there throbs a sadness;
And memory, love, and gratitude
A glory shed on every mood.

How to this hour she is sometimes seen by night in Munster.
By the foot of the old Keeper, beside the *bohreen,*
In the deep blue of night the thatched cabin is seen;
'Neath the furze-covered ledge, by the wild mountain brook,
Where the birch and the ash dimly shelter the nook,
And many's the clear star that trembles on high
O'er the thatch and the wild ash that melt in the sky.
"Shamus Oge" and old Teig are come home from the fair,
And the car stands up black with its shafts in the air,
A warbling of laughter hums over the floor,
And fragrant's the flush of the turf through the door.
Round the glow the old folk, and the colleens, and boys
Wile the hour with their stories, jokes, laughter, and noise;
Dogs stretched on the hearth with their chins on their feet lie,
To her own purring music the cat dozes sweetly;
Pretty smiles answer, coyly, while soft spins the wheel,
The bold lover's glances or whispered appeal.

Stealing in, like the leather-wings under the thatch,
A hand through the dark softly leans on the latch,
An oval face peeps through the clear deep of night,
From her jewels faint tremble blue splinters of light.
There's a stranger among us, a chill in the air,
And an awful face silently framed over there;
The green light of horror glares cold from each eye,
And laughter breaks shivering into a cry.
A flush from the fire hovers soft to the door,
In the dull void the pale lady glimmers no more.
The cow'ring dogs howl, slowly growls the white cat,
And the whisper outshivers, "God bess us! what's that?"

The sweet summer moon over Aherloe dreams,
And the Galtees, gigantic, loom cold in her beams;
From the wide flood of purple the pale peaks up-rise,
Slowly gliding like sails 'gainst the stars of the skies;
Soft moonlight is drifted on mountain and wood,
Airy voices sing faint to the drone of the flood,
As the traveller benighted flies onward in fear,
And the clink of his footsteps falls shrill on his ear.
There's a hush in the bushes, a chill in the air,
While a breath steals beside him and whispers, "Beware!"
While aslant by the oak, down the hollow ravine,
Like a flying bird's shadow smooth-gliding, is seen
Fionula the Cruel, the brightest, the worst,
With a terrible beauty the vision accurst,
Gold-filleted, sandalled, of times dead and gone—
Far-looking, and harking, pursuing, goes on;
Her white hand from her ear lifts her shadowy hair,
From the lamp of her eye floats the sheen of despair;
Her cold lips are apart, and her teeth in her smile
Glimmer death on her face with a horrible wile.
Three throbs at his heart—not a breath at his lip,
As the figure skims by like the swoop of a ship;
The breeze dies and drops like a bird on the wing,
And the pulse of the rivulet ceases to ring;
And the stars and the moon dilate o'er his head,
As they smile out an icy salute to the dead.

The traveller—alone—signs the cross on his breast,
Gasps a prayer to the saints for her weary soul's rest;
His "gospel" close pressed to the beat of his heart,
And fears still to linger, yet dreads to depart.
By the village fire crouched, his the story that night,
While his listeners around him draw pale with affright;
Till it's over the country—"God bless us, again!"
How he met Fionula in Aherloe glen.

CHARLES KINGSLEY (1819-1875)

THE WEIRD LADY

The swevens came up round Harold the Earl,
  Like motes in the sunnès beam;
And over him stood the Weird Lady,
In her charmèd castle over the sea,
  Sang "Lie thou still and dream."

"Thy steed is dead in his stall, Earl Harold,
  Since thou hast been with me;
The rust has eaten thy harness bright,
And the rats have eaten thy greyhound light,
  That was so fair and free."

Mary Mother she stooped from heaven;
She wakened Earl Harold out of his sweven,
  To don his harness on;
And over the land and over the sea
He wended abroad to his own countrie,
  A weary way to gon.

Oh but his beard was white with eld,
  Oh but his hair was gray;
He stumbled on by stock and stone,
And as he journeyed he made his moan
  Along that weary way.

Earl Harold came to his castle wall;
  The gate was burnt with fire;
Roof and rafter were fallen down,
The folk were strangers all in the town,
  And strangers all in the shire.

Earl Harold came to a house of nuns,
    And he heard the dead-bell toll;
He saw the sexton stand by a grave;
"Now Christ have mercy, who did us save,
    Upon yon fair nun's soul."

The nuns they came from the convent gate
    By one, by two, by three;
They sang for the soul of a lady bright
Who died for the love of a traitor knight:
    It was his own lady.

He stayed the corpse beside the grave;
    "A sign, a sign!" quod he.
"Mary Mother who rulest heaven,
Send me a sign if I be forgiven
    By the woman who so loved me."

A white dove out of the coffin flew;
    Earl Harold's mouth it kist;
He fell on his face, wherever he stood;
And the white dove carried his soul to God
    Or ever the bearers wist.

THE SANDS OF DEE

"O Mary, go and call the cattle home,
    And call the cattle home,
    And call the cattle home
  Across the sands of Dee";
The western wind was wild and dank with foam,
And all alone went she.

The western tide crept up along the sand,
    And o'er and o'er the sand,
    And round and round the sand,
  As far as eye could see.
The rolling mist came down and hid the land:
  And never home came she.

"Oh! is it weed, or fish, or floating hair—
    A tress of golden hair,
    A drownèd maiden's hair
  Above the nets at sea?
Was never salmon yet that shone so fair
  Among the stakes on Dee."

They rowed her in across the rolling foam,
    The cruel crawling foam,
    The cruel hungry foam,
  To her grave beside the sea:
But still the boatmen hear her call the cattle home
  Across the sands of Dee.

SYDNEY THOMPSON DOBELL (1824-1874)

KEITH OF RAVELSTON

The murmur of the mourning ghost
  That keeps the shadowy kine;
'Oh, Keith of Ravelston,
  The sorrows of thy line!'

Ravelston, Ravelston,
  The merry path that leads

Down the golden morning hill
  And through the silver meads;

Ravelston, Ravelston,
  The stile beneath the tree,
The maid that kept her mother's kine,
  The song that sang she!

She sang her song, she kept her kine,
  She sat beneath the thorn,
When Andrew Keith of Ravelston
  Rode thro' the Monday morn.

His henchmen sing, his hawk-bells ring,
  His belted jewels shine!
Oh, Keith of Ravelston,
  The sorrows of thy line!

Year after year, where Andrew came,
  Comes evening down the glade,
And still there sits a moonshine ghost
  Where sat the sunshine maid.

Her misty hair is faint and fair
  She keeps the shadowy kine;
Oh, Keith of Ravelston,
  The sorrows of thy line!

I lay my hand upon the stile,
  The stile is lone and cold;
The burnie that goes babbling by
  Says nought that can be told.

Yet, stranger! here, from year to year,
  She keeps her shadowy kine;

Oh, Keith of Ravelston,
  The sorrows of thy line!

Step out three steps, where Andrew stood—
  Why blanch thy cheeks for fear?
The ancient stile is not alone,
  'Tis not the burn I hear!

She makes her immemorial moan,
  She keeps her shadowy kine;
Oh, Keith of Ravelston,
  The sorrows of thy line!

WILLIAM ALLINGHAM (1824-1889)

THE WITCH BRIDE

A fair witch crept to a young man's side,
And he kiss'd her and took her for his bride.

But a shape came in at the dead of night,
And fill'd the room with snowy light.

And he saw how in his arms there lay
A thing more frightful than mouth may say.

And he rose in haste, and follow'd the Shape
Till morning crown'd an eastern cape.

And he girded himself and follow'd still,
When sunset sainted the western hill.

But, mocking and thwarting, clung to his side,
Weary day!—the foul Witch-Bride.

THE FAIRIES

Up the airy mountain,
  Down the rushy glen,
We daren't go a-hunting
  For fear of little men;
Wee folk, good folk,
  Trooping all together;
Green jacket, rep cap,
  And white owl's feather!

Down along the rocky shore
  Some make their home,
They live on crispy pancakes
  Of yellow tide-foam;
Some in the reeds
  Of the black mountain lake,
With frogs for their watch-dogs,
  All night awake.

High on the hill-top
  The old King sits;
He is now so old and gray
  He's nigh lost his wits.
With a bridge of white mist
  Columbkill he crosses,
On his stately journeys
  From Slieveleague to Rosses;
Or going up with music
  On cold starry nights
To sup with the Queen
  Of the gay Northern Lights.

They stole little Bridget
  For seven years long;
When she came down again
  Her friends were all gone.
They took her lightly back,
  Between the night and morrow,
They thought that she was fast asleep
  But she was dead with sorrow.
They have kept her ever since
  Deep within the lake,
On a bed of flag-leaves,
  Watching till she wake.

By the craggy hill-side,
  Through the mosses bare,
They have planted thorn-trees
  For pleasure here and there.
If any man so daring
  As dig them up in spite,
He shall find their sharpest thorns
  In his bed at night.

Up the airy mountain,
  Down the rushy glen,
We daren't go a-hunting
  For fear of little men;
Wee folk, good folk,
  Trooping all together;
Green jacket, red cap,
  And white owl's feather!

CHARLES GODFREY LELAND (1824-1903)

THE FLYING DUTCHMAN

We met the *Flying Dutchman,*
  By midnight he came,
His hull was all of hell fire,
  His sails were all aflame;
Fire on the main-top,
  Fire on the bow,
Fire on the gun-deck,
  Fire down below.

Four-and-twenty dead men,
  Those were the crew,
The devil on the bowsprit,
  Fiddled as she flew,
We gave her the broadside,
  Right in the dip,
Just like a candle,
  Went out the ship.

FITZ-JAMES O'BRIEN (1828-1862)

THE LOST STEAMSHIP

"Ho, there! Fisherman, hold your hand!
  Tell me what is that far away,—
There, where over the isle of sand
  Hangs the mist-cloud sullen and gray?
See! it rocks with a ghastly life,
  Rising and rolling through clouds of spray,
Right in the midst of the breakers' strife,—
  Tell me what is it, Fisherman, pray?"

"That, good sir, was a steamer stout
   As ever paddled around Cape Race;
And many's the wild and stormy bout
   She had with the winds, in that selfsame place;
But her time was come; and at ten o'clock
   Last night she struck on that lonesome shore;
And her sides were gnawed by the hidden rock,
   And at dawn this morning she was no more."

"Come, as you seem to know, good man,
   The terrible fate of this gallant ship,
Tell me about her all that you can;
   And here's my flask to moisten your lip.
Tell me how many she had aboard,—
   Wives, and husbands, and lovers true,—
How did it fare with her human hoard?
   Lost she many, or lost she few?"

"Master, I may not drink of your flask,
   Already too moist I feel my lip;
But I'm ready to do what else you ask,
   And spin you my yarn about the ship:
'Twas ten o'clock, as I said, last night,
   When she struck the breakers and went ashore;
And scarce had broken the morning's light
   Than she sank in twelve feet of water or more.

"But long ere this they knew her doom,
   And the captain called all hands to prayer;
And solemnly over the ocean's boom
   Their orisons wailed on the troublous air.
And round about the vessel there rose
   Tall plumes of spray as white as snow,
Like angels in their ascension clothes,
   Waiting for those who prayed below.

"So these three hundred people clung
    As well as they could to spar and rope;
With a word of prayer upon every tongue,
    Nor on any face a glimmer of hope
But there was no blubbering weak and wild,—
    Of tearful faces I saw but one,
A rough old salt, who cried like a child,
    And not for himself, but the captain's son.

"The captain stood on the quarter-deck,
    Firm, but pale, with trumpet in hand;
Sometimes he looked at the breaking wreck,
    Sometimes he sadly looked to land.
And often he smiled to cheer the crew—
    But, Lord! the smile was terrible grim—
Till over the quarter a huge sea flew;
    And that was the last they saw of him.

"I saw one young fellow with his bride,
    Standing amidships upon the wreck;
His face was white as the boiling tide,
    And she was clinging about his neck.
And I saw them try to say good-by,
    But neither could hear the other speak;
So they floated away through the sea to die—
    Shoulder to shoulder, and cheek to cheek.

"And there was a child, but eight at best,
    Who went his way in a sea she shipped;
All the while holding upon his breast
    A little pet parrot whose wings were clipped.
And as the boy and the bird went by,
    Swinging away on a tall wave's crest,
They were gripped by a man, with a drowning cry,
    And together the three went down to rest.

"And so the crew went one by one,
  Some with gladness, and few with fear;
Cold and hardship such work had done
  That few seemed frightened when death was near.
Thus every soul on board went down,—
  Sailor and passenger, little and great;
The last that sank was a man of my town,
  A capital swimmer,—the second mate."

"Now, lonely fisherman, who are you
  That say you saw this terrible wreck?
How do I know what you say is true,
  When every mortal was swept from the deck?
Where were you in that hour of death?
  How did you learn what you relate?"
His answer came in an under-breath,—
  "Master, I was the second mate!"

THE THREE GANNETS

I

On a wrinkled rock, in a distant sea,
  Three white gannets sat in the sun;
They shook the brine from their feathers so fine,
  And lazily, one by one,
They sunnily slept—while the tempest crept.

II

In a painted boat, on a distant sea,
  Three fowlers sailed merrily on,
And each took aim, as he came near the game,
  And the gannets fell, one by one,
And fluttered and died—while the tempest sighed.

III

Then a cloud came over the distant sea,
   A darkness came over the sun,
And a storm-wind smote on the painted boat,
   And the fowlers sank, one by one,
Down, down with their craft—while the tempest laughed.

THE DEMON OF THE GIBBET

There was no west, there was no east,
   No star abroad for eye to see;
And Norman spurred his jaded beast
   Hard by the terrible gallows-tree.

'O Norman, haste across this waste,—
   For something seems to follow me!'
'Cheer up, dear Maud, for, thanked be God,
   We nigh have passed the gallows-tree!'

He kissed her lip: then—spur and whip!
   And fast they fled across the lea!
But vain the heel and rowel steel,—
   For something leaped from the gallows-tree!

'Give me your cloak, your knightly cloak,
   That wrapped you oft beyond the sea;
The wind is bold, my bones are old,
   And I am cold on the gallows-tree.'

'O holy God! O dearest Maud,
   Quick, quick, some prayers,—the best that be!
A bony hand my neck has spanned,
   And tears my knightly cloak from me!'

'Give me your wine,—the red, red wine,
　　That in the flask hangs by your knee!
Ten summers burst on me accurst,
　　And I'm athirst on the gallows-tree.'

'O Maud, my life! my loving wife!
　　Have you no prayer to set us free?
My belt unclasps,—a demon grasps
　　And drags my wine-flask from my knee!'

'Give me your bride, your bonnie bride,
　　That left her nest with you to flee!
O, she hath flown to be my own,
　　For I'm alone on the gallows-tree!'

'Cling closer, Maud, and trust in God!
　　Cling close!—Ah, heaven, she slips from me!'—
A prayer, a groan, and he alone
　　Rode on that night from the gallows-tree.

DANTE GABRIEL ROSSETTI (1828-1862)

SISTER HELEN

"Why did you melt your waxen man,
　　　　Sister Helen?
To-day is the third since you began."
"The time was long, yet the time ran,
　　　　Little brother."
　　　(O Mother, Mary Mother,
Three days to-day, between Hell and Heaven!)

"But if you have done your work aright,
                    Sister Helen,
You'll let me play, for you said I might."
"Be very still in your play to-night,
                    Little brother."
            (O Mother, Mary Mother,
Third night, to-night, between Hell and Heaven!)

"You said it must melt ere vesper-bell,
                    Sister Helen;
If now it be molten, all is well."
"Even so,—nay, peace! you cannot tell,
                    Little brother."
            (O Mother, Mary Mother,
O what is this, between Hell and Heaven?)

"Oh the waxen knave was plump to-day,
                    Sister Helen;
How like dead folk he has dropped away!"
"Nay now, of the dead what can you say,
                    Little brother?"
            (O Mother, Mary Mother,
What of the dead, between Hell and Heaven?)

"See, see, the sunken pile of wood,
                    Sister Helen,
Shines through the thinned wax red as blood!"
"Nay now, when looked you yet on blood,
                    Little brother?"
            (O Mother, Mary Mother,
How pale she is, between Hell and Heaven!)

"Now close your eyes, for they're sick and sore,
                    Sister Helen,

And I'll play without the gallery door."
"Aye, let me rest,—I'll lie on the floor,
      Little brother."
    (O Mother, Mary Mother,
What rest to-night, between Hell and Heaven?)

"Here high up in the balcony,
      Sister Helen,
The moon flies face to face with me."
"Aye, look and say whatever you see,
      Little brother."
    (O Mother, Mary Mother,
What sight to-night, between Hell and Heaven?)

"Outside it's merry in the wind's wake,
      Sister Helen;
In the shaken trees the chill stars shake."
"Hush, heard you a horse-tread as you spake,
      Little brother?"
    (O Mother, Mary Mother,
What sound to-night between Hell and Heaven?)

"I hear a horse-tread, and I see,
      Sister Helen,
Three horsemen that ride terribly."
"Little brother, whence come the three,
      Little brother?"
    (O Mother, Mary Mother,
Whence should they come, between Hell and Heaven?)

"They come by the hill-verge from Boyne Bar,
      Sister Helen,
And one drays nigh, but two are afar."
"Look, look, do you know them who they are,
      Little brother?"

(O Mother, Mary Mother,
Who should they be, between Hell and Heaven?)

"Oh, it's Keith of Eastholm rides so fast,
   Sister Helen,
For I know the white mane on the blast."
"The hour has come, has come at last,
   Little brother!"
  (O Mother, Mary Mother,
Her hour at last, between Hell and Heaven!)

"He has made a sign and called Halloo!
   Sister Helen,
And he says that he would speak with you."
"Oh tell him I fear the frozen dew,
   Little brother."
  (O Mother, Mary Mother,
Why laughs she thus, between Hell and Heaven?)

"The wind is loud, but I hear him cry,
   Sister Helen,
That Keith of Ewern's like to die."
"And he and thou, and thou and I,
   Little brother."
  (O Mother, Mary Mother,
And they and we, between Hell and Heaven!)

"Three days ago, on his marriage-morn,
   Sister Helen,
He sickened, and lies since then forlorn."
"For bridegroom's side is the bride a thorn,
   Little brother?"
  (O Mother, Mary Mother,
Cold bridal cheer, between Hell and Heaven!)

"Three days and nights he has lain abed,
　　　　Sister Helen,
And he prays in torment to be dead."
"The thing may chance, if he have prayed,
　　　　Little brother!"
　　　(O Mother, Mary Mother,
If ye have prayed, between Hell and Heaven!)

"But he has not ceased to cry to-day,
　　　　Sister Helen,
That you should take your curse away."
"*My* prayer was heard,—he need but pray,
　　　　Little brother!"
　　　(O Mother, Mary Mother,
Shall God not hear, between Hell and Heaven?)

"But he says, till you take back your ban,
　　　　Sister Helen,
His soul would pass, yet never can."
"Nay then, shall I slay a living man,
　　　　Little brother?"
　　　(O Mother, Mary Mother,
A living soul, between Hell and Heaven!)

"But he calls for ever on your name,
　　　　Sister Helen,
And says that he melts before a flame."
"My heart for his pleasure fared the same,
　　　　Little brother."
　　　(O Mother, Mary Mother,
Fire at the heart, between Hell and Heaven!)

"Here's Keith of Westholm riding fast,
　　　　Sister Helen,
For I know the white plume on the blast."

"The hour, the sweet hour I forecast,
            Little brother!"
        (O Mother, Mary Mother,
Is the hour sweet, between Hell and Heaven?)

"He stops to speak, and he stills his horse,
            Sister Helen;
But his words are drowned in the wind's course."
"Nay hear, nay hear, you must hear perforce,
            Little brother!"
        (O Mother, Mary Mother,
What word between Hell and Heaven!)

"Oh he says that Keith of Ewern's cry,
            Sister Helen,
Is ever to see you ere he die."
"In all that his soul sees, there am I,
            Little brother!"
        (O Mother, Mary Mother,
The soul's one sight between Hell and Heaven!)

"He sends a ring and a broken coin,
            Sister Helen,
And bids you mind the banks of Boyne."
"What else he broke will he ever join,
            Little brother?"
        (O Mother, Mary Mother,
No, never joined, between Hell and Heaven!)

"He yields you these and craves full fain,
            Sister Helen,
You pardon him in his mortal pain."
"What else he took will he give again,
            Little brother?"
        (O Mother, Mary Mother,
Not twice to give, between Hell and Heaven!)

"He calls your name in an agony,
        Sister Helen,
That even dead Love must weep to see."
"Hate, born of Love, is blind as he,
        Little brother?"
      (O Mother, Mary Mother,
Love turned to hate, between Hell and Heaven!)

"Oh, it's Keith of Keith now that rides fast,
        Sister Helen,
For I know the white hair on the blast."
"The short, short hour will soon be past,
        Little brother!"
      (O Mother, Mary Mother,
Will soon be past, between Hell and Heaven!)

"He looks at me and he tries to speak,
        Sister Helen,
But oh! his voice is sad and weak!"
"What here should the mighty Baron seek,
        Little brother?"
      (O Mother, Mary Mother,
Is this the end, between Hell and Heaven?)

"Oh his son still cries, if you forgive,
        Sister Helen,
The body dies but the soul shall live."
"Fire shall forgive me as I forgive,
        Little brother!"
      (O Mother, Mary Mother,
As she forgives, between Hell and Heaven!)

"Oh he prays you, as his heart would rive,
        Sister Helen,
To save his dear son's soul alive."

"Fire cannot slay it, it shall thrive,
Little brother!"
(O Mother, Mary Mother,
Alas, alas, between Hell and Heaven!)

"He cries to you, kneeing in the road,
Sister Helen,
To go with him for the love of God!"
"The way is long to his son's abode,
Little brother."
(O Mother, Mary Mother,
The way is long, between Hell and Heaven!)

"A lady's here, by a dark steed brought,
Sister Helen,
So darkly clad, I saw her not."
"See her now or never see aught,
Little brother!"
(O Mother, Mary Mother,
What more to see, between Hell and Heaven?)

"Her hood falls back, and the moon shines fair,
Sister Helen,
On the Lady of Ewern's golden hair."
"Blest hour of my power and her despair,
Little brother!"
(O Mother, Mary Mother,
Hour blest and bann'd, between Hell and Heaven!)

"Pale, pale her cheeks, that in pride did glow,
Sister Helen,
Neath the bridal-wreath three days ago."
"One morn for pride and three days for woe,
Little brother!"

(O Mother, Mary Mother,
Three days, three nights, between Hell and Heaven!)

"Her clasped hands stretch from her bending head,
        Sister Helen;
With the loud wind's wail her sobs are wed."
"What wedding-strains hath her bridal-bed
        Little brother?"
    (O Mother, Mary Mother,
What strain but death's, between Hell and Heaven?)

"She may not speak, she sinks in a swoon,
        Sister Helen,
She lifts her lips and gasps on the moon."
"Oh! might I but hear her soul's blithe tune,
        Little brother!"
    (O Mother, Mary Mother,
Her woe's dumb cry, between Hell and Heaven!)

"They've caught her to Westholm's saddle-bow,
        Sister Helen,
And her moonlit hair gleams white in its flow."
"Let it turn whiter than winter snow,
        Little brother!"
    (O Mother, Mary Mother,
Woe-withered gold, between Hell and Heaven!)

"O Sister Helen, you heard the bell,
        Sister Helen,
More loud than the vesper-chime it fell."
"No vesper-chime, but a dying knell,
        Little brother!"
    (O Mother, Mary Mother,
His dying knell, between Hell and Heaven!)

"Alas! but I fear the heavy sound,
          Sister Helen;
Is it in the sky or in the ground?"
"Say, have they turned their horses round,
          Little brother?"
          (O Mother, Mary Mother,
What would she more, between Hell and Heaven?)

"They have raised the old man from his knee,
          Sister Helen,
And they ride in silence hastily."
"More fast the naked soul doth flee,
          Little brother!"
          (O Mother, Mary Mother,
The naked soul, between Hell and Heaven!)

"Flank to flank are the three steeds gone,
          Sister Helen,
But the lady's dark steed goes alone."
"And lonely her bridegroom's soul hath flown,
          Little brother."
          (O Mother, Mary Mother,
The lonely ghost, between Hell and Heaven!)

"Oh the wind is sad in the iron chill,
          Sister Helen,
And weary sad they look by the hill."
"But Keith of Ewern's sadder still,
          Little brother!"
          (O Mother, Mary Mother,
Most sad of all, between Hell and Heaven!)

"See, see, the wax has dropped from its place,
          Sister Helen!

And the flames are winning up apace!"
"Yet here they burn but for a space,
          Little brother!"
     (O Mother, Mary Mother,
Here for a space, between Hell and Heaven!)

"Ah! what white thing at the door has cross'd,
          Sister Helen?
Ah! what is this that sighs in the frost?"
"A soul that's lost as mine is lost,
          Little brother!"
     (O Mother, Mary Mother,
Lost, lost, all lost, between Hell and Heaven!)

CHRISTINA ROSSETTI (1830-1894)

GOBLIN MARKET

Morning and evening
Maids heard the goblins cry:
"Come buy our orchard fruits,
Come buy, come buy:
Apples and quinces,
Lemons and oranges,
Plump unpecked cherries,
Melons and raspberries,
Bloom-down-cheeked peaches,
Swart-headed mulberries,
Wild free-born cranberries,
Crab apples, dewberries,
Pine-apples, blackberries,
Apricots, strawberries;—

All ripe together
In summer weather,—
Morns that pass by,
Fair eves that fly;
Come buy, come buy:
Our grapes fresh from the vine,
Pomegranates full and fine,
Dates and sharp bullaces,
Rare pears and greengages,
Damsons and bilberries,
Taste them and try:
Currants and gooseberries,
Bright-fire-like barberries,
Figs to fill your mouth,
Citrons from the South,
Sweet to tongue and sound to eye;
Come buy, come buy."

Evening by evening
Among the brookside rushes,
Laura bowed her head to hear,
Lizzie veiled her blushes:
Crouching close together
In the cooling weather,
With clasping arms and cautioning lips,
With tingling cheeks and finger tips.
"Lie close," Laura said,
Pricking up her golden head:
"We must not look at goblin men,
We must not buy their fruits:
Who knows upon what soil they fed
Their hungry thirsty roots?"
"Come buy," call the goblins
Hobbling down the glen.
"Oh," cried Lizzie, "Laura, Laura,

You should not peep at goblin men."
Lizzie covered up her eyes,
Covered close lest they should look;
Laura reared her glossy head,
And whispered like the restless brook:
"Look, Lizzie, look, Lizzie,
Down the glen tramp little men.
One hauls a basket,
One bears a plate,
One lugs a golden dish
Of many pounds weight.
How fair the vine must grow
Whose grapes are so luscious;
How warm the wind must blow
Through those fruit bushes."
"No," said Lizzie: "No, no, no;
Their offers should not charm us,
Their evil gifts would harm us."
She thrust a dimpled finger
In each ear, shut eyes and ran:
Curious Laura chose to linger
Wondering at each merchant man.
One had a cat's face,
One whisked a tail,
One tramped at a rat's pace,
One crawled like a snail,
One like a wombat prowled obtuse and furry,
One like a ratel tumbled hurry skurry.
She heard a voice like voice of doves
Cooing all together:
They sounded kind and full of loves
In the pleasant weather.

Laura stretched her gleaming neck
Like a rush-imbedded swan,

Like a lily from the beck,
Like a moonlit poplar branch,
Like a vessel at the launch
When its last restraint is gone.

   Backwards up the mossy glen
Turned and trooped the goblin men,
With their shrill repeated cry,
"Come buy, come buy."
When they reached where Laura was
They stood stock still upon the moss,
Leering at each other,
Brother with queer brother;
Signalling each other,
Brother with sly brother.
One set his basket down,
One reared his plate;
One began to weave a crown
Of tendrils, leaves, and rough nuts brown
(Men sell not such in any town);
One heaved the golden weight
Of dish and fruit to offer her:
"Come buy, come buy," was still their cry.
Laura stared but did not stir,
Longed but had no money:
The whisk-tailed merchant bade her taste
In tones as smooth as honey,
The cat-faced purr'd,
The rat-paced spoke a word
Of welcome, and the snail-paced even was heard;
One parrot-voiced and jolly
Cried "Pretty Goblin" still for "Pretty Polly";—
One whistled like a bird.

But sweet-tooth Laura spoke in haste:
"Good folk, I have no coin;
To take were to purloin:
I have no copper in my purse,
I have no silver either,
And all my gold is on the furze
That shakes in windy weather
Above the rusty heather."
"You have much gold upon your head,"
They answered all together:
"Buy from us with a golden curl."
She clipped a precious golden lock,
She dropped a tear more rare than pearl,
Then sucked their fruit globes fair or red:
Sweeter than honey from the rock,
Stronger than man-rejoicing wine,
Clearer than water flowed that juice;
She never tasted such before,
How should it cloy with length of use?
She sucked and sucked and sucked the more
Fruits which that unknown orchard bore;
She sucked until her lips were sore;
Then flung the emptied rinds away
But gathered up one kernel stone,
And knew not was it night or day
As she turned home alone.

Lizzie met her at the gate
Full of wise upbraidings:
"Dear, you should not stay so late,
Twilight is not good for maidens;
Should not loiter in the glen
In the haunts of goblin men.
Do you not remember Jeanie,

How she met them in the moonlight,
Took their gifts both choice and many,
Ate their fruits and wore their flowers
Plucked from bowers
Where summer ripens at all hours?
But ever in the moonlight
She pined and pined away;
Sought them by night and day,
Found them no more but dwindled and grew grey;
Then fell with the first snow,
While to this day no grass will grow
Where she lies low:
I planted daisies there a year ago
That never blow.
You should not loiter so."
"Nay, hush," said Laura:

"Nay, hush, my sister:
I ate and ate my fill,
Yet my mouth waters still;
Tomorrow night I will
Buy more:" and kissed her:
"Have done with sorrow;
I'll bring you plums tomorrow
Fresh on their mother twigs,
Cherries worth getting;
You cannot think what figs
My teeth have met in,
What melons icy-cold
Piled on a dish of gold
Too huge for me to hold,
What peaches with a velvet nap,
Pellucid grapes without one seed:
Odorous indeed must be the mead
Whereon they grow, and pure the wave they drink

With lilies at the brink,
And sugar-sweet their sap."

   Golden head by golden head,
Like two pigeons in one nest
Folded in each other's wings,
They lay down in their curtained bed:
Like two blossoms on one stem,
Like two flakes of new-fall'n snow,
Like two wands of ivory
Tipped with gold for awful kins.
Moon and stars gazed in at them,
Wind sang to them lullaby,
Lumbering owls forbore to fly,
Not a bat flapped to and fro
Round their nest:
Cheek to cheek and breast to breast
Locked together in one nest.

   Early in the morning
When the first cock crowed his warning,
Neat like bees, as sweet and busy,
Laura rose with Lizzie:
Fetched in honey, milked the cows,
Aired and set to rights the house,
Kneaded cakes of whitest wheat,
Cakes for dainty mouths to eat,
Next churned butter, whipped up cream,
Fed their poultry, sat and sewed;
Talked as modest maidens should:
Lizzie with an open heart,
Laura in an absent dream,
One content, one sick in part;
One warbling for the mere bright day's delight,
One longing for the night.

At length the slow evening came:
They went with pitchers to the reedy brook;
Lizzie most placid in her look,
Laura most like a leaping flame.
They drew the gurgling water from its deep;
Lizzie plucked purple and rich golden flags,
Then turning homewards said: "The sunset flushes
Those furthest loftiest crags;
Come, Laura, not another maiden lags,
No wilful squirrel wags,
The beasts and birds are fast asleep."
But Laura loitered still among the rushes
And said the bank was steep.

And said the hour was early still,
The dew not fall'n, the wind not chill:
Listening ever, but not catching
The customary cry,
"Come buy, come buy,"
With its iterated jingle
Of sugar-baited words:
Not for all her watching
Once discerning even one goblin
Racing, whisking, tumbling, hobbling;
Let alone the herds
That used to tramp along the glen,
In groups or single,
Of brisk fruit-merchant men.

Till Lizzie urged, "O Laura, come;
I hear the fruit-call but I dare not look:
You should not loiter longer at this brook:
Come with me home.
The stars rise, the moon bends her arc,

Each glowworm winks her spark,
Let us get home before the night grows dark:
For clouds may gather
Though this is summer weather,
Put out the lights and drench us through;
Then if we lost our way what should we do?"

   Laura turned cold as stone
To find her sister heard that cry alone,
That goblin cry,
"Come buy our fruits, come buy."
Must she then buy no more such dainty fruit?
Must she no more such succous pasture find,
Gone deaf and blind?
Her tree of life drooped from the root:
She said not one word in her heart's sore ache;
But peering thro' the dimness, nought discerning,
Trudged home, her pitcher dripping all the way;
She crept to bed, and lay
Silent till Lizzie slept;
Then sat up in a passionate yearning,
And gnashed her teeth for baulked desire, and wept
As if her heart would break.

   Day after day, night after night,
Laura kept watch in vain
In sullen silence of exceeding pain.
She never caught again the goblin cry:
"Come buy, come buy";—
She never spied the goblin men
Hawking their fruits along the glen:
But when the moon waxed bright
Her hair grew thin and grey;
She dwindled, as the fair full moon doth turn
To swift decay and burn
Her fire away.

One day remembering her kernel-stone
She set it by a wall that faced the south;
Dewed it with tears, hoped for a root,
Watched for a waxing shoot,
But there came none;
It never saw the sun,
It never felt the trickling moisture run:
While with sunk eyes and faded mouth
She dreamed of melons, as a traveller sees
False waves in desert drouth
With a shade of leaf-crowned trees,
And burns the thirstier in the sandful breeze.

She no more swept the house,
Tended the fowls or cows,
Fetched honey, kneaded cakes of wheat,
Brought water from the brook:
But sat down listless in the chimney-nook
And would not eat.

Tender Lizzie could not bear
To watch her sister's cankerous care
Yet not to share.
She night and morning
Caught the goblins' cry:
"Come buy our orchard fruits,
Come buy, come buy:"—
Beside the brook, along the glen,
She heard the tramp of goblin men,
The voice and stir
Poor Laura could not hear;
Longed.to buy fruit to comfort her,
But feared to pay too dear.
She thought of Jeanie in her grave,

Who should have been a bride;
But who for joys brides hope to have
Fell sick and died
In her gay prime,
In earliest Winter time,
With the first glazing rime,
With the first snow-fall of crisp Winter time.

   Till Laura dwindling
Seemed knocking at Death's door:
Then Lizzie weighed no more
Better and worse;
But put a silver penny in her purse,
Kissed Laura, crossed the heath with clumps of furze
At twilight, halted by the brook:
And for the first time in her life
Began to listen and look.

   Laughed every goblin
When they spied her peeping:
Came towards her hobbling,
Flying, running, leaping,
Puffing and blowing,
Chuckling, clapping, crowing,
Clucking and gobbling,
Mopping and mowing,
Full of airs and graces,
Pulling wry faces,
Demure grimaces,
Cat-like and rat-like,
Ratel- and wombat-like,
Snail-paced in a hurry,
Parrot-voiced and whistler,
Helter skelter, hurry skurry,

Chattering like magpies,
Fluttering like pigeons,
Gliding like fishes,—
Hugged her and kissed her:
Squeezed and caressed her:
Stretched up their dishes,
Panniers, and plates:
"Look at our apples
Russet and dun,
Bob at our cherries,
Bite at our peaches,
Citrons and dates,
Grapes for the asking,
Pears red with basking
Out in the sun,
Plums on their twigs;
Pluck them and suck them,
Pomegranates, figs."—

"Good folk," said Lizzie,
Mindful of Jeanie:
"Give me much and many:"—
Held out her apron,
Tossed them her penny
"Nay, take a seat with us,
Honour and eat with us,"
They answered grinning:
"Our feast is but beginning
Night yet is early,
Warm and dew-pearly,
Wakeful and starry:
Such fruits as these
No man can carry;
Half their bloom would fly,
Half their dew would dry,

Half their flavour would pass by.
Sit down and feast with us,
Be welcome guest with us,
Cheer you and rest with us."—
"Thank you," said Lizzie: "But one waits
At home alone for me:
So without further parleying,
If you will not sell me any
Of your fruits though much and many,
Give me back my silver penny
I tossed you for a fee."—

They began to scratch their pates,
No longer wagging, purring,
But visibly demurring,
Grunting and snarling.
One called her proud,
Cross-grained, uncivil;
Their tones waxed loud,
Their looks were evil.
Lashing their tails
They trod and hustled her,
Elbowed and jostled her,
Clawed with their nails,
Barking, mewing, hissing, mocking,
Tore her gown and soiled her stocking,
Twitched her hair out by the roots,
Stamped upon her tender feet,
Held her hands and squeezed their fruits
Against her mouth to make her eat.

White and golden Lizzie stood,
Like a lily in a flood,—
Like a rock of blue-veined stone
Lashed by tides obstreperously,—

Like a beacon left alone
In a hoary roaring sea,
Sending up a golden fire,—
Like a fruit-crowned orange-tree
White with blossoms honey-sweet
Sore beset by wasp and bee,—
Like a royal virgin town
Topped with gilded dome and spire
Close beleaguered by a fleet
Mad to tug her standard down.

One may lead a horse to water,
Twenty cannot make him drink.
Though the goblins cuffed and caught her,
Coaxed and fought her,
Bullied and besought her,
Scratched her, pinched her black as ink,
Kicked and knocked her,
Mauled and mocked her,
Lizzie uttered not a word;
Would not open lip from lip
Lest they should cram a mouthful in:
But laughed in heart to feel the drip
Of juice that syruped all her face,
And lodged in dimples of her chin,
And streaked her neck which quaked like curd.
At last the evil people
Worn out by her resistance
Flung back her penny, kicked their fruit
Along whichever road they took,
Not leaving root or stone or shoot;
Some writhed into the ground,
Some dived into the brook

With ring and ripple,
Some scudded on the gale without a sound,
Some vanished in the distance.

   In a smart, ache, tingle,
Lizzie went her way;
Knew not was it night or day;
Sprang up the bank, tore thro' the furze,
Threaded copse and dingle,
And heard her penny jingle
Bouncing in her purse,—
Its bounce was music to her ear.
She ran and ran
As if she feared some goblin man
Dogged her with gibe or curse
Or something worse:
But not one goblin skurried after,
Nor was she pricked by fear;
The kind heart made her windy-paced
That urged her home quite out of breath with haste
And inward laughter.

   She cried "Laura," up the garden
"Did you miss me?
Come and kiss me.
Never mind my bruises,
Hug me, kiss me, suck my juices
Squeezed from goblin fruits for you,
Goblin pulp and goblin dew.
Eat me, drink me, love me;
Laura, make much of me:
For your sake I have braved the glen
And had to do with goblin merchant men."

Laura started from her chair,
Flung her arms up in the air,
Clutched her hair:
"Lizzie, Lizzie, have you tasted
For my sake the fruit forbidden?
Must your light like mine be hidden,
Your young life like mine be wasted,
Undone in mine undoing
And ruined in my ruin,
Thirsty-cankered, goblin-ridden?"—
She clung about her sister,
Kissed and kissed and kissed her:
Tears once again
Refreshed her shrunken eyes,
Dropping like rain
After long sultry drouth;
Shaking with anguish fear, and pain,
She kissed and kissed her with a hungry mouth.

Her lips began to scorch,
That juice was wormwood to her tongue,
She loathed the feast:
Writhing as one possessed she leaped and sung,
Rent all her robe, and wrung
Her hands in lamentable haste,
And beat her breast.
Her locks streamed like the torch
Borne by a racer at full speed,
Or like the mane of horses in their flight,
Or like an eagle when she stems the light
Straight toward the sun,
Or like a caged thing freed,
Or like a flying flag when armies run.

Swift fire spread through her veins, knocked at her heart,
Met the fire smouldering there
And overbore its lesser flame;
She gorged on bitterness without a name:
Ah! fool, to choose such part
Of soul-consuming care!
Sense failed in the mortal strife:
Like the watch-tower of a town
Which an earthquake shatters down,
Like a lightning-stricken mast,
Like a wind-uprooted tree
Spun about,
Like a foam-topped waterspout
Cast down headlong in the sea,
She fell at last;
Pleasure past and anguish past,
Is it death or is it life?

Life out of death.
That night long Lizzie watched by her,
Counted her pulse's flagging stir,
Felt for her breath,
Held water to her lips, and cooled her face
With tears and fanning leaves:
But when the first birds chirped about their eaves,
And early reapers plodded to the place
Of golden sheaves,
And dew-wet grass
Bowed in the morning winds so brisk to pass,
And new buds with new day
Opened of cup-like lilies on the stream,
Laura awoke as from a dream,
Laughed in the innocent old way,
Hugged Lizzie but not twice or thrice;

Her gleaming locks showed not one thread of grey,
Her breath was sweet as May
And light danced in her eyes.

   Days, weeks, months, years
Afterwards, when both were wives
With children of their own;
Their mother-hearts beset with fears,
Their lives bound up in tender lives;
Laura would call the little ones
And tell them of her early prime,
Those pleasant days long gone
Of not-returning time:
Would talk about the haunted glen,
The wicked, quaint fruit-merchant men,
Their fruits like honey to the throat
But poison in the blood;
(Men sell not such in any town:)
Would tell them how her sister stood
In deadly peril to do her good,
And win the fiery antidote:
Then joining hands to little hands
Would bid them cling together,
"For there is no friend like a sister
In calm or stormy weather;
To cheer one on the tedious way,
To fetch one if one goes astray,
To lift one if one totters down,
To strengthen whilst one stands."

THE GHOST'S PETITION

   "There's a footstep coming; look out and see."—
      "The leaves are falling, the wind is calling;
   No one cometh across the lea."—

"There's a footstep coming; O sister, look."—
    "The ripple flashes, the white foam dashes;
No one cometh across the brook."—

"But he promised that he would come:
    Tonight, tomorrow, in joy or sorrow,
He must keep his word, and must come home.

"For he promised that he would come;
    His word was given; from earth to heaven,
He must keep his word, and must come home.

"Go to sleep, my sweet sister Jane;
    You can slumber, who need not number
Hour after hour, in doubt and pain.

"I shall sit here awhile and watch;
    Listening, hoping for one hand groping,
In deep shadow, to find the latch."

After the dark and before the light,
    One lay sleeping, and one sat weeping,
Who had watched and wept the weary night.

After the night and before the day
    One lay sleeping; and one sat weeping—
Watching, weeping for one away.

There came a footstep climbing the stair,
    Some one standing out on the landing
Shook the door like a puff of air.—

Shook the door and in he passed.
    Did he enter? In the room center
Stood her husband; the door shut fast.

"O Robin, but you are cold—
   Chilled with the night-dew; so lily white you
Look like a stray lamb from our fold.

"O Robin, but you are late:
   Come and sit near me—sit here and cheer me."—
(Blue the flame burnt in the grate.)

"Lay not down your head on my breast:
   I cannot hold you, kind wife, nor fold you
In the shelter that you love best.

"Feel not after my clasping hand:
   I am but a shadow, come from the meadow,
Where many lie, but no tree can stand.

"We are the trees that have shed their leaves:
   Our heads lie low there, but no tears flow there;
Only I grieve for my wife who grieves.

"I could rest if you would not moan
   Hour after hour; I have no power
To shut my ears as I lie alone.

"I could rest if you would not cry,
   But there's no sleeping while you sit weeping—
Watching, weeping so bitterly."—

"Woe's me! Woe's me! For this I have heard.
   Oh night of sorrow—oh, black tomorrow!
Is it thus that you keep your word?

"Oh, you who used so to shelter me,
   Warm from the least wind—why, now the east wind
Is warmer than you, whom I quake to see.

"Oh, my husband of flesh and blood,
    For whom my mother I left, and brother,
And all I had, accounting it good,

"What do you do there, under the ground,
    In the dark hollow? I'm fain to follow.
What do you do there? What have you found?"—

"What I do there I must not tell,
    But I have plenty—kind wife, content ye:
It is well with us: it is well.

"Tender hand hath made our nest;
    Our fear is ended; our hope is blended
With present pleasure, and we have rest."

"Oh, but Robin, I'm fain to come,
    If your present days are so pleasant,
For my days are so wearisome.

"Yet I'll dry my tears for your sake:
    Why should I tease you, who cannot please you
Any more with the pains I take?"

JAMES THOMSON (1834-1882)

THE CITY OF DREADFUL NIGHT

Lo, thus, as prostrate, "In the dust I write
    My heart's deep languor and my soul's sad tears."
Yet why evoke the spectres of black night
    To blot the sunshine of exultant years?

Why disinter dead faith from mouldering hidden?
Why break the seals of mute despair unbidden,
    And wail life's discords into careless ears?

Because a cold rage seizes one at whiles
    To show the bitter old and wrinkled truth
Stripped naked of all vesture that beguiles,
    False dreams, false hopes, false masks and modes of youth:
Because it gives some sense of power and passion
In helpless impotence to try to fashion
    Our woe in living words howe'er uncouth.

Surely I write not for the hopeful young,
    Or those who deem their happiness of worth,
Or such as pasture and grow fat among
    The shows of life and feel nor doubt nor dearth,
Or pious spirits with a God above them,
To sanctify and glorify and love them,
    Or sages who foresee a heaven on earth.

For none of these I write, and none of these
    Could read the writing if they deigned to try:
So may they flourish, in their due degrees,
    On our sweet earth and in their unplaced sky.
If any cares for the weak words here written,
It must be some one desolate, Fate-smitten,
    Whose faith and hope are dead, and who would die.

Yes, here and there some weary wanderer
    In that same city of tremendous night,
Will understand the speech, and feel a stir
    Of fellowship in all-disastrous fight;
"I suffer mute and lonely, yet another
Uplifts his voice to let me know a brother
    Travels the same wild paths though out of sight."

O sad Fraternity, do I unfold
  Your dolorous mysteries shrouded from of yore?
Nay, be assured; no secret can be told
  To any who divined it not before:
None uninitiate by many a presage
Will comprehend the language of the message,
  Although proclaimed aloud for evermore.

I

The City is of Night; perchance of Death,
  But certainly of Night; for never there
Can come the lucid morning's fragrant breath
  After the dewy dawning's cold grey air;
The moon and stars may shine with scorn or pity;
The sun has never visited that city,
  For it dissolveth in the daylight fair.

Dissolveth like a dream of night away;
  Though present in distempered gloom of thought
And deadly weariness of heart all day.
  But when a dream night after night is brought
Throughout a week, and such weeks few or many
Recur each year for several years, can any
  Discern that dream from real life in aught?

For life is but a dream whose shapes return,
  Some frequently, some seldom, some by night
And some by day, some night and day: we learn,
  The while all change and many vanish quite,
In their recurrence with recurrent changes
A certain seeming order; where this ranges
  We count things real; such is memory's might.

A river girds the city west and south,
  The main north channel of a broad lagoon,

Regurging with the salt tides from the mouth;
  Waste marshes shine and glister to the moon
For leagues, then moorland black, then stony ridges;
Great piers and causeways, many noble bridges,
  Connect the town and islet suburbs strewn.

Upon an easy slope it lies at large,
  And scarcely overlaps the long curved crest
Which swells out two leagues, from the river marge.
  A trackless wilderness rolls north and west,
Savannahs, savage woods, enormous mountains,
Bleak uplands, black ravines with torrent fountains;
  And eastward rolls the shipless sea's unrest.

The city is not ruinous, although
  Great ruins of an unremembered past,
With others of a few short years ago
  More sad, are found within its precincts vast.
The street-lamps always burn; but scarce a casement
In house or place front from roof to basement
  Doth glow or gleam athwart the mirk air cast.

The street-lamps burn amidst the baleful glooms,
  Amidst the soundless solitudes immense
Of rangèd mansions dark and still as tombs.
  The silence which benumbs or strains the sense
Fulfils with awe the soul's despair unweeping:
Myriads of habitants are ever sleeping,
  Or dead, or fled from nameless pestilence!

Yet as in some necropolis you find
  Perchance one mourner to a thousand dead,
So there; worn faces that look deaf and blind
  Like tragic masks of stone. With weary tread,

Each wrapt in his own doom, they wander, wander,
Or sit foredone and desolately ponder
    Through sleepless hours with heavy drooping head.

Mature men chiefly, few in age or youth,
    A woman rarely, now and then a child:
A child! If here the heart turns sick with ruth
    To see a little one from birth defiled,
Or lame or blind, as preordained to languish
Through youthless life, think how it bleeds with anguish
    To meet one erring in that homeless wild.

They often murmur to themselves, they speak
    To one another seldom, for their woe
Broods maddening inwardly and scorns to wreak
    Itself abroad; and if at whiles it grow
To frenzy which must rave, none heeds the clamor.
Unless there waits some victim of like glamour,
    To rave in turn, who lends attentive show.

The City is of Night, but not of Sleep;
    There sweet sleep is not for the weary brain;
The pitiless hours like years and ages creep,
    A night seems termless hell. This dreadful strain
Of thought and consciousness which never ceases,
Or which some moments' stupor but increases,
    This, worse than woe, makes wretches there insane.

They leave all hope behind who enter there:
    One certitude while sane they cannot leave,
One anodyne for torture and despair;
    The certitude of Death, which no reprieve
Can put off long; and which divinely tender,
But waits the outstretched hand to promptly render
    That draught whose slumber nothing can bereave.

II

Because he seemed to walk with an intent
   I followed him; who, shadowlike and frail,
Unswervingly though slowly onward went,
   Regardless, wrapt in thought as in a veil:
Thus step for step with lonely sounding feet
We travelled many a long dim silent street.

At length he paused: a black mass in the gloom,
   A tower that merged into the heavy sky;
Around, the huddled stones of grave and tomb:
   Some old God's-acre now corruption's sty:
He murmured to himself with dull despair,
Here Faith died, poisoned by this charnel air.

Then turning to the right went on once more,
   And travelled weary roads without suspense;
And reached at last a low wall's open door,
   Whose villa gleamed beyond the foliage dense:
He gazed, and muttered with a hard despair,
Here Love died, stabbed by its own worshipped pair.

Then turning to the right resumed his march,
   And travelled streets and lanes with wondrous strength,
Until on stooping through a narrow arch
   We stood before a squalid house at length:
He gazed, and whispered with a cold despair,
Here Hope died, starved out in its utmost lair.

When he had spoken thus, before he stirred,
   I spoke, perplexed by something in the signs
Of desolation I had seen and heard
   In this drear pilgrimage to ruined shrines:
When Faith and Love and Hope are dead indeed,
Can Life still live? By what doth it proceed?

As whom his one intense thought over-powers,
  He answered coldly, Take a watch, erase
The signs and figures of the circling hours,
  Detach the hands, remove the dial-face;
The works proceed until run down; although
Bereft of purpose, void of use, still go.

Then turning to the right paced on again,
  And traversed squares and travelled streets whose glooms
Seemed more and more familiar to my ken;
  And reached that sullen temple of the tombs;
And paused to murmur with the old despair,
Here Faith died, poisoned by this charnel air.

I ceased to follow, for the knot of doubt
  Was severed sharply with a cruel knife:
He circled thus for ever tracing out
  The series of the fraction left of Life;
Perpetual recurrence in the scope
Of but three terms, dead Faith, dead Love, dead Hope.

III

Although lamps burn along the silent streets;
  Even when moonlight silvers empty squares
The dark holds countless lanes and close retreats;
  But when the night its sphereless mantle wears
The open spaces yawn with gloom abysmal,
The sombre mansions loom immense and dismal,
  The lanes are black as subterranean lairs.

And soon the eye a strange new vision learns:
  The night remains for it as dark and dense,
Yet clearly in this darkness it discerns
  As in the daylight with its natural sense;

Perceives a shade in shadow not obscurely,
Pursues a stir of black in blackness surely,
    Sees spectres also in the gloom intense.

The ear, too, with the silence vast and deep
    Becomes familiar though unreconciled;
Hears breathings as of hidden life asleep,
    And muffled throbs as of pent passions wild,
Far murmurs, speech of pity or derision;
But all more dubious than the things of vision,
    So that it knows not when it is beguiled.

No time abates the first despair and awe,
    But wonder ceases soon; the weirdest thing
Is felt least strange beneath the lawless law
    Where Death-in-Life is the eternal king;
Crushed impotent beneath this reign of terror,
Dazed with such mysteries of woe and error,
    The soul is too outworn for wondering.

IV

He stood alone within the spacious square
    Declaiming from the central grassy mound,
With head uncovered and with streaming hair,
    As if large multitudes were gathered round:
A stalwart shape, the gestures full of might,
The glances burning with unnatural light:—

As I came through the desert thus it was,
As I came through the desert: All was black,
In heaven no single star, on earth no track;
A brooding hush without a stir or note,
The air so thick it clotted in my throat;
And thus for hours; then some enormous things

Swooped past with savage cries and clanking wings:
        But I strode on austere;
        No hope could have no fear.

As I came through the desert thus it was,
As I came through the desert: Eyes of fire
Glared at me throbbing with a starved desire;
The hoarse and heavy and carnivorous breath
Was hot upon me from deep jaws of death;
Sharp claws, swift talons, fleshless fingers cold
Plucked at me from the bushes, tried to hold:
        But I strode on austere;
        No hope could have no fear.

As I came through the desert thus it was,
As I came through the desert: Lo you, there,
That hillock burning with a brazen glare;
Those myriad dusky flames with points aglow
Which writhed and hissed and darted to and fro;
A Sabbath of the Serpents, heaped pell-mell
For Devil's roll-call and some *fête* of Hell:
        Yet I strode on austere;
        No hope could have no fear.

As I came through the desert thus it was,
As I came through the desert: Meteors ran
And crossed their javelins on the black sky-span;
The zenith opened to a gulf of flame,
The dreadful thunderbolts jarred earth's fixed frame:
The ground all heaved in waves of fire that surged
And weltered round me sole there unsubmerged:
        Yet I strode on austere;
        No hope could have no fear.

As I came through the desert thus it was,
As I came through the desert: Air once more,
And I was close upon a wild sea-shore;
Enormous cliffs arose on either hand,
The deep tide thundered up a league-broad strand;
White foambelts seethed there, wan spray swept and flew;
The sky broke, moon and stars and clouds and blue:
       And I strode on austere;
       No hope could have no fear.

As I came through the desert thus it was,
As I came through the desert: On the left
The sun arose and crowned a broad crag-cleft;
There stopped and burned out black, except a rim,
A bleeding eyeless socket, red and dim;
Whereon the moon fell suddenly south-west,
And stood above the right-hand cliffs at rest:
       Still I strode on austere;
       No hope could have no fear.

As I came through the desert thus it was,
As I came through the desert: From the right
A shape came slowly with a ruddy light;
A woman with a red lamp in her hand,
Bareheaded and barefooted on that strand;
O desolation moving with such grace!
O anguish with such beauty in thy face!
       I fell as on my bier,
       Hope travailed with such fear.

As I came through the desert thus it was,
As I came through the desert: I was twain,
Two selves distinct that cannot join again;
One stood apart and knew but could not stir,
And watched the other stark in swoon and her;

And she came on, and never turned aside,
Between such sun and moon and roaring tide:
　　　And as she came more near
　　　My soul grew mad with fear.

As I came through the desert thus it was,
As I came through the desert: Hell is mild
And piteous matched with that accursèd wild;
A large black sign was on her breast that bowed,
A broad black band ran down her snow-white shroud;
That lamp she held was her own burning heart,
Whose blood-drops trickled step by step apart;
　　　The mystery was clear;
　　　Mad rage had swallowed fear.

As I came through the desert thus it was,
As I came through the desert: By the sea
She knelt and bent above that senseless me;
Those lamp-drops fell upon my white brow there,
She tried to cleanse them with her tears and hair;
She murmured words of pity, love, and woe,
She heeded not the level rushing flow:
　　　And mad with rage and fear,
　　　I stood stonebound so near.

As I came through the desert thus it was,
As I came through the desert: When the tide
Swept up to her there kneeling by my side,
She clasped that corpse-like me, and they were borne
Away, and this vile me was left forlorn;
I know the whole sea cannot quench that heart,
Or cleanse that brow, or wash those two apart:
　　　They love; their doom is drear,
　　　Yet they nor hope nor fear;
　　　But I, what do I here?

V

How he arrives there none can clearly know;
 Athwart the mountains and immense wild tracts,
Or flung a waif upon that vast sea-flow,
 Or down the river's boiling cataracts:
To reach it is as dying fever-stricken;
To leave it, slow faint birth intense pangs quicken;
 And memory swoons in both the tragic acts.

But being there one feels a citizen;
 Escape seems hopeless to the heart forlorn:
Can Death-in-Life be brought to life again?
 And yet release does come; there comes a morn
When he awakes from slumbering so sweetly
That all the world is changed for him completely,
 And he is verily as if new-born.

He scarcely can believe the blissful change.
 He weeps perchance who wept not while accurst;
Never again will he approach the range
 Infected by that evil spell now burst:
Poor wretch! who once hath paced that dolent city
Shall pace it often, doomed beyond all pity,
 With horror ever deepening from the first.

Though he possess sweet babes and loving wife,
 A home of peace by loyal friendships cheered,
And love them more than death or happy life,
 They shall avail not; he must dree his weird;
Renounce all blessings for that imprecation,
Steal forth and haunt that builded desolation,
 Of woe and terrors and thick darkness reared.

VI

I sat forlornly by the river-side,
    And watched the bridge-lamps glow like golden stars
Above the blackness of the swelling tide,
    Down which they struck rough gold in ruddier bars;
And heard the heave and splashing of the flow
Against the wall a dozen feet below.

Large elm-trees stood along that river-walk;
    And under one, a few steps from my seat,
I heard strange voices join in stranger talk,
    Although I had not heard approaching feet;
These bodiless voices in my waking dream
Flowed dark words blending with the sombre stream:—

And you have after all come back; come back.
I was about to follow on your track.
And you have failed: our spark of hope is black.

That I have failed is proved by my return:
The spark is quenched, nor ever more will burn.
But listen; and the story you shall learn.

I reached the portal common spirits fear,
And read the words above it, dark yet clear,
"Leave hope behind, all ye who enter here:"

And would have passed in, gratified to gain
That positive eternity of pain,
Instead of this insufferable inane.

A demon warder clutched me, Not so fast;
First leave your hopes behind!—But years have passed
Since I left all behind me, to the last:

You cannot count for hope, with all your wit,
This bleak despair that drives me to the Pit:
How could I seek to enter void of it?

He snarled, What thing is this which apes a soul,
And would find entrance to our gulf of dole
Without the payment of the settled toll?

Outside the gate he showed an open chest:
Here pay their entrance fees the souls unblest;
Cast in some hope, you enter with the rest.

This is Pandora's box; whose lid shall shut,
And Hell-gate too, when hopes have filled it; but
They are so thin that it will never glut.

I stood a few steps backwards, desolate;
And watched the spirits pass me to their fate,
And fling off hope, and enter at the gate.

When one casts off a load he springs upright,
Squares back his shoulders, breathes with all his might,
And briskly paces forward strong and light:

But these, as if they took some burden, bowed;
The whole frame sank; however strong and proud
Before, they crept in quite infirm and cowed.

And as they passed me, earnestly from each
A morsel of his hope I did beseech,
To pay my entrance; but all mocked my speech.

Not one would cede a tittle of his store
Though knowing that in instants three or four
He must resign the whole for evermore.

So I returned. Our destiny is fell;
For in this Limbo we must ever dwell,
Shut out alike from Heaven and Earth and Hell.

The other sighed back, Yea; but if we grope
With care through all this Limbo's dreary scope,
We yet may pick up some minute lost hope;

And, sharing it between us, entrance win,
In spite of fiends so jealous for gross sin:
Let us without delay our search begin.

VII

Some say that phantoms haunt those shadowy streets,
   And mingle freely there with sparse mankind;
And tell of ancient woes and black defeats,
   And murmur mysteries in the grave enshrined:
But others think them visions of illusion,
Or even men gone far in self-confusion;
   No man there being wholly sane in mind.

And yet a man who raves, however mad,
   Who bares his heart and tells of his own fall,
Reserves some inmost secret good or bad:
   The phantoms have no reticence at all:
The nudity of flesh will blush though tameless,
The extreme nudity of bone grins shameless,
   The unsexed skeleton mocks shroud and pall.

I have seen phantoms there that were as men
   And men that were as phantoms flit and roam;
Marked shapes that were not living to my ken,
   Caught breathings acrid as with Dead Sea foam:
The City rests for man so weird and awful,

That his intrusion there might seem unlawful,
    And phantoms there may have their proper home.

VIII

While I still lingered on that river-walk,
    And watched the tide as black as our black doom,
I heard another couple join in talk,
    And saw them to the left hand in the gloom
Seated against an elm bole on the ground,
Their eyes intent upon the stream profound.

"I never knew another man on earth
    But had some joy and solace in his life,
    Some chance of triumph in the dreadful strife:
My doom has been unmitigated dearth."

"We gaze upon the river, and we note
The various vessels large and small that float,
Ignoring every wrecked and sunken boat."

"And yet I asked no splendid dower, no spoil
    Of sway or fame or rank or even wealth;
    But homely love with common food and health,
And nightly sleep to balance daily toil."

"This all-too-humble soul would arrogate
Unto itself some signalising hate
From the supreme indifference of Fate!"

"Who is most wretched in this dolorous place?
    I think myself; yet I would rather be
    My miserable self than He, than He
Who formed such creatures to His own disgrace

"The vilest thing must be less vile than Thou
    From whom it had its being, God and Lord!
    Creator of all woe and sin! abhorred,
Malignant and implacable! I vow

"That not for all Thy power furled and unfurled,
    For all the temples to Thy glory built,
    Would I assume the ignominious guilt
Of having made such men in such a world."

"As if a Being, God or Fiend, could reign,
At once so wicked, foolish, and insane,
As to produce men when He might refrain!

"The world rolls round for ever like a mill;
It grinds out death and life and good and ill;
It has no purpose, heart or mind or will.

"While air of Space and Time's full river flow
The mill must blindly whirl unresting so:
It may be wearing out, but who can know?

"Man might know one thing were his sight less dim
That it whirls not to suit his petty whim,
That it is quite indifferent to him.

"Nay, does it treat him harshly as he saith?
It grinds him some slow years of bitter breath,
Then grinds him back into eternal death."

IX

It is full strange to him who hears and feels,
    When wandering there in some deserted street,
The booming and the jar of ponderous wheels,
    The trampling clash of heavy ironshod feet:

Who in this Venice of the Black Sea rideth?
Who in this city of the stars abideth
  To buy or sell as those in daylight sweet?

The rolling thunder seems to fill the sky
  As it comes on; the horses snort and strain,
The harness jingles, as it passes by;
  The hugeness of an overburthened wain:
A man sits nodding on the shaft or trudges
Three parts asleep beside his fellow-drudges:
  And so it rolls into the night again.

What merchandise? whence, whither, and for whom?
  Perchance it is a Fate-appointed hearse,
Bearing away to some mysterious tomb
  Or Limbo of the scornful universe
The joy, the peace, the life-hope, the abortions
Of all things good which should have been our portions
  But have been strangled by that City's curse.

X

The mansion stood apart in its own ground;
  In front thereof a fragrant garden-lawn,
High trees about it, and the whole walled round:
  The massy iron gates were both withdrawn;
And every window of its front shed light,
Portentuous in that City of the Night

But though thus lighted it was deadly still
  As all the countless bulks of solid gloom:
Perchance a congregation to fulfil
  Solemnities of silence in this doom,
Mysterious rites of dolor and despair
Permitting not a breath of chant or prayer?

Broad steps ascended to a terrace broad
  Whereon lay still light from the open door;
The hall was noble, and its aspect awed,
  Hung round with heavy black from dome to floor;
And ample stairways rose to left and right
Whose balustrades were also draped with night.

I paced from room to room, from hall to hall,
  Nor any life throughout the maze discerned;
But each was hung with its funereal pall,
  And held a shrine, around which tapers burned,
With picture or with statue or with bust,
All copied from the same fair form of dust:

A woman very young and very fair:
  Beloved by bounteous life and joy and youth,
And loving these sweet lovers, so that care
  And age and death seemed not for her in sooth:
Alike as stars, all beautiful and bright,
These shapes lit up that mausoléan night.

At length I heard a murmur as of lips,
  And reached an open oratory hung
With heaviest blackness of the whole eclipse;
  Beneath the dome a fuming censer swung;
And one lay there upon a low white bed,
With tapers burning at the foot and head:

The Lady of the images: supine,
  Deathstill, lifesweet, with folded palms she lay:
And kneeling there as at a sacred shrine
  A young man wan and worn who seemed to pray:
A crucifix of dim and ghostly white
Surmounted the large altar left in night:—

The chambers of the mansion of my heart,
In every one whereof thine image dwells,
Are black with grief eternal for thy sake.

The inmost oratory of my soul,
Wherein thou ever dwellest quick or dead,
Is black with grief eternal for thy sake.

I kneel beside thee and I clasp the cross
With eyes for ever fixed upon that face
So beautiful and dreadful in its calm.

I kneel here patient as thou liest there;
As patient as a statue carved in stone,
Of adoration and eternal grief.

While thou dost not awake I cannot move;
And something tells me thou wilt never wake,
And I alive feel turning into stone.

Most beautiful were Death to end my grief,
Most hateful to destroy the sight of thee,
Dear vision better than all death or life.

But I renounce all choice of life or death,
For either shall be ever at thy side,
And thus in bliss or woe be ever well.—

He murmured thus and thus in monotone,
    Intent upon that uncorrupted face,
Entranced except his moving lips alone:
    I glided with hushed footsteps from the place.
This was the festival that filled with light
That palace in the City of the Night.

XI

What men are they who haunt these fatal glooms,
   And fill their living mouths with dust of death,
And make their habitations in the tombs,
   And breathe eternal sighs with mortal breath,
And pierce life's pleasant veil of various error
To reach that void of darkness and old terror
   Wherein expire the lamps of hope and faith?

They have much wisdom yet they are not wise,
   They have much goodness yet they do not well,
(The fools we know have their own Paradise,
   The wicked also have their proper Hell);
They have much strength but still their doom is stronger,
Much patience but their time endureth longer,
   Much valor but life mocks it with some spell.

They are most rational and yet insane:
   An outward madness not to be controlled;
A perfect reason in the central brain,
   Which has no power, but sitteth wan and cold,
And sees the madness, and foresees as plainly
The ruin in its path, and trieth vainly
   To cheat itself refusing to behold.

And some are great in rank and wealth and power,
   And some renowned for genius and for worth;
And some are poor and mean, who brood and cower
   And shrink from notice, and accept all dearth
Of body, heart and soul, and leave to others
And boons of life: yet these and those are brothers,
   The saddest and the weariest men on earth.

XII

Our isolated units could be brought
   To act together for some common end?
For one by one, each silent with his thought,
   I marked a long loose line approach and wend
Athwart the great cathedral's cloistered square,
And slowly vanish from the moonlit air.

Then I would follow in among the last;
   And in the porch a shrouded figure stood,
Who challenged each one pausing ere he passed,
   With deep eyes burning through a blank white hood,
Whence come you in the world of life and light
To this our City of Tremendous Night?—

From pleading in a senate of rich lords
For some scant justice to our countless hordes
Who toil half-starved with scarce a human right:
I wake from daydreams to this real night.

From wandering through many a solemn scene
Of opium visions, with a heart serene
And intellect miraculously bright:
I wake from my dreams to this real night.

From making hundreds laugh and roar with glee
By my transcendent feats of mimicry,
And humor wanton as an elfish sprite:
I wake from daydreams to this real night.

From prayer and fasting in a lonely cell,
Which brought an ecstasy ineffable
Of love and adoration and delight:
I wake from daydreams to this real night.

From ruling on a splendid kingly throne
A nation which beneath my rule has grown
Year after year in wealth and arts and might:
I wake from daydreams to this real night.

From preaching to an audience fired with faith
The Lamb who died to save our souls from death,
Whose blood hath washed our scarlet sins wool-white:
I wake from daydreams to this real night.

From drinking fiery poison in a den
Crowded with tawdry girls and squalid men,
Who hoarsely laugh and curse and brawl and fight:
I wake from daydreams to this real night.

From picturing with all beauty and all grace
First Eden and the parents of our race,
A luminous rapture unto all men's sight:
I wake from daydreams to this real night.

From writing a great work with patient plan
To justify the ways of God to man,
And show how ill must fade and perish quite:
I wake from daydreams to this real night.

From desperate fighting with a little band
Against the powerful tyrants of our land,
To free our brethren in their own despite:
I wake from daydreams to this real night.

Thus, challenged by that warder sad and stern,
  Each one responded with his countersign,
Then entered the cathedral; and in turn
  I entered also, having given mine;

But lingered near until I heard no more,
And marked the closing of the massive door.

XIII

Of all things human which are strange and wild
　This is perchance the wildest and most strange,
And showeth man most utterly beguiled,
　To those who haunt that sunless City's range;
That he bemoans himself for aye, repeating
How time is deadly swift, how life is fleeting,
　How naught is constant on the earth but change.

The hours are heavy on him and the days;
　The burden of the months he scarce can bear;
And often in his secret soul he prays
　To sleep through barren periods unaware,
Arousing at some longed-for date of pleasure;
Which having passed and yielded him small treasure,
　He would outsleep another term of care.

Yet in his marvellous fancy he must make
　Quick wings for Time, and see it fly from us;
This Time which crawleth like a monstrous snake,
　Wounded and slow and very venomous;
Which creeps blindwormlike round the earth and ocean,
Distilling poison at each painful motion,
　And seems condemned to circle ever thus.

And since he cannot spend and use aright
　The little time here given him in trust,
But wasteth it in weary undelight
　Of foolish toil and trouble, strife and lust,
He naturally claimeth to inherit
The everlasting Future, that his merit
　May have full scope; as surely is most just.

O length of the intolerable hours,
  O nights that are as aeons of slow pain,
O Time, too ample for our vital powers,
  O Life, whose woeful vanities remain
Immutable for all of all our legions
Through all the centuries and in all the regions,
  Not of your speed and variance *we* complain.

We do not ask a longer term of strife,
  Weakness and weariness and nameless woes:
We do not claim renewed and endless life
  When this which is our torment here shall close,
An everlasting conscious inanition!
We yearn for speedy death in full fruition,
  Dateless oblivion and divine repose.

XIV

Large glooms were gathered in the mighty fane,
  With tinted moongleams slanting here and there;
And all was hush: no swelling organ-strain,
  No chant, no voice or murmuring of prayer;
No priests came forth, no tinkling censers fumed,
  And the high altar space was unillumed.

Around the pillars and against the walls
  Leaned men and shadows; others seemed to brood
Bent or recumbent in secluded stalls.
  Perchance they were not a great multitude
Save in that city of so lonely streets
Where one may count up every face he meets.

All patiently awaited the event
  Without a stir or sound, as if no less
Self-occupied, doomstricken, while attent.
  And then we heard a voice of solemn stress

From the dark pulpit, and our gaze there met
Two eyes which burned as never eyes burned yet:

Two steadfast and intolerable eyes
    Burning beneath a broad and rugged brow;
The head behind it of enormous size,
    And as black fir-groves in a large wind bow,
Our rooted congregation, gloom-arrayed,
By that great sad voice deep and full were swayed:—

O melancholy Brothers, dark, dark, dark!
O battling in black floods without an ark!
    O spectral wanderers of unholy Night!
My soul hath bled for you these sunless years,
With bitter blood-drops running down like tears:
    Oh, dark, dark, dark, withdrawn from joy and light!

My heart is sick with anguish for your bale!
Your woe hath been my anguish; yea, I quail
    And perish in your perishing unblest,
And I have searched the heights and depths, the scope
Of all our universe, with desperate hope
    To find some solace for your wild unrest.

And now at last authentic word I bring,
Witnessed by every dead and living thing;
    Good tidings of great joy for you, for all:
There is no God; no Fiend with names divine
Made us and tortures us; if we must pine,
    It is to satiate no Being's gall.

It was the dark delusion of a dream,
That living Person conscious and supreme,
    Whom we must curse for cursing us with life;

Whom we must curse because the life He gave
Could not be buried in the quiet grave,
  Could not be killed by poison or by knife.

This little life is all we must endure,
The grave's most holy peace is ever sure,
  We fall asleep and never wake again;
Nothing is of us but the mouldering flesh,
Whose elements dissolve and merge afresh
  In earth, air, water, plants, and other men.

We finish thus; and all our wretched race
Shall finish with its cycle, and give place
  To other beings, with their own time-doom;
Infinite aeons ere our kind began;
Infinite aeons after the last man
  Has joined the mammoth in earth's tomb and womb.

We bow down to the universal laws,
Which never had for man a special clause
  Of cruelty or kindness, love or hate;
If toads and vultures are obscene to sight,
If tigers burn with beauty and with might,
  Is it by favor or by wrath of fate?

All substance lives and struggles evermore
Through countless shapes continually at war,
  By countless interactions interknit:
If one is born a certain day on earth,
All times and forces tended to that birth,
  Not all the world could change or hinder it.

I find no hint throughout the Universe
Of good or ill, of blessing or of curse;
  I find alone Necessity Supreme;

With infinite Mystery, abysmal, dark,
Unlighted ever by the faintest spark,
　　For us the flitting shadows of a dream.

O Brothers of sad lives! they are so brief;
A few short years must bring us all relief:
　　Can we not bear these years of laboring breath?
But if you would not this poor life fulfil,
Lo, you are free to end it when you will,
　　Without the fear of waking after death.—

The organ-like vibrations of his voice
　　Thrilled through the vaulted aisles and died away;
The yearning of the tones which bade rejoice
　　Was sad and tender as a requiem lay:
Our shadowy congregation rested still
As brooding on that "End it when you will."

XV

Wherever men are gathered, all the air
　　Is charged with human feeling, human thought;
Each shout and cry and laugh, each curse and prayer,
　　Are into its vibrations surely wrought;
Unspoken passion, wordless meditation,
Are breathed into it with our respiration;
　　It is with our life fraught and over-fraught.

So that no man there breathes earth's simple breath,
　　As if alone on mountains or wide seas;
But nourishes warm life or hastens death
　　With joys and sorrows, health and foul disease,
Wisdom and folly, good and evil labors,
Incessant of his multitudinous neighbors;
　　He in his turn affecting all of these.

That City's atmosphere is dark and dense,
  Although not many exiles wander there,
With many a potent evil influence,
  Each adding poison to the poisoned air;
Infections of unutterable sadness,
Infections of incalculable madness,
  Infections of incurable despair.

XVI

Our shadowy congregation rested still,
  As musing on that message we had heard
And brooding on that "End it when you will";
  Perchance awaiting yet some other word;
When keen as lightning through a muffled sky
Sprang forth a shrill and lamentable cry:—

The man speaks sooth, alas! the man speaks sooth:
  We have no personal life beyond the grave;
There is no God; Fate knows nor wrath nor ruth:
  Can I find here the comfort which I crave?

In all eternity I had one chance,
  One few years' term of gracious human life:
The splendors of the intellect's advance,
  The sweetness of the home with babes and wife;

The social pleasures with their genial wit;
  The fascination of the worlds of art,
The glories of the worlds of nature, lit
  By large imagination's glowing heart;

The rapture of mere being, full of health;
  The careless childhood and the ardent youth,
The strenuous manhood winning various wealth,
  The reverend age serene with life's long truth:

All the sublime prerogatives of Man;
    The storied memories of the times of old,
The patient tracking of the world's great plan
    Through sequences and changes myriad-fold.

This chance was never offered me before;
    For me the infinite Past is blank and dumb:
This chance recurreth never, nevermore;
    Blank, blank for me the infinite To-come.

And this sole chance was frustrate from my birth,
    A mockery, a delusion; and my breath
Of noble human life upon this earth
    So racks me that I sigh for senseless death.

My wine of life is poison mixed with gall,
    My noonday passes in a nightmare dream,
I worse than lose the years which are my all:
    What can console me for the loss supreme?

Speak not of comfort where no comfort is,
    Speak not at all: can words make foul things fair?
Our life's a cheat, our death a black abyss:
    Hush and be mute envisaging despair.—

This vehement voice came from the northern aisle,
    Rapid and shrill to its abrupt harsh close;
And none gave answer for a certain while,
    For words must shrink from these most wordless woes;
At last the pulpit speaker simply said,
With humid eyes and thoughtful drooping head:—

My Brother, my poor Brothers, it is thus;
This life itself holds nothing good for us,
    But it ends soon and nevermore can be;

And we knew nothing of it ere our birth,
And shall know nothing when consigned to earth:
  I ponder these thoughts and they comfort me.

XVII

How the moon triumphs through the endless nights!
  How the stars throb and glitter as they wheel
Their thick processions of supernal lights
  Around the blue vault obdurate as steel!
And men regard with passionate awe and yearning
The mighty marching and the golden burning,
  And think the heavens respond to what they feel.

Boats gliding like dark shadows of a dream,
  Are glorified from vision as they pass
The quivering moonbridge on the deep black stream;
  Cold windows kindle their dead glooms of glass
To restless crystals; cornice, dome, and column
Emerge from chaos in the splendor solemn;
  Like faëry lakes gleam lawns of dewy grass.

With such a living light these dead eyes shine,
  These eyes of sightless heaven, that as we gaze
We read a pity, tremulous, divine,
  Or cold majestic scorn in their pure rays:
Fond man! they are not haughty, are not tender;
There is no heart or mind in all their splendor,
  They thread mere puppets all their marvellous maze.

If we could near them with the flight unflown,
  We should but find them worlds as sad as this,
Or suns all self-consuming like our own
  Enringed by planet worlds as much amiss:

They wax and wane through fusion and confusion;
The spheres eternal are a grand illusion,
 The empyréan is a void abyss.

XVIII

I wandered in a suburb of the north,
 And reached a spot whence three close lanes led down,
Beneath thick trees and hedgerows winding forth
 Like deep brook channels, deep and dark and lown:
The air above was wan with misty light,
The dull grey south showed one vague blur of white.

I took the left-hand lane and slowly trod
 Its earthen footpath, brushing as I went
The humid leafage; and my feet were shod
 With heavy languor, and my frame down-bent,
With infinite sleepless weariness outworn,
So many nights I thus had paced forlorn.

After a hundred steps I grew aware
 Of something crawling in the lane below;
It seemed a wounded creature prostrate there
 That sobbed with pangs in making progress slow,
The hind limbs stretched to push, the fore limbs then
To drag; for it would die in its own den.

But coming level with it I discerned
 That it had been a man; for at my tread
It stopped in its sore travail and half-turned,
 Leaning upon its right, and raised its head,
And with the left hand twitched back as in ire
Long grey unreverend locks befouled with mire.

A haggard filthy face with bloodshot eyes,
  An infamy for manhood to behold.
He gasped all trembling, What, you want my prize?
  You leave, to rob me, wine and lust and gold
And all that men go mad upon, since you
Have traced my sacred secret of the clue?

You think that I am weak and must submit;
  Yet I but scratch you with this poisoned blade,
And you are dead as if I clove with it
  That false fierce greedy heart. Betrayed! betrayed!
I fling this phial if you seek to pass,
And you are forthwith shrivelled up like grass.

And then with sudden change, Take thought! take thought!
  Have pity on me! it is mine alone.
If you could find, it would avail you naught;
  Seek elsewhere on the pathway of your own:
For who of mortal or immortal race
The lifetrack of another can retrace?

Did you know my agony and toil!
  Two lanes diverge up yonder from this lane;
My thin blood marks the long length of their soil;
  Such clue I left, who sought my clue in vain:
My hands and knees are worn both flesh and bone;
I cannot move but with continual moan.

But I am in the very way at last
  To find the long-lost broken golden thread
Which reunites my present with my past,
  If you but go your own way. And I said,
I will retire as soon as you have told
Whereunto leadeth this lost thread of gold.

And so you know it not! he hissed with scorn;
　　I feared you, imbecile! It leads me back
From this accursèd night without a morn,
　　And through the deserts which have else no track,
And through vast wastes of horror-haunted time,
　　To Eden innocence in Eden's clime:

And I become a nursling soft and pure,
　　An infant cradled on its mother's knee,
Without a past, love-cherished and secure;
　　Which if it saw this loathsome present Me,
Would plunge its face into the pillowing breast,
And scream abhorrence hard to lull to rest.

He turned to grope; and I retiring brushed
　　Thin shreds of gossamer from off my face,
And mused, His life would grow, the germ uncrushed;
　　He should to antenatal night retrace,
And hide his elements in that large womb
Beyond the reach of man-evolving Doom.

And even thus, what weary way were planned,
　　To seek oblivion through the far-off gate
Of birth, when that of death is close at hand!
　　For this is law, if law there be in Fate:
What never has been, yet may have its when;
The thing which has been, never is again.

XIX

The mighty river flowing dark and deep,
　　With ebb and flood from the remote seatides
Vague-sounding through the City's sleepless sleep,
　　Is named the River of the Suicides;

For night by night some lorn wretch over-weary,
And shuddering from the future yet more dreary,
　　Within its cold secure oblivion hides.

One plunges from a bridge's parapet,
　　As by some blind and sudden frenzy hurled;
Another wades in slow with purpose set
　　Until the waters are above him furled;
Another in a boat with dream-like motion
Glides drifting down into the desert ocean,
　　To stare or sink from out the desert world.

They perish from their suffering surely thus,
　　For none beholding them attempts to save,
The while each thinks how soon, solicitous,
　　He may seek refuge in the self-same wave;
Some hour when tired of ever-vain endurance
Impatience will forerun the sweet assurance
　　Of perfect peace eventual in the grave.

When this poor tragic-farce has palled us long,
　　Why actors and spectators do we stay?—
To fill our so-short *rôles* out right or wrong;
　　To see what shifts are yet in the dull play
For our illusion; to refrain from grieving
Dear foolish friends by our untimely leaving:
　　But those asleep at home, how blest are they!

Yet it is but for one night after all:
　　What matters one brief night of dreary pain?
When after it the weary eyelids fall
　　Upon the weary eyes and wasted brain;
And all sad scenes and thoughts and feelings vanish
In that sweet sleep no power can ever banish,
　　That one best sleep which never wakes again.

XX

I sat me weary on a pillar's base,
    And leaned against the shaft; for broad moonlight
O'erflowed the peacefulness of cloistered space,
    A shore of shadow slanting from the right:
The great cathedral's western front stood there,
A wave-worn rock in that calm sea of air.

Before it, opposite my place of rest,
    Two figures faced each other, large, austere:
A couchant sphinx in shadow to the breast,
    An angel standing in the moonlight clear;
So mighty by magnificence of form,
They were not dwarfed beneath that mass enorm.

Upon the cross-hilt of a naked sword
    The angel's hands, as prompt to smite, were held;
His vigilant intense regard was poured
    Upon the creature placidly unquelled,
Whose front was set at level gaze which took
No heed of aught, a solemn trance-like look.

And as I pondered these opposèd shapes
    My eyelids sank in stupor, that dull swoon
Which drugs and with a leaden mantle drapes
    The outworn to worse weariness. But soon
A sharp and clashing noise the stillness broke,
And from the evil lethargy I woke.

The angel's wings had fallen, stone on stone,
    And lay there shattered; hence the sudden sound:
A warrior leaning on his sword alone
    Now watched the sphinx with that regard profound;
The sphinx unchanged looked forthright, as aware
Of nothing in the vast abyss of air.

Again I sank in that repose unsweet,
  Again a clashing noise my slumber rent;
The warrior's sword lay broken at his feet:
  An unarmed man with raised hands impotent
Now stood before the sphinx, which ever kept
Such mien as if with open eyes it slept.

My eyelids sank in spite of wonder grown;
  A louder crash upstartled me in dread:
The man had fallen forward, stone on stone,
  And lay there shattered, with his trunkless head
Between the monster's large quiescent paws,
Beneath its grand front changeless as life's laws.

The moon had circled westward full and bright,
  And made the temple-front a mystic dream,
And bathed the whole enclosure with its light,
  The sworded angel's wrecks, the sphinx supreme:
I pondered long that cold majestic face
Whose vision seemed of infinite void space.

XXI

Anear the centre of that northern crest
  Stands out a level upland bleak and bare,
From which the city east and south and west
  Sinks gently in long waves; and thronèd there
An Image sits, stupendous, superhuman,
The bronge colossus of a wingèd Woman,
  Upon a graded granite base foursquare.

Low-seated she leans forward massively,
  With cheek on clenched left hand, the fore-arm's might
Erect, its elbow on her rounded knee;
  Across a clasped book in her lap the right

Upholds a pair of compasses; she gazes
With full set eyes, but wandering thick mazes
    Of sombre thought behold no outward sight.

Words cannot picture her; but all men know
    That solemn sketch the pure sad artist wrought
Three centuries and threescore years ago,
    With phantasies of his peculiar thought:
The instruments of carpentry and science
Scattered about her feet, in strange alliance
    With the keen wolf-hound sleeping undistraught;

Scales, hour-glass, bell, and magic-square above;
    The grave and solid infant perched beside,
With open winglets that might bear a dove,
    Intent upon its tablets, heavy-eyed;
Her folded wings as of a mighty eagle,
But all too impotent to lift the regal
    Robustness of her earth-born strength and pride;

And with those wings, and that light wreath which seems
    To mock her grand head and the knotted frown
Of forehead charged with baleful thoughts and dreams,
    The household bunch of keys, the housewife's gown
Voluminous, indented, and yet rigid
As if a shell of burnished metal frigid;
    The feet thick shod to tread all weakness down;

The comet hanging o'er the waste dark seas,
    The massy rainbow curved in front of it,
Beyond the village with the masts and trees;
    The snaky imp, dog-headed, from the Pit,
Bearing upon its batlike leathern pinions
Her name unfolded in the sun's dominion,
    The "Melencolia" that transcends all wit.

Thus has the artist copied her, and thus
  Surrounded to expound her form sublime,
Her fate heroic and calamitous;
  Fronting the dreadful mysteries of Time,
Unvanquished in defeat and desolation,
Undaunted in the hopeless conflagration
  Of the day setting on her baffled prime.

Baffled and beaten back she works on still,
  Weary and sick of soul she works the more,
Sustained by her indomitable will;
  The hands shall fashion and the brain shall pore
And all her sorrow shall be turned to labor,
Till death the friend-foe piercing with his sabre
  That mighty heart of hearts ends bitter war.

But as if blacker night could dawn on night,
  With tenfold gloom on moonless night unstarred,
A sense more tragic than defeat and blight,
  More desperate than strife with hope debarred,
More fatal than the adamantine Never
Encompassing her passionate endeavor
  Dawns glooming in her tenebrous regard:

The sense that every struggle brings defeat
  Because Fate holds no prize to crown success
That all the oracles are dumb or cheat
  Because they have no secret to express;
That none can pierce the vast black veil uncertain
Because there is no light beyond the curtain;
  That all is vanity and nothingness.

Titanic from her high throne in the north,
  That City's sombre Patroness and Queen,
In bronze sublimity she gazes forth
  Over her Capital of teen and threne,

Over the river with its isles and bridges,
The marsh and moorland, to the stern rock-ridges,
  Confronting them with a coëval mien.

The moving moon and stars from east to west
  Circle before her in the sea of air;
Shadows and gleams glide round her solemn rest.
  Her subjects often gaze up to her there:
The strong to drink new strength of iron endurance,
The weak new terrors; all, renewed assurance
  And confirmation of the old despair.

WILLIAM MORRIS (1834-1896)

THE WIND

Ah! no, no, it is nothing, surely nothing at all,
Only the wild-going wind round by the garden-wall,
For the dawn just now is breaking, the wind beginning to fall.

> *Wind, wind! thou art sad, art thou kind?*
> *Wind, wind, unhappy! thou art blind,*
> *Yet still thou wanderest the lily-seed to find.*

So I will sit, and think and think of the days gone by,
Never moving my chair for fear the dogs should cry,
Making no noise at all while the flambeau burns awry.

For my chair is heavy and carved, and with sweeping green behind
It is hung, and the dragons thereon grin out in the gusts of the
    wind;
On its folds an orange lies, with a deep gash cut in the rind.

Wind, wind! thou art sad, art thou kind?
Wind, wind, unhappy! thou art blind,
Yet still thou wanderest the lily-seed to find.

If I move my chair it will scream, and the orange will roll out far,
And the faint yellow juice ooze out like blood from a wizard's jar;
And the dogs will howl for those who went last month to the war.

Wind, wind! thou art sad, art thou kind?
Wind, wind, unhappy! thou art blind,
Yet still thou wanderest the lily-seed to find.

So I will sit and think of love that is over and past,
O! so long ago—yes, I will be quiet at last;
Whether I like it or not, a grim half-slumber is cast

Over my worn old brains, that touches the roots of my heart,
And above my half-shut eyes the blue roof 'gins to part,
And show the blue spring sky, till I am ready to start

From out of the green-hung chair; but something keeps me still,
And I fall in a dream that I walk'd with her on the side of a hill,
Dotted—for was it not spring?—with tufts of the daffodil.

Wind, wind! thou art sad, art thou kind?
Wind, wind, unhappy! thou art blind,
Yet still thou wanderest the lily-seed to find.

And Margaret as she walk'd held a painted book in her hand;
Her finger kept the place; I caught her, we both did stand
Face to face, on the top of the highest hill in the land.

Wind, wind! thou art sad, art thou kind?
Wind, wind, unhappy! thou art blind,
Yet still thou wanderest the lily-seed to find.

I held to her long bare arms, but she shudder'd away from me,
While the flush went out of her face as her head fell back on a tree,
And a spasm caught her mouth, fearful for me to see;

And still I held to her arms till her shoulder touch'd my mail,
Weeping she totter'd forward, so glad that I should prevail,
And her hair went over my robe, like a gold flag over a sail.

> *Wind, wind! thou art sad, art thou kind?*
> *Wind, wind, unhappy! thou art blind,*
> *Yet still thou wanderest the lily-seed to find.*

I kiss'd her hard by the ear, and she kiss'd me on the brow,
And then lay down on the grass, where the mark on the moss is now,
And spread her arms out wide while I went down below.

> *Wind, wind! thou art sad, art thou kind?*
> *Wind, wind, unhappy! thou art blind,*
> *Yet still thou wanderest the lily-seed to find.*

And then I walk'd for a space to and fro on the side of the hill,
Till I gather'd and held in my arms great sheaves of the daffodil,
And when I came again my Margaret lay there still.

I piled them high and high above her heaving breast,
How they were caught and held in her loose ungirded vest!
But one beneath her arm died, happy so to be prest!

> *Wind, wind! thou art sad, art thou kind?*
> *Wind, wind, unhappy! thou art blind,*
> *Yet still thou wanderest the lily-seed to find.*

Again I turn'd my back and went away for an hour;
She said no word when I came again, so, flower by flower,
I counted the daffodils over, and cast them languidly lower.

Wind, wind! thou art sad, art thou kind?
Wind, wind, unhappy! thou art blind,
Yet still thou wanderest the lily-seed to find.

My dry hands shook and shook as the green gown show'd again,
Clear'd from the yellow flowers, and I grew hollow with pain,
And on to us both there fell from the sun-shower drops of rain.

Wind, wind! thou art sad, art thou kind?
Wind, wind, unhappy! thou art blind,
Yet still thou wanderest the lily-seed to find.

Alas! alas! there was blood on the very quiet breast,
Blood lay in the many folds of the loose ungirded vest,
Blood lay upon her arm where the flower had been prest.

I shriek'd and leapt from my chair, and the orange roll'd out far,
The faint yellow juice oozed out like blood from a wizard's jar;
And then in march'd the ghosts of those that had gone to the war.

I knew them by the arms that I was used to paint
Upon their long thin shields; but the colours were all grown faint,
And faint upon their banner was Olaf, king and saint.

Wind, wind! thou art sad, art thou kind?
Wind, wind, unhappy! thou art blind,
Yet still thou wanderest the lily-seed to find.

RICHARD GARNETT (1835-1906)

THE HIGHWAYMAN'S GHOST

Twelve o'clock—a misty night—
Glimpsing hints of buried light—
Six years strung in an iron chain—
Time I stood on the ground again!

So—by your leave! Slip, easy enough,
Withered wrists from the rusty cuff.
The old chain rattles, the old wood groans,
O the clatter of clacking bones!

Here I am, uncoated, unhatted,
Shirt all mildewed, hair all matted,
Sockets that each have royally
Fed the crow with a precious eye.

O for slashing Bess the brown!
Where, old lass, have they earthed thee down?
Sobb'st beneath a carrier's thong?
Strain'st a coalman's cart along?

Shame to foot it!—must be so.
See, the mists are smitten below;
Over the moorland, wide away,
Moonshine pours her watery day.

There the long white-dusted track,
There a crawling speck of black.
The Northern mail, ha, ha! and he
There on the box is Anthony.

Coachman I scared him from brown or grey,
Witness he lied my blood way.
Haste, Fred! haste, boy! never fail!
Now or never! catch the mail!

The horses plunge, and sweating stop.
Dead falls Tony, neck and crop.
Nay, good guard, small profit thus,
Shooting ghosts with a blunderbuss!

Crash wheel! coach over! How it rains
Hampers, ladies, wigs, and canes!
O the spoil! to sack it and lock it!
But, woe is me, I have never a pocket!

ROBERT BUCHANAN (1841-1901)

THE BALLAD OF JUDAS ISCARIOT

'Twas the body of Judas Iscariot
  Lay in the Field of Blood;
'Twas the soul of Judas Iscariot
  Beside the body stood.

Black was the earth by night,
  And black was the sky;
Black, black were the broken clouds,
  Tho' red moon went by.

'Twas the body of Judas Iscariot
  Strangled and dead lay there;
'Twas the soul of Judas Iscariot
  Look'd on it in despair.

The breath of the world came and went
  Like a sick man's in rest;
Drop by drop on the world's eyes
  The dews fell cool and blest.

Then the soul of Judas Iscariot
  Did make a gentle moan—
"I will bury underneath the ground
  My flesh and blood and bone.

"I will bury deep beneath the soil,
  Lest mortals look thereon,
And when the wolf and raven come
  The body will be gone!

"The stones of the field are sharp as steel,
  And hard and cold, Got wot;
And I must bear my body hence
  Until I find a spot!"

'Twas the soul of Judas Iscariot,
  So grim, and gaunt, and gray,
Raised the body of Judas Iscariot,
  And carried it away.

And as he bare it from the field
  Its touch was cold as ice,
And the ivory teeth within the jaw
  Rattled aloud, like dice.

As the soul of Judas Iscariot
  Carried its load with pain,
The Eye of Heaven, like a lanthorn's eye,
  Opened and shut again.

Half he walk'd, and half he seem'd
Lifted on the cold wind;
He did not turn, for chilly hands
Were pushing from behind.

The first place that he came unto
   It was the open wold,
And underneath were prickly whins,
   And a wind that blew so cold.

The next place that he came unto
   It was a stagnant pool,
And when he threw the body in
   It floated light as wool.

He drew the body on his back,
   And it was dripping chill,
And the next place he came unto
   Was a Cross upon a hill.

A Cross upon the windy hill,
   And a cross on either side,
Three skeletons that swing thereon,
   Who had been crucified.

And on the middle cross bar sat
   A white Dove slumbering;
Dim it sat in the dim light,
   With its head beneath its wing.

And underneath the middle cross
   A grave yawn'd wide and vast,
But the soul of Judas Iscariot
   Shiver'd, and glided past.

The fourth place that he came unto
  It was the Brig of Dread,
And the great torrents rushing down
  Were deep, and swift, and red.

He dared not fling the body in
  For fear of faces dim,
And arms were waved in the wild water
  To thrust it back to him.

'Twas the soul of Judas Iscariot
  Turned from the Brig of Dread,
And the dreadful foam of the wild water
  Had splashed the body red.

For days and nights he wandered on,
  Upon an open plain,
And the days went by like blinding mist,
  And the nights like rushing rain.

For days and nights he wandered on,
  All thro' the Wood of Woe;
And the nights went by like moaning wind,
  And the days like drifting snow.

'Twas the soul of Judas Iscariot
  Came with a weary face—
Alone, alone, and all alone,
  Alone in a lonely place!

He wandered east, he wandered west,
  And heard no human sound;
For months and years, in grief and tears,
  He wandered round and round.

For months and years, in grief and tears,
  He walked the silent night;
Then the soul of Judas Iscariot
  Perceived a far-off light.

A far-off light across the waste,
  As dim as dim might be,
That came and went like the lighthouse gleam
  On a black night at sea.

'Twas the soul of Judas Iscariot
  Crawl'd to the distant gleam;
And the rain came down, and the rain was blown
  Against him with a scream.

For days and nights he wandered on,
  Push'd on by hands behind;
And the days went by like black, black rain,
  And the nights like rushing wind.

'Twas the soul of Judas Iscariot,
  Strange, and sad, and tall
Stood alone at dead of night
  Before a lighted hall.

And the wold was white with snow,
  And his foot-marks black and damp,
And the ghost of the silvern moon arose,
  Holding her yellow lamp.

And the icicles were on the eaves,
  And the walls were deep with white,
And the shadows of the guests within
  Pass'd on the window light.

The shadows of the wedding guests
  Did strangely come and go,
And the body of Judas Iscariot
  Lay stretch'd along the snow.

The body of Judas Iscariot
  Lay stretched along the snow;
'Twas the soul of Judas Iscariot
  Ran swiftly to and fro.

To and fro, and up and down,
  He ran so swiftly there,
As round and round the frozen pole
  Glideth the lean white bear.

'Twas the Bridegroom sat at the table-head,
  And the lights burnt bright and clear—
"Oh, who is that," the Bridegroom said,
  "Whose weary feet I hear?"

'Twas one looked from the lighted hall,
  And answered soft and slow,
"It is a wolf runs up and down
  With a black track in the snow."

The Bridegroom in his robe of white
  Sat at the table-head—
"Oh, who is that who moans without?"
  The blessèd Bridegroom said.

'Twas one looked from the lighted hall,
  And answered fierce and low,
" 'Tis the soul of Judas Iscariot
  Gliding to and fro."

'Twas the soul of Judas Iscariot
　　Did hush itself and stand,
And saw the Bridegroom at the door
　　With a light in his hand.

The Bridegroom stood in the open door,
　　And he was clad in white,
And far within the Lord's Supper
　　Was spread so broad and bright.

The Bridegroom shaded his eyes and look'd,
　　And his face was bright to see—
"What dost thou here at the Lord's Supper
　　With thy body's sins?" said he.

'Twas the soul of Judas Iscariot
　　Stood black, and sad, and bare—
"I have wandered many nights and days:
　　There is no light elsewhere."

'Twas the wedding guests cried out within,
　　And their eyes were fierce and bright—
"Scourge the soul of Judas Iscariot
　　Away into the night!"

The Bridegroom stood in the open door,
　　And he waved hands still and slow,
And the third time that he waved his hands
　　The air was thick with snow.

And of every flake of falling snow,
　　Before it touch'd the ground,
There came a dove, and a thousand doves
　　Made sweet sound.

'Twas the body of Judas Iscariot
    Floated away full fleet,
And the wings of the doves that bare it off
    Were like its winding-sheet.

'Twas the Bridegroom stood at the open door,
    And beckon'd, smiling sweet;
'Twas the soul of Judas Iscariot
    Stole in, and fell at his feet.

"The holy supper is spread within,
    And the many candles shine,
And I have waited long for thee
    Before I poured the wine!"

The supper wine is poured at last,
    The lights burn bright and fair,
Iscariot washes the Bridegroom's feet
    And dries them with his hair.

A. P. GRAVES (1846-1931)

THE SONG OF THE GHOST

When all were dreaming but Pastheen Power,
A light came streaming beneath her bower,
A heavy foot at her door delayed,
A heavy hand on the latch was laid.

"Now who dare venture at this dark hour,
Unbid to enter my maiden bower?"
"Dear Pastheen, open the door to me,
And your true lover you'll surely see."

"My true lover, so tall and brave,
Lives exiled over the angry wave."
"Your true love's body lies on the bier,
His faithful spirit is with you here."

"His look was cheerful, his voice was gay;
Your speech is fearful, your face is grey;
And sad and sunken your eye of blue,
But Patrick, Patrick, alas! 'tis you."

Ere dawn was breaking she heard below
The two cocks shaking their wings to crow.
"O hush you, hush you, both red and grey,
Or you will hurry my love away.

"O hush your crowing, both grey and red,
Or he'll be going to join the dead;
O cease from calling his ghost to mould,
And I'll come crowning your combs with gold.

When all were dreaming but Pastheen Power.
A light went streaming from out her bower,
And on the morrow when they awoke,
They knew that sorrow her heart had broke.

JAMES WHITCOMB RILEY (1849-1916)

A GLIMPSE OF PAN

I caught but a glimpse of him. Summer was here,
And I strayed from the town and its dust and heat,
And walked in a wood, while the noon was near,
Where the shadows were cool, and the atmosphere

Was misty with fragrances stirred by my feet
From surges of blossoms that billowed sheer
    Of the grasses, green and sweet.

And I peered through a vista of leaning trees,
    Tressed with long tangles of vines that swept
To the face of a river, that answered these
With vines in a wave like the vines in the breeze,
    Till the yearning lips of the ripples crept
And kissed them, with quavering ecstacies,
    And wistfully laughed and wept.

And there, like a dream in a swoon, I swear
    I saw Pan lying,—his limbs in the dew
And the shade, and his face in the dazzle and glare
Of the glad sunshine; while everywhere,
    Over, across, and around him blew
Filmy dragon-flies hither and there,
    And little white butterflies, two and two,
In eddies of odorous air.

THE WITCH OF ERKMURDEN

I

Who cantereth forth in the night so late—
    So late in the night, and so nigh the dawn?
'Tis The Witch of Erkmurden who leapeth the gate
Of the old churchyard where the three Sprites wait
    Till the whir of her broom is gone.

And who peereth down from the belfry tall,
    With the ghost-white face and the ghastly stare,
With lean hands clinched in the grated wall
Where the red vine rasps and the rank leaves fall,
    And the clock-stroke drowns his prayer?

II

The wee babe wails, and the storm grows loud,
   Nor deeper the dark of the night may be,
For the lightning's claw, with a great wet cloud,
Hath wiped the moon and the wild-eyed crowd
   Of the stars out wrathfully.

Knuckled and kinked as the hunchback shade
   Of a thorn-tree bendeth the beldam old
Over the couch where the mother-maid,
With her prayerful eyes, and the babe are laid,
   Waiting the doom untold.

"Mother, O Mother, I only crave
Mercy for him and the babe—not me!"
"Hush! for it maketh my brain to rave
Of my two white shrouds, and my one wide grave,
   And a mound for my children three."

"Mother, O Mother, I only pray
   Pity for him who is son to thee
And more than my brother.—" "Wilt hush, I say!
Though I meet thee not at the Judgment Day,
   I will bury my children three!"

"Then hark! O Mother, I hear his cry—
   Hear his curse from the churchtower now,—
'Ride thou witch till thy hate shall die,
Yet hell as Heaven eternally
   Be sealed to such as thou!'"

An infant's wail—then a laugh, god wot,
   That strangled the echoes of deepest hell;
And a thousand shuttles of lightning shot,
And the moon bulged out like a great red blot,
   And a shower of blood-stars fell.

III

There is one wide grave scooped under the eaves—
    Under the eaves as they weep and weep;
And, veiled by the mist that the dead storm weaves,
The hag bends low, and the earth receives
    Mother and child asleep.

There's the print of the hand at either throat,
    And the frothy ooze at the lips of each,
But both smile up where the new stars float,
And the moon sails out like a silver boat
    Unloosed from a stormy beach.

IV

Bright was the morn when the sexton gray
    Twirled the rope of the old church-bell,—
But it answered not, and he tugged away—
And lo, at his feet a dead man lay—
    Dropped down with a single knell.

And the scared wight found, in the lean hand gripped,
    A scrip which read: "O the grave is wide,
But it empty waits, for the low eaves dripped
Their prayerful tears, and the three Sprites slipped
    Away with my babe and bride."

LIZETTE WOODWORTH REESE (1856-1935)

A WINDY NIGHT

Should Ellen from the rectory come,
Or from the grey farms Nan or Mark,

Then will they find my house gone dumb,
Drained to the ribs of all but dark.

Ellen, white mullein on its stalk
Knows her parish, shop and stall;
Smelling of apples, Nan will talk
Of weathers, crops; Mark not at all.

Not I that shaped there in the night,
Slumped down within the knobbed green chair,
That thing left in the fagot-light,
To mumble welcome, stare and stare.

For here, the bellowing lanes are out;
Roofs crack; each window is a cry;
Afar, afar, with dimming shout,
Orion's hounds race down the sky.

Beyond the pools of ghosts they race;
The Dead troop out as they go by,
And point them down the whirling space;
Orion hunts and with him I!

ROADS

Wild pear trees shout up Tinges Lane;
Through the tall dusk they shout;
Through the tall dusk the wild trees run
And hack the candles out.

Down Oxford Road by the great thorn—
Of two men's height the stalk—
White as its white in the sagged grass,
The Dead Folk come and talk.

Over a pot in the Old York Lane,
There stoops a scarlet witch;
This night one man dies in his bed,
And one down in a ditch.

AN APRIL GHOST

All the ghosts I ever knew,
  White, and thinly calling,
Come into the house with you
  When the dew is falling.

All of youth that ever died,
  In the Springtime weather,
In the windy April tide,
  Climb the dusk together.

For a moment, lad and maid
  Stand up there all lonely;
In a moment fade and fade—
  You are left, you only.

BITTERS

Hyssop from a grave's edge,
  Yarrow from spent lane,
Everlasting from a wood
  Wrecked in a dark rain.

Light the seven fagots now,
  Make them seven times hot;
Brew the sad herbs leaf and stalk
  For the scarlet pot.

Peering griefs, spites, dust of dreams
  Cast in one by one;
Drag the wild moon down, to watch
  Till the stuff is done!

They that drink of this will know
  Sharp and choking breath;
Every day of every year
  Smell the mold of Death.

A. E. HOUSMAN (1859-1936)

THE TRUE LOVER

The lad came to the door at night,
  When lovers crown their vows,
And whistled soft and out of sight
  In shadow of the boughs.

'I shall not vex you with my face
  Henceforth, my love, for aye;
So take me in your arms a space
  Before the east is grey.

'When I from hence away am past
  I shall not find a bride,
And you shall be the first and last
  I ever lay beside.'

She heard and went and knew not why;
  Her heart to his she laid;
Light was the air beneath the sky
  But dark under the shade.

'Oh do you breathe, lad, that your breast
   Seems not to rise and fall,
And here upon my bosom prest
   There beats no heart at all?'

'Oh loud, my girl, it once would knock,
   You should have felt it then;
But since for you I stopped the clock
   It never goes again.'

'Oh lad, what is it, lad, that drips
   Wet from your neck on mine?
What is it falling on my lips,
   My lad, that tastes of brine?'

Oh like enough 'tis blood, my dear,
   For when the knife has slit
The throat across from ear to ear
   'Twill bleed because of it.'

Under the stars the air was light
   But dark below the boughs,
The still air of the speechless night,
   When lovers crown their vows.

JOSÉ ASUNCIÓN SILVA (1865-1896)

LAZARUS

"Come, Lazarus!" the Savior
cried to him, and out of that black tomb
the corpse arose still in its windingsheet,

smelled, felt, saw, grew aware, uttered a cry,
and wept with happiness.

And four months later, among the many shadows
of the dark twilight, in the darker silence
of place and time, among the quiet tombs
of an old cemetery,
this Lazarus was sobbing there alone,
envying the dead.
    —Translated by Anthony Boucher

DORA SIGERSON SHORTER (1866-1918)

ALL-SOULS' NIGHT

O mother, mother, I swept the hearth, I set his chair and the white
    board spread,
I prayed for his coming to our kind Lady when Death's doors would
    let out the dead;
A strange wind rattled the window-pane, and down the lane a dog
    howled on,
I called his name and the candle flame burnt dim, pressed a hand the
    door-latch upon.
Deelish! Deelish! my woe forever that I could not sever coward flesh
    from fear.
I called his name and the pale ghost came; but I was afraid to meet my
    dear.

O mother, mother, in tears I checked the sad hours past of the year
    that's o'er,
Till by God's grace I might see his face and hear the sound of his
    voice once more;

The chair I set from the cold and wet, he took when he came from
　unknown skies
Of the land of the dead, on my bent brown head I felt the reproach
　of his saddened eyes;
I closed my lids on my heart's desire, crouched by the fire, my voice
　was dumb.
At my clean-swept hearth he had no mirth, and at my table he broke
　no crumb.
Deelish! Deelish! my woe forever that I could not sever coward flesh
　from fear.
His chair put aside when the young cock cried, and I was afraid to
　meet my dear.

THE FAIR LITTLE MAIDEN

"There is one at the door, Wolfe O'Driscoll,
　At the door, who bids you to come!"
"Who is he that wakes me in the darkness,
　Calling when all the world is dumb?"

"Six horses has he to his carriage,
　Six horses blacker than the night,
And their twelve red eyes in the shadows—
　Twelve lamps he carries for his light;

"His coach is a hearse black and mouldy,
　Within a coffin open wide:
He asks for your soul, Wolfe O'Driscoll,
　Who doth call at the door outside."

"Who let him thro' the gates of my gardens,
　Where stronger bolts have never been?"
"The father of the fair little maiden
　You drove to her grave deep and green."

"And who let him pass through the courtyard,
  Loosening the bar and the chain?"
"Who but the brother of the maiden
  Who lies in the cold and the rain!"

"Then who drew the bolts at the portal,
  And into my house bade him go?"
"The mother of the poor young maiden
  Who lies in her youth all so low."

"Who stands, that he dare not enter,
  The door of my chamber, between?"
"O, the ghost of the fair little maiden
  Who lies in the churchyard green."

THE FETCH

"What make you so late at the trysting?
What caused you so long to be?
For a weary time I have waited
From the hour you promised me."

"I would I were here by your side, love,
Full many an hour ago,
For a thing I passed on the roadway
All mournful and so slow."

"And what have you passed on the roadside
That kept you so long and late?"
"It is weary the time behind me
Since I left my father's gate.

"As I hastened on in the gloaming
By the road to you to-night,
There I saw the corpse of a young maid
All clad in a shroud of white."

"And was she some comrade cherished,
Or was she a sister dead,
That you left thus your own beloved
Till the trysting-hour had fled?"

"Oh, I would that I could discover,
But never did I see her face,
And I knew I must turn and follow
Till I came to her resting place."

"And did it go up by the town path,
Did it go down by the lake?
I know there are but the two churchyards
Where a corpse its rest may take."

"They did not go up by the town path,
Nor stopped by the lake their feet,
They buried the corpse all silently
Where the four cross-roads do meet."

"And was it so strange a sight, then,
That you should go like a child,
Thus to leave me wait all forgotten—
By a passing sight beguiled?"

" 'Twas my name that I heard them whisper,
Each mourner that passed by me;
And I had to follow their footsteps,
Though their faces I could not see."

"And right well I should like to know, now,
Who might be this fair young maid,
So come with me, my own true love,
If you be not afraid."

He did not go down by the lakeside,
He did not go by the town,
But carried her to the four cross-roads,
And he there did set her down.

"Now, I see no track of a foot here,
I see no mark of a spade,
And I know right well in this white road
That never a grave was made."

And he took her hand in his right hand
And led her to town away,
And there he questioned the good old priest,
Did he bury a maid that day.

And he took her hand in his right hand,
Down to the church by the lake,
And there he questioned the pale young priest
If a maiden her life did take.

But neither had heard of a new grave
In all the parish around,
And no one could tell of a young maid
Thus put in unholy ground.

So he loosed her hand from his hand,
And turned on his heel away,
And, "I know now you are false," he said,
"From the lie you told to-day."

And she said, "Alas! what evil thing
Did to-night my senses take?"
She knelt her down by the water-side
And wept as her heart would break.

And she said, "Oh, what fairy sight then
Was it thus my grief to see?
I will sleep well 'neath the still water,
Since my love has turned from me."

And her love he went to the north land,
And far to the south went he,
And her distant voice he still could hear
Call weeping so bitterly.

And he could not rest in the daytime,
He could not sleep in the night,
So he hastened back to the old road,
With the trysting place in sight.

What first he heard was his own love's name,
And keening both loud and long,
What first he saw was his love's dear face,
At the head of a mourning throng.

And all white she was as the dead are,
And never a move made she,
But passed him by in her lone black pall,
Still sleeping so peacefully.

And all cold she was as the dead are,
And never a word she spake,
When they said, "Unholy is her grave
For she her life did take."

And silent she was as the dead are,
And never a cry she made,
When there came, more sad than the keening,
The ring of a digging spade.

No rest she had in the old town church,
    No grave by the lake so sweet,
They buried her in unholy ground,
    Where the four cross-roads do meet.

THE FAIRY THORN-TREE

"This is an evil night to go, my sister,
    To the thorn-tree across the fairy rath,
Will you not wait till Hallow Eve is over?
    For many are the dangers in your path!"

"I may not wait till Hallow Eve is over,
    I shall be there before the night is fled,
For, brother, I am weary for my lover,
    And I must see him once, alive or dead.

"I've prayed to heaven, but it would not listen,
    I'll call thrice in the devil's name to-night,
Be it a live man that shall come to hear me,
    Or but a corpse, all clad in snowy white."

. . . .

She had drawn on her silken hose and garter,
    Her crimson petticoat was kilted high,
She trod her way amid the bog and brambles,
    Until the fairy-tree she stood near-by.

When first she cried the devil's name so loudly
    She listened, but she heard no sound at all;
When twice she cried, she thought from out the darkness
    She heard the echo of a light footfall.

When last she cried her voice came in a whisper,
    She trembled in her loneliness and fright;
Before her stood a shrouded, mighty figure,
    In sombre garments blacker than the night.

"And if you be my own true love," she questioned,
    "I fear you! Speak you quickly unto me."
"O, I am not your own true love," it answered,
    "He drifts without a grave upon the sea."

"If he be dead, then gladly will I follow
    Down the black stairs of death into the grave."
"Your lover calls you for a place to rest him
    From the eternal tossing of the wave."

"I'll make my love a bed both wide and hollow,
    A grave wherein we both may ever sleep."
"What give you for his body fair and slender,
    To draw it from the dangers of the deep?"

"I'll give you both my silver comb and earrings,
    I'll give you all my little treasure store."
"I will but take what living thing comes forward,
    The first to meet you, passing to your door."

"O may my little dog be first to meet me,
    So loose my lover from your dreaded hold."
"What will you give me for the heart that loved you,
    The heart that I hold chained and frozen cold?"

"My own betrothed ring I give you gladly,
    My ring of pearls—and every one a tear?"
"I will but have what other living creature
    That second in your pathway shall appear."

"To buy this heart, to warm my love to living,
    I pray my pony meet me on return."
"And now, for his young soul what will you give me,
    His soul that night and day doth fret and burn?"

"You will not have my silver comb and earrings,
    You will not have my ring of precious stone;
O, nothing have I left to promise to you,
    But give my soul to buy him back his own."

All woefully she wept, and stepping homeward,
    Bemoaned aloud her dark and cruel fate;
"O, come," she cried, "my little dog to meet me,
    And you, my horse, be browsing at the gate."

Right hastily she pushed by bush and bramble,
    Chased by a fear that made her footsteps fleet,
And as she ran she met her little brother,
    Then her old father coming her to meet.

"O brother, little brother," cried she, weeping,
    "Well you said of fairy-tree beware,
For precious things are bought and sold ere midnight,
    On Hallow Eve, by those who barter there."

She went alone into the little chapel,
    And knelt before the holy Virgin's shrine,
She wept, "O Mother Mary, pray you for me,
    To save those two most gentle souls of thine."

And as she prayed, behold the holy statue
    Spoke to her, saying, "Little can I aid,
God's ways are just, and you have dared to question
    His judgment on this soul; you bought—and paid.

"For that one soul, your father and your brother,
    Your own immortal life you bartered; then,
Yet one chance is allowed—your sure repentance,
    Give back his heart you made to live again."

"For these two souls—my father and my brother—
    I give his heart back into death's cold land,
Never again to warm his dead, sweet body,
    Or beat to madness underneath my hand."

"And for your soul—to save it from its sorrow,
    You must drive back his soul into the night,
Back into righteous punishment and justice,
    Or lose your chance of everlasting light."

"O never shall I drive him back to anguish,
    My soul shall suffer, letting his go free."
She rose, and weeping, left the little chapel,
    Went forward blindly till she reached the sea.

She dug a grave within the surf and shingle,
    A dark, cold bed, made very deep and wide,
She laid her down all stiff and stretched for burial,
    Right in the pathway of the rising tide.

First tossed into her waiting arms the restless
    Loud waves, a woman very grey and cold,
Within her bed she stood upright so quickly,
    And loosed her fingers from the dead hands' hold.

The second who upon her heart had rested
    From out the storm, a baby chill and stark,
With one long sob she drew it on her bosom,
    Then thrust it out again into the dark.

The last who came so slow was her own lover;
    She kissed his icy face on cheek and chin,
"O cold shall be your house to-night, belovèd,
    O cold the bed that we must sleep within.

"And heavy, heavy, on our lips so faithful
      And on our hearts, shall lie our own roof-tree."
And as she spoke the bitter tears were falling
      On his still face, all salter than the sea.

"And oh," she said, "if for a little moment
      You knew, my cold, dead love, that I was by,
That my soul goes into the utter darkness
      When yours comes forth—and mine goes in to die."

And as she wept she kissed his frozen forehead,
      Laid her warm lips upon his mouth so chill,
With no response—and then the waters flowing
      Into their grave, grew heavy, deep, and still.

.   .   .   .

And so, 'tis said, if to that fairy thorn-tree
      You dare to go, you see her ghost so lone,
She prays for love of her that you will aid her,
      And give your soul to buy her back her own.

EDWIN ARLINGTON ROBINSON (1869-1935)

LUKE HAVERGAL

Go to the western gate, Luke Havergal,
There where the vines cling crimson on the wall,
And in the twilight wait for what will come.
The leaves will whisper there of her, and some,
Like flying words, will strike you as they fall;
But go, and if you listen she will call.
Go to the western gate, Luke Havergal—
Luke Havergal.

No, there is not a dawn in eastern skies
To rift the fiery night that's in your eyes;
But there, where western glooms are gathering,
The dark will end the dark, if anything:
God slays Himself with every leaf that flies,
And hell is more than half of paradise.
No, there is not a dawn in eastern skies—
In eastern skies.

Out of a grave I come to tell you this,
Out of a grave I come to quench the kiss
That flames upon your forehead with a glow
That blinds you to the way that you must go.
Yes, there is yet one way to where she is,
Bitter, but one that faith may never miss.
Out of a grave I come to tell you this—
To tell you this.

There is the western gate, Luke Havergal,
There are the crimson leaves upon the wall.
Go, for the winds are tearing them away,—
Nor think to riddle the dead words they say,
Nor any more to feel them as they fall;
But go, and if you trust her she will call.
There is the western gate, Luke Havergal—
Luke Havergal.

ARTHUR GUITERMAN (1871-1943)

THE SUPERSTITIOUS GHOST

I'm such a quiet little ghost,
  Demure and inoffensive,
The other spirits say I'm most
  Absurdly apprehensive.

Through all the merry hours of night
I'm uniformly cheerful;
I love the dark; but in the light,
   I own I'm rather fearful.

Each dawn I cower down in bed,
   In every brightness seeing,
That weird uncanny form of dread—
   An awful Human Being!

Of course I'm told they can't exist,
   That Nature would not let them:
But Willy Spook, the Humanist,
   Declares that he has met them!

He says they do not glide like us,
   But walk in eerie paces;
They're solid, not diaphanous,
   With arms! and legs!! and faces!!!

And some are beggars, some are kings,
   Some have and some are wanting,
They squander time in doing things,
   Instead of simply haunting.

They talk of "art," the horrid crew,
   And things they call "ambitions."—
Oh, yes, I know as well as you
   They're only superstitions.

But should the dreadful day arrive
   When, starting up, I see one,
I'm sure 'twill scare me quite alive;
   And then—Oh, then I'll be one!

THE LISTENERS

"Is there anybody there?" said the Traveller,
  Knocking on the moonlit door;
And his horse in the silence champed the grasses
  Of the forest's ferny floor:
And a bird flew up out of the turret,
Above the Traveller's head:
And he smote upon the door again a second time;
  "Is there anybody there?" he said.
But no one descended to the Traveller;
  No head from the leaf-fringed sill
Leaned over and looked into his grey eyes,
  Where he stood perplexed and still.
But only a host of phantom listeners
  That dwelt in the lone house then
Stood listening in the quiet of the moonlight
  To that voice from the world of men:
Stood thronging the faint moonbeams on the dark stair,
  That goes down to the empty hall,
Hearkening in an air stirred and shaken
  By the lonely Traveller's call.
And he felt in his heart their strangeness,
  Their stillness answering his cry,
While his horse moved, cropping the dark turf,
  'Neath the starred and leafy sky;
For he suddenly smote on the door, even
  Louder, and lifted his head:—
"Tell them I came, and no one answered,
  That I kept my word," he said.
Never the least stir made the listeners,
  Though every word he spake

Fell echoing through the shadowiness of the still house
  From the one man left awake:
Ay, they heard his foot upon the stirrup,
  And the sound of iron on stone,
And how the silence surged softly backward,
  When the plunging hoofs were gone.

THE LITTLE GREEN ORCHARD

Someone is always sitting there,
                In the little green orchard;
    Even when the sun is high
    In noon's unclouded sky,
    And faintly droning goes
    The bee from rose to rose,
Some one in shadow is sitting there,
                In the little green orchard.

Yes, and when twilight's falling softly
                On the little green orchard;
    When the gray dew distils
    And every flower cup fills;
    When the last blackbird says,
    "What—what!" and goes her way—ssh!
I have heard voices calling softly
                In the little green orchard.

Not that I am afraid of being there,
                In the little green orchard;
    Why, when the moon's been bright,
    Shedding her lonesome light,
    And moths like ghosties come,
    And the horned snail leaves home:
I've stayed there, whispering and listening there,
                In the little green orchard.

Only it's strange to be feeling there,
     In the little green orchard;
Whether you paint or draw,
Dig, hammer, chop or saw,
When you are most alone,
All but the silence gone . . .
Someone is waiting and watching there,
     In the little green orchard.

THE GHOST

"Who knocks?"　"I, who was beautiful,
Beyond all dreams to restore,
I, from the roots of the dark thorn am hither,
And knock on the door."

"Who speaks?"　"I,—once was my speech
Sweet as the bird's on the air.
When echo lurks by the waters to heed;
'Tis I speak thee fair."

"Dark is the hour!"　"Aye, and cold."
"Lone is my house."　"Ah, but mine?"
"Sight, touch, lips, eyes yearn in vain."
"Long dead these to thine . . ."

Silence.　Still faint on the porch
Brake the flames of the stars.
In gloom groped a hope-wearied hand
Over keys, bolts and bars.

A face peered.　All the grey night
In chaos of vacancy shone;
Nought but vast Sorrow was there—
The sweet cheat gone.

AMY LOWELL (1874-1925)

A DRACULA OF THE HILLS

Yes, I can understan' ther's a sort o' pleasure collectin' old customs
An' linin' 'em up like a card o' butterflies.
Some on 'em's real quaint, I dessay,
But lookin's one thing an' livin's another.
Folks don't figger on th' quaintness o' th' things they're doin',
Ther' ain't no knick-knack about it then, I guess.
Times is changed since my young days,
Don't seem like th' same world I used to live in.
What with th' telephones an' th' automobiles,
An' city folks rampin' all over th' place Summers,
Lots o' things has kind o' faded out.
But I remember some queer goin's on;
They seem queer 'nough to me now, lookin' back.
We had good times a-plenty, nat'rally,
But they're all jumbled up together when I think on 'em,
I can't git aholt o' one more'n another,
While ther's some fearful strange things I can't never lose a mite of,
No matter how I try.
I'd like to forgit 'bout Florella Perry,
But I ain't never be'n able to.
I don't know as you'd call it a custom,
'Twarn't th' first time th' like had happened, I know,
But ther' ain't never no such doin's nowadays.
Do the Lord's ways change, I wonder?
Superstition, you call it—but I don't know.
Seein's believin' all th' world over,
An' 'twas my own father seed
An' others besides him.
I didn't, 'cause I was a young girl an' not let,
But I watched th' beginnin's;

An' what my eyes didn't see, my ears heerd,
An' that afore other folks' seein' was cold, as you might say.
'Twas all of forty year ago;
I was jest a slip of a girl drawn' toward th' beau stage but not yit ther'.
One day I'd be thinkin' o' nothin' but ribbons,
An' th' next I'd go coastin' bellybumps all afternoon with th' boys.
Florella made me a woman for fair;
P'raps that was a good thing, 'twas time for it,
But I be'n a woman long 'nough now
An' I kind o' like to look back to what went afore.
I warn't livin' here then;
My husband was a Rockridge man
An' I come here when I married.
I was raised t'other side o' Bear Mountain to Penowasset.
Father kep' th' store ther'.
They thought a heap o' him in th' town
An' I had a happy childhood.
We didn't live over th' shop,
But quite along by th' end o' th' village
In a house my mother got from her father.
We had a couple o' fields an' a wood lot
An' kep' a hired man.
Father used to drive back an' forth in a buggy mornin's an' evenin's
But mother an' me didn't miss for neighbors.
Jared Pierce owned a fine big farm just beyond us,
An' Joe Perry's was t'other side th' road.
Florella was Joe's wife,
An' a real pretty creatur she was,
Fragile as a chiney plate
An' bright an' tidy as a June pink in sunshine.
She loved flowers;
Her door-yard was like a nosegay from May till October.
I never see sich flowers as hers;
Nobody else couldn't make 'em bloom so,

Even when she give 'em th' seeds.
Her snowdrops was al'ays first up in th' Spring,
An' it took more'n a couple o' frosts to kill her late asters.
Th' way we knew she was ill was when th' garden begun to git weedy.
She an' Joe'd be'n married 'bout seven year then,
An' My! but they'd be'n happy!
Exceptin' for not havin' a child, I don't think ther' was a thing they
    wanted.
An' then Florella took sick.
It come with a cough one Winter,
An' she couldn't seem to git back her stren'th.
Come plantin' time, she couldn't do it.
Joe done his best, but that year th' garden warn't nothin' perticlar.
Florella used to set in her rocker on th' piazza lookin' at it an' cryin'.
Many's th' time I've slipped over an' done a little rakin' for her.
At first she liked me to do it,
But after a while she said to let it alone;
Ef it warn't her garden, she said, she didn't care nothin' 'bout it.
She spoke almost fierce, I thought, an' I didn't go over agin for quite a
    spell.
When I did, Florella had took to her bed.
She was a queer kind of invalid. You couldn't seem to help her any.
She'd let you do things an' thank you,
But she al'ays seemed angry that you had to come.
One day I was dustin' her room, an' she said to me:
"Becky, I ain't a-goin' to die."
" 'Course you ain't, Florella," says I,
"Whatever put that into your head?"
She flared up at that.
" 'Tain't no use lyin' to me, Becky Wales, I know I'm dyin'.
But I won't die. You'll see.
I'll find some way o' livin'.
Even ef they bury me, I'll live.
You can't kill me, I ain't th' kind to kill.

I'll live! I'll live, I tell you,
Ef ther's a Devil to help me do it!"
She screamed this out at me, settin' up in bed
An' p'intin' with her finger.
I was so scared I had to grab a chair to keep from fallin',
An' Joe come runnin' in from th' barn.
He took her in his arms an' soothed her,
An' she bust out cryin' an' sunk into a little heap in th' big bed
So's you couldn't hardly see her, she was so thin.
Joe sent me home. He said not to mind Florella,
That she was flighty an' didn't know what she was sayin'.
Well, after that things got worse.
Florella had spell after spell;
You could hear her cryin' an' hollerin' way down th' road.
It was al'ays th' same thing: she wouldn't die,
Nobody could make her die.
'Twas awful pitiful to hear her takin' on.
Sometimes she'd moan an' moan,
An' then she'd break out crazy mad an' angry, screamin' for life.
Joe was at his wits' end.
Dr. Smilie said ther' warn't nothin' to do for her
'Cept give her quietin' draughts.
But Florella wouldn't take 'em;
She said they was a little death,
An' she'd throw down th' cup every time they give it to her.
Then she took a notion to see Anabel Flesche.
She was a queer sort of woman, was Anabel,
She lived in a little shed of a place over Chester way.
Some said she had Indian blood in her,
Anyway she was learn'd in herbs an' semples;
She claimed to know jest when to pick 'em,
An' she talked a lot o' foolishness about th' full o' th' moon,
An' three hours before dawn, an' th' dew o' th' second Friday,
An' things like that.

Well, Florella had her in,

An' she made her camomile teas an' lotions, out o' leaves an' plants
    she'd gathered,

An' fussed around with bits o' wax an' string,

But Florella didn't change none.

She kep' sinkin' an' sinkin',

An' th' cryin' spells got to comin' oftener.

She cried most o' th' time then.

I used to set in th' stair winder

When I'd oughter be'n in bed, listenin'.

It made my flesh creep to hear her poor cracked voice declarin' she
    wouldn't die,

An' all th' time she was dyin' plain as pikestaff.

I never see nobody so hungry for life;

She was jest starvin' for it.

Why, even when ther' warn't nothing' lef' of her but eyes an' bones,

She'd talk an' talk 'bout th' life she'd a right to, an' she was goin' to
    have, come what or nothin'!

It was kind o' lonesome out our way then;

Most o' th' passin' got to go by th' Brook Road.

'Twarn't so handy by a good two mile,

But nobody couldn't a-bear to hear Florella

Callin' an' wailin'.

You couldn't count ten th' times she was still.

'Twas a awful witchin' sound, comin' through th' night th' way it did;

I know I got all frazzled out losin' my sleep for hearin' it.

Mother an' Mis' Pierce used to take it in turns to watch her,

An' 'twas a real kindness to do it,

It wore th' nerves so.

One Saturday afternoon Mis' Pierce was with her,

When all of a suddint she jumped out o' bed,

Cryin' she was goin' int' th' garden,

That she was well now an' wouldn't be kep' back no more.

Mis' Pierce caught her just as she was goin' through th' door

An' ther' was a struggle, I guess.

Joe heerd where he was out in th' yard hoein' beans.

He was scared to death, an' jest heaved his hoe up onto his shoulder

An' run in as he was.

Florella seed him comin' with th' hoe up on his shoulder,

An' she screamed a fearful wild scream:

"You too, Joe!" she said,

"You want to kill me same as th' others?

But you shan't do it.

I'll live to spite you,

I'll live because o' you."

She was mockin', an' grinnin', and' coughin',

An' menacin' him with her finger,

An' her head joggin' back an' forth from shoulder to
     shoulder like a rag-doll's.

Mis' Pierce run'd over an' tell'd Mother soon's she
     could git a minit,

An' them was her very words.

Now Florella loved Joe as only a rare few women do
     love;

But she was jest plumb crazy by this time,

Worryin' 'bout th' life was leavin' her, an' all eat up
     with consumption.

But it didn't make no diff'rence to Joe,

He loved her al'ays.

He jest picked her up an' laid her back in bed,

An' she went off unconscious an' never come to.

She died that night.

I mind it well, 'cause the' whippoorwills 'd be'n so loud
     th' night before;

When I'd heerd 'em I'd thought Florella's time was come.

I've al'ays hated funerals,

I can't a-bear to look on a corpse

An Florella's was dretful.

Not that she warn't pretty;

She was. Even her sickness hadn't sp'iled her beauty.
She was like herself in a glass, somehow,
An old glass where you don't see real clear.
'Twas like music to look at her,
Only for her mouth.
Ther' was a queer, awful smile 'bout her mouth.
It made her look jeery, not a bit th' way Florella used
    to look.
Ef I shut my eyes I can see that face now,
Blue, an' thin, an' th' lips all twisted up an' froze so.
I guess I've seen that face in my mind every day for
    forty year, more or less.
Well, they buried her, an' we girls set pansies an'
    lobelia all about her grave
An' took turns tendin' 'em, week by week.
I'd loved Florella,
An', when she was dead, I rec'llected her as she was
    'fore her sickness come
An' forgot th' rest.
Two years is a long time to watch a person die,
An' Joe'd done more nussin' than most husbands.
He kind o' pined when 'twas all finished,
But th' neighbors kep' a-droppin' in to see him,
An' Mother an' Mis' Pierce did him up every so often,
An' bimeby he got aholt of himself,
An' seemed to be gittin' on nicely.
He was a proper good farmer
An' things was goin' well with him,
All' ceptin' his sorrow, which nothin' couldn't lift,
    nat'rally,
When th' next Winter he caught a bad cold.
I guess he let it go too far afore he saw th' doctor;
Anyhow it got a good settle on him an' he couldn't
    shake it off.
Nobody'd have thought much of it, I guess, but for

Florella beginnin' th' same way.
Joe warn't concerned, he said he'd be all right come
    Spring,
But he warn't. He'd try to do his work as usual,
But soon he'd give over an' set down.
He was real patient, but he didn't git no better.
Dr. Smilie begun to look grave.
One day I went over with a bowl o' soup from Mother.
Joe was settin' in th' garden, by a bed o' portulaca;
They's cruel bright flowers, an' Joe looked so grey
    beside 'em
I got a start to see him.
"Becky," says he, "I know you loved Florella,
An' I should like you to have her flowers," says he.
"I've willed th' farm to my brother over to Hills-
    borough,
But you can dig up th' flowers afore he takes possession."
"Joe," I said, "Joe—" an' I couldn't get out another
    word for th' life o' me.
"Yes," he went on, "o' course I'm goin'. I've give her
    all I could, but it can't last.
Anabel Flesche was here yesterday, an' she told me.
I'm glad to ease her any, you know that,
But it can't last."
Glad to ease Anabel Flesche—I thought,
But I know'd he didn't mean that.
I run right home an' told Mother, an' she told
    Father,
An' that evenin' they druv down to Dr. Smilie's.
The doctor 'lowed 'twas consumption, but he was angry
    enough 'bout Anabel Flesche.
"I'll see that hussy stops her trapesin'," he said,
"Rilin' up a sick man with her witch stories," he said.
"I'll witch her, I'll run her out o' town if she comes
    agin."

Anabel didn't come agin, but I guess she done it th'
    first time,
For Joe didn't seem to take int'rest in gittin' well.
When a man don't want to live, he don't live, an' that's
    gospel.
Joe went down hill so fast that by Midsummer ther'
    warn't no hope.
I used to set with him a good deal,
An' 'twas queer how diff'rent he was to Florella.
I think he was th' quietest man I ever see.
He didn't seem to have no pleasure 'cept in speakin'
    'bout Florella.
By times he told me everythin':
How he courted her, an' what he said, an' th' way she
    looked when he brought her home.
I got awful near life for a young girl with th' things he
    told me.
I've be'n married an' widowed since, but I don't know as I
    ever got nearer to things than Joe's talk brought me.
Men ain't alike, an' women ain't alike, an' marriages
    is th' most unlike of all.
My marriage, when it come, was no more like Joe's an'
    Florella's
Than a piney's like a cabbage.
But this ain't my story.
"Florella had a strong will," says Joe to me one after-
    noon.
Autumn had come by then, an' some o' th' leaves had
    fell,
An' those that hung on were so bright they seemed to
    fairly smarten up th' sun.
Joe was layin' in his bed with a patchwork quilt over
    him,
A lovely one 'twas, the State House Steps pattern;

Florella'd made it, she was wonderful clever with her
    needle.
The' whole room was a blaze o' sunshine.
Right on the' chimbley hung a picture o' Florella
Some travellin' artist had painted th' year she was
    married.
I don't suppose city folk would have made much
    of it,
But I thought 'twas a sweet pretty thing, an' th'
    spon-image o' Florella.
"Florella had a mighty strong will," says Joe agin.
"She owned me body an' soul, an' that was a rare pride
    to me."
I couldn't figger what to answer, so I didn't.
"I guess she owns me still," he says, an' I don't know
    ef he was really talkin' to me.
"I'm glad she does. It's got to be both o' us, all or
    neither, together."
He smiled at that, very slow an' tired, almost as though
    it hurt his lips to do it.
"Perhaps you don't understand, little Becky," said he.
I don't know whether I did or not, an' I didn't have a
    chance to say,
For all of a sudden crash down come Florella's picture
    on th' floor with th' cord broke.
I jumped nearly out o' my skin, I expect I screamed
    too,
But Joe didn't so much as shiver.
"Yes," he said, lookin' at me with his steady smile,
"This proves it. You mark my words. It can't go on
    much longer. Poor Florella!"
He sighed then an' layed down, an' I thought he went
    to sleep.
I picked up th' picture, but th' glass had cut it badly,

All about th' mouth too.
It made it look th' way Florella's corpse did an' give
    me a turn.
I was afeerd Joe'd see it when he waked up,
So I set it with its face aginst th' wall.
But I needn't have bothered, for Joe never waked up.
When Mother come, she didn't think he looked right,
An' she sent for Dr. Smilie.
He warn't dead when th' doctor got ther',
But he was unconscious an' hardly breathin';
He stayed like that for a day an' a night
An' then 'twas all over.
All over for Joe, yes,
But not for us.
About a week after th' funeral, Father met Anabel
    Flesche.
"So Joe Perry's dead," whined Anabel, an' Father was
    sure th' old hag looked pleased.
He only said "Yes, he's dead," an' was pushin' on
    when Anabel stopped him.
"Florella's a determined woman," she cackled, "ain't
    you afeerd she'll try somebody else?"
"What th' Hell do you mean?" cried out Father.
"She loved life," said Anabel, in a queer, sly way,
"Joe's gone, but ther's others."
Father was so angry he couldn't trust himself to
    speak,
He jest touched up his horse an' druv on.
But what Anabel said rankled.
He an' Mother talked it over that night.
I warn't supposed to hear, but I did.
I was all shook up with th' things had happened
An' I daresn't stay in bed alone with nobody near,
So I used to creep out an' set on th' stairs

Till Father an' Mother come up.

It comforted me to know they was in th' next room,

An' I could sleep then.

Mother was real strict, an' I was al'ays sent to bed at
     nine;

They'd come up 'bout ten, an' I'd set that hour on th'
     stairs

Where I could look int' th' kitchen an' see 'em.

That's how I come to hear.

Afterwards I 'lowed I knew, an' they told me every-
     thin'.

Well, to make a long story short,

Father an' Jared Pierce went straight to th' Selectmen,

An told 'em what Anabel was hintin'.

Then some old people rec'llected things which had
     happened years ago,

An', puttin' two an' two together, they decided to see
     for themselves.

The Selectmen was all ther', an' Father, an' Jared
     Pierce;

They did it at night so's not to scare folks.

I warn't ther', but Father told it so I think I seen it:

Th' leaves blowin' an' sidlin' down,

Th' lantern light jerkin' 'long th' ground,

Th' noise o' th' pickaxes an' spades.

The got up th' coffin an' opened it.

Florella's body was all gone to dust,

Though 'twarnt' much more'n a year she'd be'n
     buried,

But her heart was as fresh as a livin' person's,

Father said it glittered like a garnet when they took
     th' lid off th' coffin.

It was so 'live, it seemed to beat almost.

Father said a light come from it so strong it made
     shadows

Much heavier than th' lantern shadows an' runnin' in
    a diff'rent direction.
Oh, they burnt it; they al'ays do in such cases,
Nobody's safe till it's burnt.
Now, sir, will you tell me how such things used to be?
They don't happen now, seemingly, but this happened.
You can see Joe's grave over to Penowasset Buryin'-
    ground
Ef you go that way.
The church-members wouldn't let Florella's ashes be
    put back in hers,
So you won't find that.
Only an open space with a maple in th' middle of it;
They planted th' tree so's no one wouldn't ever be
    buried in that spot agin.

THE PAPER IN THE GATE-LEGGED TABLE

Richardson, Erik Follows, Reed and I
Were all comparing notes on our vacations
One evening after dinner. Richardson
Had been to Labrador on a coasting steamer
And run across a half a dozen whales
In the mating season. He has an eye for colour
And picturesque detail, his flashing ocean
And his superb, preoccupied great whales
Love-hunted into fighting, was a thing
I might not have forgotten, but—you'll see,
We'd something bigger even than his whales
To occupy us later on. Tom Reed
Had climbed Mount Everest and broken his leg
And crawled and starved for near a week before
A searching party found him. I had been
Playing the miner for socialistic reasons,

And I thought I had a pretty tale to tell
Until I heard the others. I began,
A bit puffed up to start with, then came Reed,
Then Richardson, the last was Erik Follows.
I rather think he'd needed his vacation
More than the rest of us; he worked so hard.
A doctor can work himself down to bare nerves
If he's in love with his profession, and Follows
Cared more for his than any man I know.
An alienist has many leads to follow,
But Erik's leads all seemed to follow him;
They ran him down a dozen times a day
And even tracked him into his vacations.
That's why we'd left his tale until the last,
For he was sure to have encountered something.
He had; he showed it to us. A gate-legged table
Of old maghogany, as soft as skin,
The colour of maple-syrup, with slender legs,
And just a touch of brass to liven it—
The round-ringed handle of its one small drawer.
And out of this drawer it came, the amazing thing.
A little, pigskin-bound, octavo booklet,
Ruled for accounts, but kept for notes, it seemed.
Half of the pages were blank, the rest were scrawled
With a large, oafish sort of pencil-writing,
So blurred and rubbed, it hardly could be read.
But Follows had read it; you see it was a lead.
"Well?"—we all said, for we could see at once
That Follows had a clue which stretched away
From just this note-book. "Well"—he said at last,
"I took a little trip into the Berkshires
Last Autumn in my car. One afternoon
I chanced to pass a farm-house where an auction
Was being held, and went in just for fun.

It was a pretty place. A little brook
Nuzzled its way along a boggy meadow
Behind a barn with a ship weather-vane,
Which should have struck me, but somehow it didn't,
And, just beyond, one of those odd-shaped hills
You see in Hiroshige's prints ran up,
A slope of hemlocks, right into the sky.
The house was low and wide, with both its porches
So thickly covered with Virginia creeper
The lattice laths might have been creeper-stems.
The crimson of the leaves in the Autumn sunlight
Against the old white paint was strangely cheerful.
I liked the place at once; it seemed a shame
To scatter all the queer, comfortable old things
Had been there for so long. I stopped to look
A moment at the crowd, trampling the garden
And shuffling through the house, then I went in
And bought that table in a sort of pity
That all these things spread round were up for sale.
The old stock ended—it was the usual story—
Gone West, or dead, no one to keep the farm.
I bought the table, ordered it expressed,
Pondered the natural queries which an auction
Always arouses for a day or so,
And finished out my trip without adventure.
Without adventure, yes, that was to come.
It must have been at least two weeks before
I found a moment to unbox my table.
I set it up, dusted it, opened the leaves,
And in the drawer I found this diary;
For that is what it is, a diary.
There is no date, but I can tell you now
The notes were made in eighteen eighty-nine.
But I don't know who wrote them. There's no name;

And that, I think, I never shall discover.
The diary begins—I'll read it to you,
Just a few pages, and then tell the rest."
He picked the book up from the table and read
Slowly and quietly, yet it rang my nerves
It was so still and horrible.

                                    "My God!
Why have they sent me up here to the grass?
Sent me to live among the hateful grass!
The terrible, creeping, creeping, pitiless grass!
What is this thing, this gorging, endless thing,
Moving so slowly that it baffles sight,
But never stopping either night or day?
We mow it down, and in a week again
It covers all the place we have laid bare.
Man builds his roads through grass. With breaking toil,
With sweat and muscle-ache he forces his way
Across the earth. He shears the grasses down
And keeps them there with infinite stress of wheels,
But if he pauses in his travelling,
If for a space he rests, worn with fatigue,
The ravening grass has run across his paths
And choked them utterly away. Oh, God!
The chatter, chatter, chatter, of the grass!
I hear it in the night crying for men
To feed its vitals with their own. I see
It crawling toward this thin, unstable house,
Thrusting its clutching fingers through the boards,
Swallowing the poor weak flowers in their beds.
What is this house? A flimsy, man-made thing
Besieged on all sides by the gluttonous grass.
They speak of spears of grass, but I see bellies
Bellies which feed on man-blood; feet which suck
Entrails of human beings. I am mad,

Tortured to see this island of a house
Waiting to be engulfed. And they have sent
Me here for rest! Oh, Fools! Fools! I, alone—
The myraids of grass are more than I.
I cannot eat, for I will feed no grass.
I cannot sleep for listening to it drink
And fortify its waiting strength with dew.
They tell me to go sit upon the hill
Under the hemlocks where no grass can grow.
But do not trees themselves flourish on graves?
They laugh, the farmer and his sons, they do not think
Of the fat, waving grass that I have seen
In the churchyard. I often go to watch
How green, how wicked green, it grows just there.

*   *   *   *   *   *

Last night I heard a little quiet noise,
A wood-pecker noise, but very, very soft,
And it was in the middle of the night.
I listened for hours till the grey light came,
And then it stopped, and then at last I slept."

*   *   *   *   *   *

The doctor paused, but not one of us spoke.
He turned some pages over and went on:
"I hear it now on almost every night
And all day long my head aches. Lack of sleep,
I know. And that is very bad, for when
I do not sleep, my hearing is so sharp
I very nearly catch the words they say,
The grasses. Only not quite, not quite; and this
Hearing and not is piercing my head through,
Burning it up with irons, hot and cold,
So that I break out in a chilly sweat.
The farmer's wife tells me I'm looking badly,
Should go out more. But that I will not do.
I never go out now. The grass is there.

I have no money; the town doctors saw
To that. 'No care at all,' they said, 'just grow
As the grass grows.' I laughed, oh, I did laugh!
And still they sent me here to rest. My ears!
My ears! They hurt with all the noise. The tapping
Is louder every night. It seems as though
It tried to drown the whimper of the grass,
But nothing can do that. And I can't go
Away, I have no money, not a cent.
I cannot walk, for I must walk through grass.
I've whittled bits of wood to stop my ears,
But, with them in, I think I hear the leaves
Of some dead tree stuttering out my name
In a ghoulish whisper. So I take them out.
The tapping is better, even the stealthy, licking
Murmur which comes from all that tide of grass.

    *   *   *   *   *   *

I've found it out at last. I made them tell me.
I threatened them one evening with a knife,
And said I'd go to bed like a good boy
When once they'd told. It seems that, years ago,
Fifty years or a hundred, I don't remember,
An old sea-captain came up here to live.
He'd left the sea, and as his daughter was married
To the man who owned this place, they took him home
To die, whenever that might happen. But he
Was marvellously afraid of just this dying,
Because he felt like me about the grass.
He used to swear that it should never get him,
And begged his daughter to cast him in the sea.
But she, a decent, quiet woman, was shocked,
And he could never make her give her promise.
At length he hit upon a compromise

And made the two of them agree to it.
His coffin was to be slung from a high beam
Beneath the roof-peak of the barn, and left
To rot and crumble. When they'd given their words,
He had that vane I've often wondered at
Set up there on the barn, he liked to watch
The wind-flaws veer it round and round, he said,
And they were satisfied and never thought
Beyond his reason. But I know more than they.
I know he set it for a sign, a symbol,
A monument. He died at last quite happy
Believing he had overcome the grass.
Way up under the roof-peak swung the coffin,
And mostly folk forgot that it was there.
It gathered dust and cobwebs and grew dim,
You couldn't rightly see it when you looked,
For all the chaff and hayseed floating round
Made a kind of blur to any one below.
But, one day, many years after that time,
The farmer's son, going to feed the horses,
Heard a loud, intermittent sort of banging
Under the roof, and when he took the ladder
And climbed up there to see, he found·a strap
Had given way, and the coffin hung head down
Suspended by the other, and there it teetered
To and fro with every gust of wind
When the barn-door was open. So he said
He'd fix it in the morning. But that night
He woke to hear a rap-tap-tapping, so like
A hammer—but that was a foolish thought,
He knew directly what the thing must be,
Some stanchion broken loose in the high wind.
It was a stormy night, so he decided
He'd leave the shutter, or whatever it was,

Until next day, and fell asleep again.
But in the morning when he went to see
About the coffin, it was all nailed up
As firm as could be with a harness-strap.
They thought that very odd, they little knew
What men can do who have the fear of grass,
What fear can make men do although they're dead.
But I have found a hero I can worship.
Napoleon, Julius Caesar, what are these?
They never ruled the grass, it sucked them up
And drank their brains, and overscored their towns.
O rare and mighty Captain, here's my hand.
Mightier than all men have been before!
Dominant Master, even over grass!
Not by the accident of death at sea,
But by compelling force in your own soul
To be forever above these miles of grass,
As no one ever in the world has been.
I feel a leaping fervour to join my hand
With yours, to grasp your bony, brittle fingers
Unstained by grass-roots. To-morrow I will go
And offer sacrifices to your manes.
How soaring my thoughts are released at last
From all the demon grasses that have gnawed
At them these months past! Now I go to bed,
And I shall sleep to-night.

            *   *   *   *   *   *

Oh, merciless God! The coffin is not there!
They tell me it crumbled many years ago,
And where the bones are no one knows. A jelly-fish
With oozing, pulpy brain, a worthless polyp
Tossed in the air by a Devil-God for fun,
That's what I am, and have been, ever to think
One could cheat grass! The squirming, oily grass!
It waited, lapping round and round the walls

Of the old barn to catch him as he fell.
The terrible, blind grass, feeling its way
With little patting hands. Feeling its way
Slowly, horribly, over all mankind.
There is no safety anywhere at all
For any people. The clapboards of this house
Will peel off one by one, the floor will crack
And through the cracks will come the grinning grass.
My legs will find it stifling them in nets,
My open hands be shut with thongs of grass,
My mouth will hold its roots, my nose its heads,
And in my ears the clatter of its laughter
Will burst my brain and cleave my senseless skull.
I cannot wait and watch, the strain is fire
Stretching and shrivelling me till my bones twist
And drive their needle ends out through my flesh,
And all I see is blood struck through with green,
The bloated green of over-nourished grass.
You dastard God, who set this hideous thing
Upon us! Curse you! Curse you! And all this
Foul, beastly, eating Earth. You shall not have me,
I'll die before I'm eaten. I'll squeeze my hands
About my neck until my eyes spit out
And after them the blood which is my life.
I cannot do it, my fingers are too thin.
But I will find a way to strengthen them,
I'll think of nothing but how to find a way,
I'll kill myself with thinking—"

                                    Follows stopped,
And closed the book. "That entry is the last,"
He said, quite simply, "but there's more to tell.
For I went back to Oakfield—that was the nearest
Village to the farm—and found a man
Who'd known the Crawfords in the eighteen eighties.

And when I asked him if they'd had a boarder,
He said, 'Oh, yes, a poor demented fellow,
Sent up there for the quiet of the country.'
He'd been there just about three months, he told me,
And then, one day when no one was about,
He'd hanged himself by an old harness-strap
To one of the barn beams. He said no more.
Perhaps he did not know about the coffin,
And clearly he knew nothing of the man.
I think I've learned a salutary lesson.
I might myself have been one of those doctors
Prescribing easily 'Rest in the country.'
But, all the same, I wish I'd had a chance
To try my hand. And even as I say it,
I realize what harpies science makes us.
I pity him profoundly—yet a case
Like his to perish on a harness-strap!
Gool Lord, what brutes we are! And now let's talk
Of something cheerful. Richardson, your whales—"

HAUNTED

See! He trails his toes
Through the long streaks of moonlight,
And the nails of his fingers glitter;
They claw and flash among the tree-tops.
His lips suck at my open window,
And his breath creeps about my body
And lies in pools under my knees.
I can see his mouth sway and wobble,
Sticking itself against the window-jambs,
But the moonlight is bright on the floor,
Without a shadow.
Hark! A hare is strangling in the forest,
And the wind tears a shutter from the wall.

ROBERT FROST (1875-   )

THE WITCH OF COÖS

I stayed the night for shelter at a farm
Behind the mountain, with a mother and son,
Two old-believers. They did all the talking.

Mother. Folks think a witch who has familiar spirits
She could call up to pass a winter evening,
But won't, should be burned at the stake or something.
Summoning spirits isn't "Button, button,
Who's got the button," I would have them know.

Son. Mother can make a common table rear
And kick with two legs like an army mule.

Mother. And when I've done it, what good have I done?
Rather than tip a table for you, let me
Tell you what Ralle the Sioux Control once told me.
He said the dead had souls, but when I asked him
How could that be—I thought the dead were souls,
He broke my trance. Don't that make you suspicious
That there's something the dead are keeping back?
Yes, there's something the dead are keeping back.

Son. You wouldn't want to tell him what we have
Up attic, mother?

Mother. Bones—a skeleton.

Son. But the headboard of mother's bed is pushed
Against the attic door: the door is nailed.
It's harmless. Mother hears it in the night

Halting perplexed behind the barrier
Of door and headboard. Where it wants to get
Is back into the cellar where it came from.

Mother. We'll never let them, will we, son! We'll never!

Son. It left the cellar forty years ago
And carried itself like a pile of dishes
Up one flight from the cellar to the kitchen,
Another from the kitchen to the bedroom,
Another from the bedroom to the attic,
Right past both father and mother, and neither stopped it.
Father had gone upstairs; mother was downstairs.
I was a baby: I don't know where I was.

Mother. The only fault my husband found with me—
I went to sleep before I went to bed,
Especially in winter when the bed
Might just as well be ice and the clothes snow.
The night the bones came up the cellar-stairs
Toffile had gone to bed alone and left me,
But left an open door to cool the room off
So as to sort of turn me out of it.
I was just coming to myself enough
To wonder where the cold was coming from,
When I heard Toffile upstairs in the bedroom
And thought I heard him downstairs in the cellar.
The board we had laid down to walk dry-shod on
When there was water in the cellar in spring
Struck the hard cellar bottom. And then someone
Began the stairs, two footsteps for each step,
The way a man with one leg and a crutch,
Or a little child, comes up. It wasn't Toffile:
It wasn't anyone who could be there.

The bulkhead double-doors were double-locked
And swollen tight and buried under snow.
The cellar windows were banked up with sawdust
And swollen tight and buried under snow.
It was the bones. I knew them—and good reason.
My first impulse was to get to the knob
And hold the door. But the bones didn't try
The door; they halted helpless on the landing,
Waiting for things to happen in their favor.
The faintest restless rustling ran all through them.
I never could have done the thing I did
If the wish hadn't been too strong in me
To see how they were mounted for this walk.
I had a vision of them put together
Not like a man, but like a chandelier.
So suddenly I flung the door wide on him.
A moment he stood balancing with emotion,
And all but lost himself. (A tongue of fire
Flashed out and licked along his upper teeth.
Smoke rolled inside the sockets of his eyes.)
Then he came at me with one hand outstretched,
The way he did in life once; but this time
I struck the hand off brittle on the floor,
And fell back from him on the floor myself.
The finger-pieces slid in all directions.
(Where did I see one of those pieces lately?
Hand me my button-box—it must be there.)
I sat up on the floor and shouted, "Toffile,
It's coming up to you." It had its choice
Of the door to the cellar or the hall.
It took the hall door for the novelty,
And set off briskly for so slow a thing,
Still going every which way in the joints, though,
So that it looked like lightning or a scribble,

From the slap I had just now given its hand.
I listened till it almost climbed the stairs
From the hall to the only finished bedroom,
Before I got up to do anything;
Then ran and shouted, "Shut the bedroom door,
Toffile, for my sake!" "Company?" he said,
"Don't make me get up; I'm too warm in bed."
So lying forward weakly on the handrail
I pushed myself upstairs, and in the light
(The kitchen had been dark) I had to own
I could see nothing. "Toffile, I don't see it.
It's with us in the room though. It's the bones."
"What bones?" "The cellar bones—out of the grave."
That made him throw his bare legs out of bed
And sit up by me and take hold of me.
I wanted to put out the light and see
If I could see it, or else mow the room,
With our arms at the level of our knees,
And bring the chalk-pile down. "I'll tell you what—
It's looking for another door to try.
The uncommonly deep snow has made him think
Of his old song, *The Wild Colonial Boy,*
He always used to sing along the tote-road.
He's after an open door to get out-doors.
Let's trap him with an open door up attic."
Toffile agreed to that, and sure enough,
Almost the moment he was given an opening,
The steps began to climb the attic stairs.
I heard them. Toffile didn't seem to hear them.
"Quick!" I slammed to the door and held the knob.
"Toffile, get nails." I made him nail the door shut,
And push the headboard of the bed against it.
Then we asked was there anything
Up attic that we'd ever want again.

The attic was less to us than the cellar.
If the bones liked the attic, let them have it.
Let them stay in the attic. When they sometimes
Come down the stairs at night and stand perplexed
Behind the door and headboard of the bed,
Brushing their chalky skull with chalky fingers,
With sounds like the dry rattling of a shutter,
That's what I sit up in the dark to say—
To no one any more since Toffile died.
Let them stay in the attic since they went there.
I promised Toffile to be cruel to them
For helping them be cruel once to him.

Son. We think they had a grave down in the cellar.

Mother. We know they had a grave down in the cellar.

Son. We never could find out whose bones they were.

Mother. Yes, we could too, son. Tell the truth for once.
They were a man's his father killed for me.
I mean a man he killed instead of me.
The least I could do was to help dig their grave.
We were about it one night in the cellar.
Son knows the story: but 'twas not for him
To tell the truth, suppose the time had come.
Son looks surprised to see me end a lie
We'd kept all these years between ourselves
So as to have it ready for outsiders.
But tonight I don't care enough to lie—
I don't remember why I ever cared.
Toffile, if he were here, I don't believe
Could tell you why he ever cared himself . . .

She hadn't found the finger-bone she wanted
Among the buttons poured out in her lap.
I verified the name next morning: Toffile.
The rural letter-box said Toffile Lajway.

JOSEPHINE DASKAM BACON (1876-   )

THE LITTLE DEAD CHILD

When all but her were sleeping fast,
   And the night was nearly fled,
The little dead child came up the stair
   And stood by his mother's bed.

"Ah, God!" she cried, "the nights are three,
   And yet I have not slept!"
The little dead child he sat him down,
   And sank his head and wept.

"And is it thou, my little dead child,
   Come in from out the storm?
Ah, lie thou back against my heart,
   And I will keep thee warm!"

That is long ago, mother,
   Long and long ago!
Shall I grow warm who lay three nights
   Beneath the winter snow?

"Hast thou not heard the old nurse weep?
   She sings to us no more;
And thy brothers leave the broken toys
   And whisper in the door."

That is far away, mother,
  Far and far away!
Above my head the stone is white,
  My hands forget to play.

"What wilt thou then, my little dead child,
  Since here thou may'st not lie?
Ah, me! that snow should be thy sheet,
  And winds thy lullaby!"

Down within my grave, mother,
  I heard, I know not how,
"Go up to God, thou little child,
  Go up and meet him now!"

That is far to fare, mother,
  Far and far to fare!
I come for thee to carry me
  The way from here to there.

"Oh, hold thy peace, my little dead child.
  My heart will break in me!
Thy way to God thou must go alone,
  I may not carry thee!"

The cock crew out the early dawn
  Ere she could stay her moan;
She heard the cry of a little child,
  Upon his way alone.

JOYCE KILMER (1886-1918)

DAVE LILLY

There's a brook on the side of Greylock that used to be full of trout,
But there's nothing there now but minnows; they say it is all fished out.
I fished there many a Summer day some twenty years ago,
And I never quit without getting a mess of a dozen or so.

There was a man, Dave Lilly, who lived on the North Adams road,
And he spent all his time fishing, while his neighbors reaped and sowed.
He was the luckiest fisherman in the Berkshire hills, I think.
And when he didn't go fishing he'd sit in the tavern and drink.

Well, Dave is dead and buried and nobody cares very much;
They have no use in Greylock for drunkards and loafers and such,
But I always liked Dave Lilly, he was pleasant as you could wish,
He was shiftless and good-for-nothing, but he certainly could fish.

The other night I was walking up the hill from Williamstown
And I came to the brook I mentioned, and I stopped on the bridge
  and sat down.
I looked at the blackened water with its little flecks of white,
And I heard it ripple and whisper in the still of the Summer night.

And after I'd been there a minute it seemed to me I could feel
The presence of someone near me, and I heard the hum of a reel.
And the water was churned and broken, and something was brought
  to land
By a twist and a flirt of a shadowy rod in a deft and shadowy hand.

I scrambled down to the brookside and hunted all about;
There wasn't a sign of a fisherman; there wasn't a sign of a trout.
But I heard somebody chuckle behind the hollow oak
And I got a whiff of tobacco like Lilly used to smoke.

It's fifteen years, they tell me, since anyone fished that brook;
And there's nothing in it but minnows that nibble the bait off your hook.
But before the sun has risen and after the moon has set
I know that it's full of ghostly trout for Lilly's ghost to get.

I guess I'll go to the tavern and get a bottle of rye
And leave it down by the hollow oak, where Lilly's ghost went by.
I meant to go up on the hillside and try to find his grave
And put some flowers on it—but this will be better for Dave.

WILLIAM ROSE BENÉT (1886-   )

THE SORCERESS OF THE MOON

Its gates are griffin-guarded gates,
Its towers of yellow ivory hewn.
Resplendent glints each sparkling stud
Of rubies red as pigeon's blood,
Of pearls as white as the swan's neck,
Of diamonds without flaw or fleck
That crust its towers, and glitter thence
Along its cloudy battlements.
And far within its portals waits
The sorceress of the moon.

This palace I have seen afar
When crimson, gold, and purple cloud
Made all the west a blaze of flame,
Ere twilight from her cloisters came
To walk the heavens with nunlike pace
And downcast eyes and wistful face.
Then all its wonder crumbling lies
In splendid wreckage on the skies.

But now—ah, see! Its raptures rise
Impossible and proud.

So fling a bridle of delight
Upon the wildest dream of all,
And, as Mahomet 'strode the back
Of the white beast called Alborac,
We too shall thunder up the west
With rich caparison and crest,
Wind horn before those marvelous gates,
Daring their guard, and find who waits
Withdrawn in splendor infinite
In that vast presence-hall.

Her brows would make the calla gray.
Her hair is soft and dark as night.
Her purple dais canopy
Bears stars in golden broidery.
She wields a slight and silvern wand
To summon spirits from beyond.
And all the wandering winds in tune
Sing to the sorceress of the moon
With airiest music, and alway
Swoon in her haze of light.

Yet hers are griffin-guarded gates.
Minds in her presence madden soon.
Her gaze is strange; and to sustain
Her glamorous eyes means joy and pain
Mixed in such wise, the soul is caught
Spellbound, bewildered passing thought.
O glance not long, but shun her sight
While still the heart desires delight,
Where deep within the sunset waits
The sorceress of the moon!

221B

Here dwell together still two men of note
Who never lived and so can never die:
How very near they seem, yet how remote
That age before the world went all awry.
But still the game's afoot for those with ears
Attuned to catch the distant view-halloo:
England is England yet, for all our fears—
Only those things the heart *believes* are true.

A yellow fog swirls past the window-pane
As night descends upon this fabled street:
A lonely hansom splashes through the rain,
The ghostly gas lamps fail at twenty feet.
Here, though the world explode, these two survive,
And it is always eighteen ninety-five.

CHANGELING

The gallows tree is straight and tall
Save for a single jutting limb. . . .
And from a spot across the road
I watched the tortured legs of him
Who dangled there. . . .

        The hangman laughed,
So merry was the sight withal.
The hangman's daughter, standing near,
Was lovely as a waterfall;
Her yellow hair streamed over her,
Her symmetry was starkly limned. . . .
I loathed and loved her, and it seemed

Her scarlet roses glowed and dimmed
As my wild eyes upon her fed.
Her glance was free and bold, I thought. . . .
Our tryst was secret, when the dark
Had fallen, where the corpse hung taut
In the red moon. . . .

                  The cursèd babe
Was hideous as Hell, and we
Shrieked as we knew the twisted face
Of him that decked the gallows tree.

VISITATION

The trull came out of nothing and was there;
That is the truth, you may depend upon it.
You could have knocked me over with a sonnet—
She said she didn't have a thing to wear.
And that was true enough, for she was bare
From Ballymena all the way to Connaught,
Except for something reckless like a bonnet—
I looked at her and said, "Well, I declare!"

But something cold was sneaking up my spine;
Perhaps I was a little scared, at that:
At any rate the creature must be banished.
"Look here," I said, "is this your room or mine?
"I don't believe in ghosts," I told her flat.
"Ah, well," said she, "there's them that does!"
   and vanished.

LEGEND

(For Mary Hope)

She went into the wood where serpents are,
Into the wood with silent darkness crowned.

The black teeth of the forest hemmed her round,
But still her feet led onward toward the star.
The forest crushed the wind in arms of sound. . . .
"Geritza!" still his voice cried from afar.

Into the distance of her footsteps crept
All that had gone before and that was dead.
Adders were in the forest, he had said. . . .
Under her feet the evil grasses slept.
"Geritza!" still his voice called. Overhead
The star burned whitely as he stood and wept.

She crossed the black stream where the adders float;
Only the star looked back to where he stood.
"Geritza!" But the voices of the flood
Tossed the white crumbling echo of his note.
Fear spread itself between him and the wood:
The silence was a snake around his throat.

GOOSEFLESH

Sometimes,
Reading late in my bookroom,
I look quickly to the window,
With a cold feeling that I am being watched;
And there is the Night
Peering in. . . .

*

Once, at midnight,
I crept to the edge of all things
And looked over;
But the darkness was there
Too!

*

You, there—
Behind the curtain!
Are you aware that you
Bulge?

                    *

We are alike in this,
Silence,
That we would speak
If we could.

                    *

Ah, Death,
Is it you?
Walk softly, please,
And the neighbors will not know
Until morning.

EXTRAORDINARY VISIT

The rocket was as sleek as any ship:
I looked around to see that all was right—
My dressing gown and slippers for the trip,
My "Reader's Digest" and electric light.
I counted all the presents up again—
Ten-cent cigars for Uncle George and Dad,
The lemon drops for Minnie, "Little Men"
For Freddie Smith; and Mamma's heating-pad.

At last the moment came; the crowd was numb,
The music ceased. Then as I raised my hand
And gave the Sign—two fingers and a thumb—
The rocket leapt and thrust away the land.
With one lone shriek, at quarter past eleven,
At awful speed we shot away for Heaven.

SEA STORY

Man and boy—said the old Sailor—
I've sailed the Thirty Seas
(Who told you there was only seven?)
And never seen a Ghost Ship;
But mermaids, bless you, is another story.
Glory be, I remember once,
It was in the Bay of Biscay,
Or maybe off the coast of Devon,
Nine of the little darlings came aboard,
Cute little tricks with slapsy shining tails;
Only one lipstick and a harmonica between 'em—
Sirens they said they was.
Ah, sir, that was an occasion, no mistake!
That very night the Captain died in my arms—
Like a brother he was!
Listening for his heartbeat,
Under his shirt I sees the name of "Molly"
Tattooed on his stomick,
And I almost passes out.
Little Molly Jelstrup
That had been my childhood sweetheart!
I tell you I was shocked, sir:
Many's the time I wished I hadn't killed him,
So I could ask him what became of Molly.
But there it was, you understand,
And a bad business too—
The Captain dead, and every day
Provisions getting lower in the locker.
God forgive me for what I done!
There was my little mermaids, nine of 'em,
Playing in the pool like happy dolphins.
Innocent as you please.
Well, sir, I baited me a hook with bacon rind,

And then—
Cover your eyes, sir!—
I fishes up them little mers
And eats 'em one by one!
Tender? Yes, sir, they was that;
That's exactly what they was.
Tender as a maiden's heart,
Like chicken, sir, if you know what I mean:
I kissed the last one before I done her in.
And then the weeks went past;
No ship, no land, no food,
And no more dancing girls.
I tell you it was tough, sir,
Until that day a little island
Comes bouncing out o' the sea
Like a colored motion pitcher
I seen in Brooklyn once—
Volcanic action they calls it.
And there I was, sir, on that little island
For twenty years!
It warn't so bad, you understand;
Just lonesome like, with only the water and the crabs,
And now and then a tiger burning bright.
But it do get on a seaman's nerves,
And so one day I writes a little note—
In blood it was, on a torn piece of hanky—
And puts it in a empty bottle,
And says a little prayer,
And heaves it into the sea.
That was forty years ago, shipmate,
And from that day to this
I ain't never been discovered!
Sometimes I wonder if I'm still there,
I'd kind of like to know;

But listen,
Put your ear down close:
I remember where that island is!
I've got it written in this little book—
Latitude 25° 4′ *South, longitude* 130° 8′ *West.*
That's it, sir, that's the place;
That's where I am this very minute,
Like as not;
Dying of thirst,I shouldn't wonder,
And this pretty little grog shop
Eight thousand miles away.
Dying of thirst belike,
And not a sail on the horizon!
Dying of—well, now, thankee, sir;
The same to you, sir, and
I'll take the same.

ROY HELTON (1886-   )

LONESOME WATER

Drank lonesome water:
Warn't but a tad then
Up in a laurel thick
Digging for sang;
Came on a place where
The stones were hollow.
Something below them
Tinkled and rang.

Dug whar I heard it
Drippling below me;
Should a knowd better.

Should a been wise;
Leant down and drank it,
Clutching and gripping
The over hung cliv
With the ferns in my eyes.

Twarn't no tame water
I knowd in a minute;
Must a been laying there
Projecting round
Since winter went home;
Must a laid like a cushion
Whar the feet of the blossoms
Was tucked in the ground.

Tasted of heart leaf
And that smells the sweetest,
Paw paw and spice bush
And wild briar rose;
Must a been counting
The heels of the spruce pines,
And neighboring round
Whar angelica grows.

I'd drunk lonesome water
I knowed in a minute:
Never larnt nothing
From then till today;
Nothing worth larning;
Nothing worth knowing,
I'm bound to the hills
And I can't get away.

Mean sort of dried up old
Ground hoggy fellow,
Laying out cold here

Watching the sky;
Pore as a hipporwill,
Bent like a grass blade;
Counting up stars
Till they count too high.

I know whar the gray foxes
Uses up yander:
Know what'll cure ye
Of tisic or chills,
But I never been way from here,
Never got going;
I've drunk lonesome water.
I'm bound to the hills.

OLD CHRISTMAS

"Where are you coming from, Lomey Carter,
  So airly over the snow?
And what's them pretties you got in your hand,
  And where you aiming to go?

"Step in, Honey: Old Christmas morning
  I ain't got nothing much;
Maybe a bite of sweetness and corn bread,
  A little ham meat and such.

"But come in, Honey! Sally Anne Barton's
  Hungering after your face.
Wait till I light my candle up:
  Set down! There's your old place.

"Now where you been so airly this morning?"
  "Graveyard, Sally Anne.
Up by the trace in the salt lick meadows
  Where Taulbe kilt my man."

"Taulbe ain't to home this morning . . .
   I can't scratch up a light:
Dampness gets on the heads of the matches;
   But I'll blow up the embers bright."

"Needn't trouble. I won't be stopping:
   Going a long ways still."
"You didn't see nothing, Lomey Carter,
   Up on the graveyard hill?"

"What should I see there, Sally Anne Barton?"
   "Well, sperits do walk last night."
"There were an elder bush a-blooming
   While the moon still give some light."

"Yes, elder bushes, they bloom, Old Christmas,
   And critters kneel down in their straw.
Anything else up in the graveyard?"
   "One thing more I saw:

I saw my man with his head all bleeding
   Where Taulbe's shot went through."
"What did he say?" *"He stooped and kissed me."*
   "What did he say to you?"

"Said, Lord Jesus forguv your Taulbe;
   But he told me another word;
He said it soft when he stooped and kissed me.
   That were the last I heard."

"Taulbe ain't to home this morning."
"I know that, Sally Anne,
For I kilt him, coming down through the meadow
   Where Taulbe kilt my man.

"I met him upon the meadow trace
  When the moon were fainting fast,
And I had my dead man's rifle gun
  And kilt him as he come past."

"But I heard two shots." *"'Twas his was second:*
  He shot me 'fore he died:
You'll find us at daybreak, Sally Anne Barton:
  I'm lying there dead at his side."

HOWARD PHILLIPS LOVECRAFT (1890-1937)

PSYCHOPOMPOS

I am He who howls in the night;
  I am He who moans in the snow;
I am He who hath never seen light;
  I am He who mounts from below.

My car is the car of Death;
  My wings are the wings of dread;
My breath is the north wind's breath;
  My prey are the cold and the dead.

In old Auvergne, when schools were poor and few,
And peasants fancy'd what they scarcely knew,
When lords and gentry shunn'd their Monarch's throne
For solitary castles of their own,
There dwelt a man of rank, whose fortress stood
In the hush'd twilight of a hoary wood.
De Blois his name; his lineage high and vast,

A proud memorial of an honor'd past;
But curious swains would whisper now and then
That Sieur De Blois was not as other men.
In person dark and lean, with glossy hair,
And gleaming teeth that he would often bare,
With piercing eye, and stealthy roving glance,
And tongue that clipt the soft, sweet speech of France;
The Sieur was little lov'd and seldom seen,
So close he kept within his own demesne.
The castle servants, few, discreet, and old,
Full many a tale of strangeness might have told;
But bow'd with years, they rarely left the door
Wherein their sires and grandsires serv'd before.
Thus gossip rose, as gossip rises best,
When mystery imparts a keener zest;
Seclusion oft the poison tongue attracts,
And scandal prospers on a dearth of facts.
'Twas said, the Sieur had more than once been spy'd
Alone at midnight by the river's side,
With aspect so uncouth, and gaze so strange,
That rustics cross'd themselves to see the change;
Yet none, when pressed, could clearly say or know
Just what it was, or why they trembled so.
De Blois, as rumor whisper'd, fear'd to pray,
Nor us'd his chapel on the Sabbath day;
Howe'er this may have been, 'twas known at least
His household had no chaplain, monk, or priest.
But if the Master liv'd in dubious fame,
Twice fear'd and hated was his noble Dame;
As dark as he, in features wild and proud,
And with a weird supernal grace endow'd,
The haughty mistress scorn'd the rural train
Who sought to learn her source, but sought in vain.
Old women call'd her eyes too bright by half,
And nervous children shiver'd at her laugh;

Richard, the dwarf (whose word had little weight),
Vow'd she was like a serpent in her gait,
Whilst ancient Pierre (the aged often err)
Laid all her husband's mystery to her.
Still more absurd were those odd mutter'd things
That calumny to curious list'ners brings;
Those subtle slanders, told with downcast face,
And muffled voice . . . those tales no man may trace;
Tales that the faith of old wives can command,
Though always heard at sixth or seventh hand.
Thus village legend darkly would imply
That Dame De Blois possess'd an evil eye;
Or going further, furtively suggest
A lurking spark of sorcery in her breast;
Old Mère Allard (herself half witch) once said
The lady's glance work'd strangely on the dead.
So liv'd the pair, like many another two
That shun the crowd, and shrink from public view.
They scorn'd the doubts by ev'ry peasant shown,
And ask'd but one thing . . . to be let alone!

'Twas Candlemas, the dreariest time of year,
With fall long gone, and spring too far to cheer,
When little Jean, the bailiff's son and heir,
Fell sick and threw the doctors in despair.
A child so stout and strong that few would think
An hour might carry him to death's dark brink,
Yet pale he lay, through hidden was the cause,
And Galens search'd in vain through Nature's laws.
But stricken sadness could not quite suppress
The roving thought, or wrinkled grandam's guess:
Though spoke by stealth, 'twas known to half a score
That Dame De Blois rode by the day before;
She had (they said) with glances weird and wild
Paus'd by the gate to view the prattling child,

Nor did they like the smile which seem'd to trace
New lines of evil on her proud, dark face.
These things they whisper'd, when the mother's cry
Told of the end . . . the gentle soul gone by;
In genuine grief the kindly watcher wept,
Whilst the lov'd babe with saints and angels slept.
The village priest his simple rites went through,
And good Michel nail'd up the box of yew;
Around the corpse the holy candles burn'd,
The mourners sighed, the parents dumbly yearn'd.
Then one by one each sought his humble bed,
And left the lonely mother with her dead.
Late in the night it was, when o'er the vale
The storm king swept with pandemoniac gale;
Deep pil'd the cruel snow, yet strange to tell,
The lightning sputter'd while the white flakes fell;
A hideous presence seem'd abroad to steal,
And terror sounded in the thunder's peal.
Within the house of grief the tapers glow'd
Whilst the poor mother bow'd beneath her load;
Her salty eyes too tired now to weep,
Too pain'd to see, too sad to close in sleep..
The clock struck three, above the tempest heard,
When something near the lifeless infant stirr'd;
Some slipp'ry thing, that flopp'd in awkward way,
And climb'd the table where the coffin lay,
With scaly convolutions strove to find
The cold, still clay that death had left behind.
The nodding mother hears . . . starts broad awake . . .
Empower'd to reason, yet too stunn'd to shake;
The pois'nous thing she sees, and nimbly foils
The ghoulish purpose of the quiv'ring coils:
With ready ax the serpent's head she cleaves,
And thrills with savage triumph whilst she grieves.

The injur'd reptile hissing glides from sight,
And hides it cloven carcass in the night.

The weeks slipp'd by, and gossip's tongue began
To call the Sieur De Blois an alter'd man;
With curious mien he oft would pace along
The village street, and eye the gaping throng.
Yet whilst he showed himself as ne'er before,
His wild-eyed lady was observ'd no more.
In course of time, 'twas scarce thought odd or ill
That he his ears with village lore should fill;
Nor was the town with special rumor rife
When he sought out the bailiff and his wife:
Their tale of sorrow, with its ghastly end,
Was told, indeed, by ev'ry wond'ring friend
The Sieur heard all, and low'ring rode away,
Nor was he seen again for many a day.

When vernal sunshine shed its cheering glow,
And genial zephyrs blew away the snow,
To frighten'd swains a horror was reveal'd
In the damp herbage of a melting field.
There (half preserved by winter's frigid bed)
Lay the dark Dame De Blois, untimely dead;
By some assassin's stroke most foully slain,
Her shapely brow and temples cleft in twain.
Reluctant hands the dismal burden bore
To the stone arches of the husband's door,
Where silent serfs the ghastly thing receiv'd,
Trembling with fright, but less amaz'd than griev'd;
The Sieur his dame beheld with blazing eyes,
And shook with anger, more than with surprize.
(At least 'tis thus the stupid peasants told
Their wide-mouth'd wives when they the tale unroll'd.)

The village wonder'd why De Blois had kept
His spouse's loss unmention'd and unwept,
Nor were there lacking sland'rous tongues to claim
That the dark master was himself to blame.
But village talk could scarcely hope to solve
A crime so deep, and thus the months revolve:
The rural train repeat the gruesome tale,
And gape and marvel more than they bewail.

Swift flew the sun, and winter once again
With icy talons gripp'd the frigid plain.
December brought its store of Christmas cheer,
And grateful peasants hail'd the op'ning year;
But by the hearth as Candlemas drew nigh,
The whisp'ring ancients spoke of things gone by.
Few had forgot the dark demoniac lore
Of things that came the Candlemas before,
And many a crone intently ey'd the house
Where dwelt the sadden'd bailiff and his spouse.
At last the day arriv'd, the sky o'erspread
With dark'ning messengers and clouds of lead;
Each neighb'ring grove Æolian warnings sigh'd,
And thick'ning terrors broadcast seem'd to bide.
The good folk, though they knew not why, would run
Swift past the bailiff's door, the scene to shun;
Within the house the grieving couple wept,
And mourn'd the child who now for ever slept.
On rush'd the dusk in doubly hideous form,
Borne on the pinions of the gath'ring storm;
Unusual murmurs fill'd the rainless wind,
And hast'ning travelers fear'd to glance behind.
Mad o'er the hills the demon tempest tore;
The rising river lash'd the troubled shore;
Black through the night the awful storm god prowl'd,

And froze the list'ners' life-blood as he howled;
Gigantic trees like supple rushes sway'd,
Whilst for his home the trembling cotter pray'd.
Now falls a sudden lull amidst the gale;
With less'ning force the circling currents wail;
Far down the stream that laves the neighb'ring mead
Burst a new ululation, wildly key'd;
The peasant train a frantic mien assume,
And huddle closer in the spectral gloom:
To each strain'd ear the truth too well is known,
For that dread sound can come from wolves alone!
The rustics close attend, when ere they think,
A lupine army swarms the river's brink;
From out the waters leap a howling train
That rend the air, and scatter o'er the plain:
With flaming orbs the frothing creatures fly,
And chant with hellish voice their hungry cry.
First of the pack a mighty monster leaps
With fearless tread, and martial order keeps;
Th' attendant wolves his yelping tones obey,
And form in columns for the coming fray:
No frighten'd swain they harm, but silent bound
With a fix'd purpose o'er the frozen ground.
Straight course the monsters through the village street,
Unholy vigor in their flying feet;
Through half-shut blinds the shelter'd peasants peer,
And wax in wonder as they lose in fear.
Th' excited pack at last their goal perceive,
And the vex'd air with deaf'ning clamor cleave;
The churls, astonish'd, watch th' unnatural herd
Flock round a cottage at the leader's word:
Quick spreads the fearsome fact, by rumor blown,
That the doom'd cottage is the bailiff's own!
Round and around the howling demons glide,

Whilst the fierce leader scales the vine-clad side;
The frantic wind its horrid wail renews,
And mutters madly through the leafless yews.
In the frail house the bailiff calmly waits
The rav'ning horde, and trusts th' impartial Fates,
But the wan wife revives with curious mien
Another monster and an older scene;
Amidst th' increasing wind that rocks the walls,
The dame to him the serpent's deed recalls:
Then as a nameless thought fills both their minds,
The bare-fang'd leader crashes through the blinds.
Across the room, with murd'rous fury rife,
Leaps the mad wolf, and seizes on the wife;
With strange intent he drags his shrieking prey
Close to the spot where once the coffin lay.
Wilder and wilder roars the mounting gale
That sweeps the hills and hurtles through the vale;
The ill-made cottage shakes, the pack without
Dance with new fury in demoniac rout.
Quick as his thought, the valiant bailiff stands
Above the wolf, a weapon in his heads;
The ready ax that served a year before,
Now serves as well to slay one monster more.
The creature drops inert, with shatter'd head,
Full on the floor, and silent as the dead;
The rescu'd wife recalls the dire alarms,
And faints from terror in her husband's arms.
But as he holds her, all the cottage quakes,
And with full force the titan tempest breaks:
Down crash the walls, and o'er their shrinking forms
Burst the mad revels of the storm of storms.
Th' encircling wolves advance with ghastly pace,
Hunger and murder in each gleaming face,
But as they close, from out the hideous night
Flashes a bolt of unexpected light:

The vivid scene to ev'ry eye appears,
And peasants shiver with returning fears.
Above the wreck the scatheless chimney stays,
Its outline glimm'ring in the fitful rays,
Whilst o'er the hearth still hangs the houshold shrine,
The Savior's image and the Cross divine!
Round the blest spot a lambent radiance glows,
And shields the cotters from their stealthy foes:
Each monstrous creature marks the wondrous glare,
Droops, fades, and vanishes in empty air!
The village train with startled eyes adore,
And count their beads in rev'rence o'er and o'er.
Now fades the light, and dies the raging blast,
The hour of dread and reign of horror past.
Pallid and bruis'd, from out his toppled walls
The panting bailiff with his good wife crawls:
Kind hands attend them. whilst o'er all the town
A strange sweet peace of spirit settles down.
Wonder and fear are still'd in soothing sleep,
As through the breaking clouds the moon rays peep.

Here paus'd the prattling grandam in her speech,
Confus'd with age, the tale half out of reach;
The list'ning guest, impatient for a clue,
Fears 'tis not one tale, but a blend of two;
He fain would know how far'd the widow'd lord
Whose eery ways th' initial theme afford,
And marvels that the crone so quick should slight
His fate, to babble of the wolf-rack'd night.
The old wife, press'd, for greater clearness strives,
Nods wisely, and her scatter'd wits revives;
Yet strangely lingers on her latter tale
Of wolf and bailiff, miracle and gale.
When (quoth the crone) the dawn's bright radiance bath'd
Th' eventful scene, so late in terror swath'd,

The chatt'ring churls that sought the ruin'd cot
Found a new marvel in the gruesome spot.
From fallen walls a trail of gory red,
As of the stricken wolf, erratic led;
O'er road and mead the new-dript crimson wound,
Till lost amidst the neighb'ring swampy ground:
With wonder unappeas'd the peasants burn'd,
For what the quicksand takes is ne'er return'd.

Once more the grandam, with a knowing eye,
Stops in her tale, to watch a hawk soar by;
The weary list'ner, baffled, seeks anew
For some plain statement, or enlight'ning clue.
Th' indulgent crone attends the puzzled plea,
Yet strangely mutters o'er the mystery.
The Sieur? Ah, yes . . . that morning all in vain
His shaking servants scour'd the frozen plain;
No man had seen him since he rode away
In silence on the dark preceding day,
His horse, wild-eyed with some unusual fright,
Came wand'ring from the river bank that night.
His hunting-hound, that mourn'd with piteous woe,
Howl'd by the quicksand swamp, his grief to show.
The village folk thought much, but utter'd less;
The servants' search wore out in emptiness:
For Sieur De Blois (the old wife's tale is o'er)
Was lost to mortal sight forevermore.

FUNGI FROM YUGGOTH

I. The Book

The place was dark and dusty and half-lost
In tangles of old alleys near the quays,
Reeking of strange things brought in from the seas,
And with queer curls of fog that west winds tossed.
Small lozenge panes, obscured by smoke and frost
Just showed the books, in piles like twisted trees,
Rotting from floor to roof—congeries
Of crumbling elder lore at little cost.

I entered, charmed, and from a cobwebbed heap
Took up the nearest tome and thumbed it through,
Trembling at curious words that seemed to keep
Some secret, monstrous if one only knew.
Then, looking for some seller old in craft,
I could find nothing but a voice that laughed.

II. Pursuit

I held the book beneath my coat, at pains
To hide the thing from sight in such a place;
Hurrying through the ancient harbour lanes
With often-turning head and nervous pace.
Dull, furtive windows in old tottering brick
Peered at me oddly as I hastened by,
And thinking what they sheltered, I grew sick
For a redeeming glimpse of clean blue sky.

No one had seen me take the thing—but still
A blank laugh echoed in my whirling head,
And I could guess what nighted worlds of ill
Lurked in that volume I had coveted.
The way grew strange—the walls alike and madding—
And far behind me, unseen feet were padding.

III. *The Key*

I do not know what windings in the waste
Of those strange sea-lanes brought me home once more
But on my porch I trembled, white with haste
To get inside and bolt the heavy door.
I had the book that told the hidden way
Across the void and through the space-hung screens
That hold the undimensioned worlds at bay.
And keep lost aeons to their own demesnes.

At last the key was mine to those vague visions
Of sunset spires and twilight woods that brood
Dim in the gulfs beyond this earth's precisions,
Lurking as Memories of infinitude.
The key was mine, but as I sat there mumbling,
The attic window shook with a faint fumbling.

IV. *Recognition*

The day had come again, when as a child
I saw—just once—that hollow of old oaks,
Grey with a ground-mist that enfolds and chokes
The slinking shapes which madness has defiled.
It was the same—an herbage rank and wild
Clings round an altar whose carved sign invokes
That Nameless One to whom a thousand smokes
Rose, aeons gone, from unclean towers up-piled.

I saw the body spread on that dank stone,
And knew those things which feasted were not men;
I knew this strange, grey world was not my own,
But Yuggoth, past the starry voids—and then
The body shrieked at me with a dead cry,
And all too late I knew that it was I!

V. Homecoming

The daemon said that he would take me home
To the pale, shadowy land I half-recalled
As a high place of stair and terrace, walled
With marble balustrades that sky-winds comb,
While miles below a maze of dome on dome
And tower on tower beside a sea lies sprawled.
Once more, he told me, I would stand enthralled
On those old heights, and hear the far-off foam.

All this he promised, and through sunset's gate
He swept me, past the lapping lakes of flame,
And red-gold thrones of gods without a name
Who shriek in fear at some impending fate.
Then a black gulf with sea-sounds in the night:
"Here was your home," he mocked, "when you had sight!"

VI. The Lamp

We found the lamp inside those hollow cliffs
Whose chiselled sign no priest in Thebes could read,
And from whose caverns frightened hieroglyphs
Warned every living creature of earth's breed.
No more was there—just that one brazen bowl
With traces of a curious oil within;
Fretted with some obscurely patterned scroll,
And symbols hinting vaguely of strange sin.

Little the fears of forty centuries meant
To us as we bore off our slender spoil,
And when we scanned it in our darkened tent
We struck a match to test the ancient oil.
It blazed—great God! . . . But the vast shapes we saw
In that mad flash have seared our lives with awe.

VII. Zaman's Hill

The great hill hung close over the old town,
A precipice against the main street's end;
Green, tall, and wooded, looking darkly down
Upon the steeple at the highway bend.
Two hundred years the whispers had been heard
About what happened on the man-shunned slope—
Tales of an oddly mangled deer or bird,
Or of lost boys whose kin had ceased to hope.

One day the mail-man found no village there,
Nor were its folk or houses seen again;
People came out from Aylesbury to stare—
Yet they all told the mail-man it was plain
That he was mad for saying he had spied
The great hill's gluttonous eyes, and jaws stretched wide.

VIII. The Port

Ten miles from Arkham I had struck the trail
That rides the cliff-edge over Boynton Beach,
And hoped that just at sunset I could reach
The crest that looks on Innsmouth in the vale.
Far out at sea was a retreating sail,
White as hard years of ancient winds could bleach,
But evil with some portent beyond speech,
So that I did not wave my hand or hail.

Sails out of Innsmouth! Echoing old renown
Of long-dead times, but now a too-swift night
Is closing in, and I have reached the height
Whence I so often scan the distant town.
The spires and roofs are there—but look! The gloom
Sinks on dark lanes, as lightless as the tomb!

IX. The Courtyard

It was the city I had known before;
The ancient, leprous town where mongrel throngs
Chant to strange gods, and beat unhallowed gongs
In crypts beneath foul alleys near the shore.
The rotting, fish-eyed houses leered at me
From where they leaned, drunk and half-animate,
As edging through the filth I passed the gate
To the black courtyard where the man would be.

The dark walls closed me in, and loud I cursed
That ever I had come to such a den,
When suddenly a score of windows burst
Into wild light, and swarmed with dancing men:
Mad, soundless revels of the dragging dead—
And not a corpse had either hands or head!

X. The Pigeon-Flyers

They took me slumming, where gaunt walls of brick
Bulge outward with a viscous stored-up evil,
And twisted faces, thronging foul and thick,
Wink messages to alien god and devil.
A million fires were blazing in the streets,
And from flat roofs a furtive few would fly
Bedraggled birds into the yawning sky
While hidden drums droned on with measured beats.

I knew those fires were brewing monstrous things,
And that those birds of space had been *Outside*—
I guessed to what dark planet's crypts they plied,
And what they brought from Thok beneath their wings.
The others laughed—till struck too mute to speak
By what they glimpsed in one bird's evil beak.

XI. The Well

Farmer Seth Atwood was past eighty when
He tried to sink that deep well by his door,
With only Eb to help him bore and bore.
We laughed, and hoped he'd soon be sane again.
And yet, instead, young Eb went crazy, too,
So that they shipped him to the county farm.
Seth bricked the well-mouth up as tight as glue—
Then hacked an artery in his gnarled left arm.

After the funeral we felt bound to get
Out to that well and rip the bricks away,
But all we saw were iron hand-holds set
Down a black hole deeper than we could say.
And yet we put the bricks back—for we found
The hole too deep for any line to sound.

XII. The Howler

They told me not to take the Briggs' Hill path
That used to be the highroad through to Zoar,
For Goody Watkins, hanged in seventeen-four,
Had left a certain monstrous aftermath.
Yet when I disobeyed, and had in view
The vine-hung cottage by the great rock slope,
I could not think of elms or hempen rope,
But wondered why the house still seemed so new.

Stopping a while to watch the fading day,
I heard faint howls, as from a room upstairs,
When through the ivied panes one sunset ray
Struck in, and caught the howler unawares.
I glimpsed—and ran in frenzy from the place,
And from a four-pawed thing with human face.

XIII. Hesperia

The winter sunset, flaming beyond spires
And chimneys half-detached from this dull sphere,
Opens great gates to some forgotten year
Of elder splendours and divine desires.
Expectant wonders burn in those rich fires,
Adventure-fraught, and not untinged with fear;
A row of sphinxes where the way leads clear
Toward walls and turrets quivering to far lyres.

It is the land where beauty's meaning flowers;
Where every unplaced memory has a source;
Where the great river Time begins its course
Down the vast void in starlit streams of hours.
Dreams bring us close—but ancient lore repeats
That human tread has never soiled these streets.

XIV. Star-Winds

It is a certain hour of twilight glooms,
Mostly in autumn, when the star-wind pours
Down hilltop streets, deserted out-of-doors,
But showing early lamplight from snug rooms.
The dead leaves rush in strange, fantastic twists,
And chimney-smoke whirls around with alien grace
Heeding geometries of outer space,
While Fomalhaut peers in through southward mists.

This is the hour when moonstruck poets know
What fungi sprout in Yuggoth, and what scents
And tints of flowers fill Nithon's continents,
Such as in no poor earthly garden blow.
Yet for each dream these winds to us convey,
A dozen more of ours they sweep away!

XV. *Antarktos*

Deep in my dream the great bird whispered queerly
Of the black cone amid the polar waste;
Pushing above the ice-sheet lone and drearly,
By storm-crazed aeons battered and defaced.
Hither no living earth-shapes take their courses,
And only pale auroras and faint suns
Glow on that pitted rock, whose primal sources
Are guessed at dimly by the Elder Ones.

If men should glimpse it, they would merely wonder
What tricky mound of Nature's build they spied;
But the bird told of vaster parts, that under
The mile-deep ice-shroud crouch and brood and hide.
God help the dreamer whose mad visions show
Those dead eyes set in crystal gulfs below!

XVI. *The Window*

The house was old, with tangled wings outthrown,
Of which no one could ever half keep track,
And in a small room somewhat near the back
Was an odd window sealed with ancient stone.
There, in a dream-plagued childhood, quite alone
I used to go, where night reigned vague and black;
Parting the cobwebs with a curious lack
Of fear, and with a wonder each time grown.

One later day I brought the masons there
To find what view my dim forbears had shunned,
But as they pierced the stone, a rush of air
Burst from the alien voids that yawned beyond.
They fled—but I peered through and found unrolled
All the wild worlds of which my dreams had told.

XVII. A Memory

There were great steppes, and rocky table-lands
Stretching half-limitless in starlit night,
With alien campfires shedding feeble light
On beasts with tinkling bells, in shaggy bands.
Far to the south the plain sloped low and wide
To a dark zigzag line of wall that lay
Like a huge python of some primal day
Which endless time had chilled and petrified.

I shivered oddly in the cold, thin air,
And wondered where I was and how I came,
When a cloaked form against a campfire's glare
Rose and approached, and called me by my name.
Staring at that dead face beneath the hood,
I ceased to hope—because I understood.

XVIII. The Gardens of Yin

Beyond that wall, whose ancient masonry
Reached almost to the sky in moss-thick towers,
There would be terraced gardens, rich with flowers,
And flutter of bird and butterfly and bee.
There would be walks, and bridges arching over
Warm lotus-pools reflecting temple eaves,
And cherry-trees with delicate boughs and leaves
Against a pink sky where the herons hover.

All would be there, for had not old dreams flung
Open the gate to that stone-lanterned maze
Where drowsy streams spin out their winding ways,
Trailed by green vines from bending branches hung?
I hurried—but when the wall rose, grim and great,
I found there was no longer any gate.

XIX. The Bells

Year after year I heard that faint, far ringing
Of deep-toned bells on the black midnight wind;
Peals from no steeple I could ever find,
But strange, as if across some great void winging.
I searched my dreams and memories for a clue,
And thought of all the chimes my visions carried;
Of quiet Innsmouth, where the white gulls tarried
Around an ancient spire that once I knew.

Always perplexed I heard those far notes fallng,
Till one March night the bleak rains splashing cold
Beckoned me back through gateways of recalling
To elder towers where the mad clappers tolled.
They tolled—but from the sunless tides that pour
Through sunken valleys on the sea's dead floor.

XX. Night-Gaunts

Out of what crypt they crawl, I cannot tell,
But every night I see the rubbery things,
Black, horned, and slender, with membranous wings,
And tails that bear the bifid barb of hell.
They come in legions on the north wind's swell
With obscene clutch that titillates and stings,
Snatching me off on monstrous voyagings
To grey worlds hidden deep in nightmare's well.

Over the jagged peaks of Thok they sweep,
Heedless of all the cries I try to make,
And down the nether pits to that foul lake
Where the puffed shoggoths splash in doubtful sleep.
But oh! If only they would make some sound,
Or wear a face where faces should be found!

XXI. Nyarlathotep

And at the last from inner Egypt came
The strange dark One to whom the fellahs bowed;
Silent and lean and cryptically proud,
And wrapped in fabrics red as sunset flame.
Throngs pressed around, frantic for his commands,
But leaving, could not tell what they had heard;
While through the nations spread the awestruck word
That wild beasts followed him and licked his hands.

Soon from the sea noxious birth began;
Forgotten lands with weedy spires of gold;
The ground was cleft, and mad auroras rolled
Down on the quaking citadels of man.
Then, crushing what he chanced to mould in play,
The idiot Chaos blew Earth's dust away.

XXII. Azathoth

Out in the mindless void the daemon bore me,
Past the bright clusters of dimensioned space,
Till neither time nor matter stretched before me,
But only Chaos, without form or place.
Here the vast Lord of All in darkness muttered
Things he had dreamed but could not understand,
While near him shapeless bat-things flopped and fluttered
In idiot vortices that ray-streams fanned.

They danced insanely to the high, thin whining
Of a cracked flute clutched in a monstrous paw,
Whence flow the aimless waves whose chance combining
Gives each frail cosmos its eternal law.
"I am His Messenger," the daemon said,
As in contempt he struck his Master's head.

XXIII. Mirage

I do not know if ever it existed—
That lost world floating dimly on Time's stream—
And yet I see it often, violet-misted,
And shimmering at the back of some vague dream.
There were strange towers and curious lapping rivers,
Labyrinths of wonder, and low vaults of light,
And bough-crossed skies of flame, like that which quivers
Wistfully just before a winter's night.

Great moors led off to sedgy shores unpeopled,
Where vast birds wheeled, while on a windswept hill
There was a village, ancient and white-steepled,
With evening chimes for which I listen still.
I do not know what land it is—or dare
Ask when or why I was, or will be, there.

XXIV. The Canal

Somewhere in dream there is an evil place
Where tall, deserted buildings crowd along
A deep, black, narrow channel, reeking strong
Of frightful things whence oily currents race.
Lanes with old walls half-meeting overhead
Wind off to streets one may or may not know,
And feeble moonlight sheds a spectral glow
Over long rows of windows, dark and dead.

There are no footfalls, and the soft sound
Is of the oily water as it glides
Under stone bridges, and along the sides
Of its deep flume, to some vague ocean bound.
None lives to tell when that stream washed away
Its dream-lost region from the world of clay.

XXV. St. Toad's

"Beware St. Toad's cracked chimes!" I heard him scream
As I plunged into those mad lanes that wind
In labyrinths obscure and undefined
South of the river where old centuries dream.
He was a furtive figure, bent and ragged,
And in a flash had staggered out of sight,
So still I burrowed onward in the night
Toward where more roof-lines rose, malign and jagged.

No guide-book told of what was lurking here—
But now I heard another old man shriek:
"Beware St. Toad's cracked chimes!" And growing weak,
I paused, when a third greybeard croaked in fear:
"Beware St. Toad's cracked chimes!" Aghast, I fled—
Till suddenly that black spire loomed ahead.

XXVI. The Familiars

John Whateley lived about a mile from town,
Up where the hills begin to huddle thick;
We never thought his wits were very quick,
Seeing the way he let his farm run down.
He used to waste his time on some queer books
He'd found around the attic of his place,
Till funny lines got creased into his face,
And folks all said they didn't like his looks.

When he began those night-howls we declared
He'd better be locked up away from harm,
So three men from the Aylesbury town farm
Went for him—but came back alone and scared.
They'd found him talking to two crouching things
That at their step flew off on great black wings.

XXVII. *The Elder Pharos*

From Leng, where rocky peaks climb bleak and bare
Under cold stars obscure to human sight,
There shoots at dusk a single beam of light
Whose far blue rays make shepherds whine in prayer.
They say (though none has been there) that it comes
Out of a pharos in a tower of stone,
Where the last Elder One lives on alone,
Talking to Chaos with the beat of drums.

The Thing, they whisper, wears a silken mask
Of yellow, whose queer folds appear to hide
A face not of this earth, though none dares ask
Just what those features are, which bulge inside.
Many, in man's first youth, sought out that glow,
But what they found, no one will ever know.

XXVIII. *Expectancy*

I cannot tell why some things hold for me
A sense of unplumbed marvels to befall,
Or of a rift in the horizon's wall
Opening to worlds where only gods can be.
There is a breathless, vague expectancy,
As of vast ancient pomps I half-recall,
Or wild adventures, uncorporeal,
Ecstasy-fraught, and as a day-dream free.

It is in sunsets and strange city spires,
Old villages and woods and misty downs,
South winds, the sea, low hills, and lighted towns,
Old gardens, half-heard songs, and the moon's fires.
But though its lure alone makes life worth living,
None gains or guesses what it hints at giving.

XXIX. Nostalgia

Once every year, in autumn's wistful glow,
The birds fly out over an ocean waste,
Calling and chattering in a joyous haste
To reach some land their inner memories know.
Great terraced gardens where bright blossoms blow,
And lines of mangoes luscious to the taste,
And temple-groves with branches interlaced
Over cool paths—all these their vague dreams show.

They search the sea for marks of their old shore—
For the tall city, white and turreted—
But only empty waters stretch ahead,
So that at last they turn away once more.
Yet sunken deep where alien polyps throng,
The old towers miss their lost, remembered song.

XXX. Background

I never can be tied to raw, new things,
For I first saw the light in an old town,
Where from my window huddled roofs sloped down
To a quaint harbour rich with visionings.
Streets with carved doorways where the sunset beams
Flooded old fanlights and small window-panes,
And Georgian steeples topped with gilded vanes—
These were the sights that shaped my childhood dreams.

Such treasures, left from times of cautious leaven,
Cannot but loose the hold of flimsier wraiths
That flit with shifting ways and muddled faiths
Across the changeless walls of earth and heaven.
They cut the moment's thongs and leave me free
To stand alone before eternity.

XXXI. *The Dweller*

It had been old when Babylon was new;
None knows how long it slept beneath that mound,
Where in the end our questing shovels found
Its granite blocks and brought it back to view.
There were vast pavements and foundation-walls,
And crumbling slabs and statues, carved to show
Fantastic beings of some long ago
Past anything the world of man recalls.

And then we saw those stone steps leading down
Through a choked gate of graven dolomite
To some black haven of eternal night
Where elder signs and primal secrets frown.
We cleared a path—but raced in mad retreat
When from below we heard those clumping feet.

XXXII. *Alienation*

His solid flesh had never been away,
For each dawn found him in his usual place,
But every night his spirit loved to race
Through gulfs and worlds remote from common day.
He had seen Yaddith, yet retained his mind,
And come back safely from the Ghooric zone,
When one still night across curved space was thrown
That beckoning piping from the voids behind.

He waked that morning as an older man,
And nothing since has looked the same to him.
Objects around float nebulous and dim—
False phantom trifles of some vaster plan.
His folk and friends are now an alien throng
To which he struggles vainly to belong.

XXXIII. Harbour Whistles

Over old roofs and past decaying spires
The harbour whistles chant all through the night;
Throats from strange ports, and beaches far and white,
And fabulous oceans, ranged in motley choirs.
Each to the other alien and unknown,
Yet all, by some obscurely-focussed force
From brooding gulfs beyond the Zodiac's course,
Fused into one mysterious cosmic drone.

Through shadowy dreams they send a marching line
Of still more shadowy shapes and hints and views;
Echoes from outer voids, and subtle clues
To things which they themselves cannot define.
And always in that chorus, faintly blent,
We catch some notes no earth-ship ever sent.

XXXIV. Recapture

The way led down a dark, half-wooded heath
Where moss-grey boulders humped above the mould,
And curious drops, disquieting and cold,
Sprayed up from unseen streams in gulfs beneath.
There was no wind, nor any trace of sound
In puzzling shrub, or alien-featured tree,
Nor any view before—till suddenly,
Straight in my path, I saw a monstrous mound.

Half to the sky those steep sides loomed upspread,
Rank-grassed, and cluttered by a crumbling flight
Of lava stairs that scaled the fear-topped height
In steps too vast for any human tread.
I shrieked—and *knew* what primal star and year
Had sucked me back from man's dream-transient sphere!

XXXV. *Evening Star*

I saw it from that hidden, silent place
Where the old wood half shuts the meadow in.
It shone through all the sunset's glories—thin
At first, but with a slowly-brightening face.
Night came, and that lone beacon, amber-hued,
Beat on my sight as never it did of old;
The evening star, but grown a thousandfold
More haunting in this hush and solitude.

It traced strange pictures on the quivering air—
Half-memories that had always filled my eyes—
Vast towers and gardens; curious seas and skies
Of some dim life—I never could tell where.
But now I knew that through the cosmic dome
Those rays were calling from my far, lost home.

XXXVI. *Continuity*

There is in certain ancient things a trace
Of some dim essence—more than form or weight;
A tenuous aether, indeterminate,
Yet linked with all the laws of time and space.
A faint, veiled sign of continuities
That outward eyes can never quite descry;
Of locked dimensions harbouring years gone by,
And out of reach except for hidden keys.

It moves me most when slanting sunbeams glow
On old farm buildings set against a hill,
And paint with life the shapes which linger still
From centuries less a dream that this we know.
In that strange light I feel I am not far
From the fixt mass whose sides the ages are.

THE MESSENGER

The Thing, he said, would come that night at three
From the old churchyard on the hill below;
But crouching by an oak fire's wholesome glow,
I tried to tell myself it could not be.
Surely, I mused, it was a pleasantry
Devised by one who did not truly know
The Elder Sign, bequeathed from long ago,
That sets the fumbling forms of darkness free.
He had not meant it—no—but still I lit
Another lamp as starry Leo climbed
Out of the Seekonk, and a steeple chimed
Three—and the firelight faded, bit by bit.
Then at the door that cautious rattling came—
And the mad truth devoured me like a flame!

THE ANCIENT TRACK

There was no hand to hold me back
That night I found the ancient track
Over the hill, and strained to see
The fields that teased my memory.
This tree, that wall—I knew them well,
And all the roofs and orchards fell
Familiarly upon my mind
As from a past not far behind.
I knew what shadows would be cast
When the late moon came up at last
From back of Zaman's Hill, and how
The vale would shine three hours from now.
And when the path grew steep and high,
And seemed to end against the sky,
I had no fear of what might rest

Beyond that silhouetted crest.
Straight on I walked, while all the night
Grew pale with phosphorescent light,
And wall and farmhouse gable glowed
Unearthly by the climbing road.
There was the milestone that I knew—
"Two miles to Dunwich"—now the view
Of distant spire and roofs would dawn
With ten more upward paces gone. . . .

There was no hand to hold me back
That night I found the ancient track,
And reached the crest to see outspread
A valley of the lost and dead:
And over Zaman's Hill the horn
Of a malignant moon was born,
To light the weeds and vines that grew
On ruined walls I never knew.
The fox-fire glowed in field and bog,
And unknown waters spewed a fog
Whose curling talons mocked the thought
That I had ever known this spot.
Too well I saw from the mad scene
That my loved past had never been—
Nor was I now upon the trail
Descending to that long dead vale.
Around was fog—ahead, the spray
Of star-streams in the Milky Way. . . .
There was no hand to hold me back
That night I found the ancient track.

ROBERT P. TRISTRAM COFFIN (1892-   )

THE WARNING

The little screech owl sits polite
In the middle of the night
   And tells you gently, over, over,
   You are wisest under cover
Of your roof. Things rooted drink
More than walking things can think
   From the cup of night and take
   More pleasure than the sun can make.

You had best not be abroad
When a tree might seem a god
   Naked in vast company.
   There are things you best not see.
Better keep your eyes within
The little day a light can spin.
   Better in, the owl politely
   Warns and warns you, lightly, lightly.

CLARK ASHTON SMITH (1893-   )

THE ELDRITCH DARK

Now as the twilight's doubtful interval
   Closes with night's accomplished certainty,
   A wizard wind goes crying eerily;
And in the glade unsteady shadows crawl,
Timed to the trees, whose voices rear and fall

As with some dreadful witches' ecstasy,
   Flung upward to the dark, whence glitters free
The crooked moon, impendent over all.

Twin veils of covering cloud and silence thrown
   Across the movement and the sound of things,
     Make blank the night, till in the broken west
The moon's ensanguined blade awhile is shown . . .
     The night grows whole again . . . The shadows rest,
   Gathered beneath a greater shadow's wings.

WARNING

Hast heard the voices of the fen,
That softly sing a lethal rune
Where reeds have caught the fallen moon—
A song more sweet than conium is,
Or honey-blended cannabis,
To draw the dreaming feet of men
On ways where none goes forth again?

Beneath the closely woven grass,
The coiling syrt, more soft and deep
Than some divan where lovers sleep,
Is fain of all that wander there;
And arms that glimmer, vague and bare,
Beckon within the lone morass
Where only dead things dwell and pass.

Beware! the voices float and fall
Half-heard, and haply sweet to thee
As are the runes of memory
And murmurs of a voice foreknown
In days when love dwelt not alone:

Beware! for where the voices call,
Slow waters weave thy charnel pall.

THE HASHISH-EATER

Bow down: I am the emperor of dreams;
I crown me with the million-coloured sun
Of secret worlds incredible, and take
Their trailing skies for vestment, when I soar,
Throned on the mounting zenith, and illume
The spaceward-flown horizons infinite.
Like rampant monsters roaring for their glut,
The fiery-crested oceans rise and rise,
By jealous moons maleficently urged
To follow me forever; mountains horned
With peaks of sharpest adamant, and mawed
With sulphur-lit volcanoes lava-langued,
Usurp the skies with thunder, but in vain;
And continents of serpent-shapen trees,
With slimy trunks that lengthen league by league,
Pursue my flight through ages spurned to fire
By that supreme ascendance. Sorcerers,
And evil kings predominantly armed
With scrolls of fulvous dragon-skin, whereon
Are worm-like runes of ever-twisting flame,
Would stay me; and the sirens of the stars,
With foam-light songs from silver fragrance wrought,
Would lure me to their crystal reefs; and moons
Where viper-eyed, senescent devils dwell,
With antic gnomes abominably wise,
Heave up their icy horns across my way:
But naught deters me from the goal ordained
By suns, and aeons, and immortal wars,
And sung by moons and motes; the goal whose name
Is all the secret of forgotten glyphs,

By sinful gods in torrid rubies writ
For ending of a brazen book; the goal
Whereat my soaring ecstasy may stand,
In amplest heavens multiplied to hold
My hordes of thunder-vested avatars,
And Promethèan armies of my thought,
That brandish claspèd levins. There I call
My memories, intolerably clad
In light the peaks of paradise may wear,
And lead the Armageddon of my dreams,
Whose instant shout of triumph is become
Immensity's own music: For their feet
Are founded on innumerable worlds,
Remote in alien epochs, and their arms
Upraised, are columns potent to exalt
With ease ineffable the countless thrones
Of all the gods that are and gods to be,
Or bear the seats of Asmadai and Set
Above the seventh paradise.

                                        Supreme
In culminant omniscience manifold,
And served by senses multitudinous,
Far-posted on the shifting walls of time,
With eyes that roam the star-unwinnowed fields
Of utter night and chaos, I convoke
The Babel of their visions, and attend
At once their myriad witness: I behold,
In Ombos, where the fallen Titans dwell,
With mountain-builded walls, and gulfs for moat,
The secret cleft that cunning dwarves have dug
Beneath an alp-like buttress; and I list,
Too late, the clang of adamantine gongs,
Dinned by their drowsy guardians, whose feet

Have felt the wasp-like sting of little knives,
Embrued with slobber of the basilisk,
Or juice of wounded upas. And I see,
In gardens of a crimson-litten world
The sacred flow'r with lips of purple flesh,
And silver-lashed, vermillion-lidded eyes
Of torpid azure; whom his furtive priests
At moonless eve in terror seek to slay,
With bubbling grails of sacrificial blood
That hide a hueless poison. And I read,
Upon the tongue of a forgotten sphinx,
The annulling word a spiteful demon wrote
With gall of slain chimeras; and I know
What pentacles the lunar wizards use,
That once allured the gulf-returning roc,
With ten great wings of furlèd storm, to pause
Midmost an alabaster mount; and there,
With boulder-weighted webs of dragons'-gut,
Uplift by cranes a captive giant built,
They wound the monstrous, moonquake-throbbing bird,
And plucked, from off his sabre-taloned feet,
Uranian sapphires fast in frozen blood,
With amethysts from Mars. I lean to read,
With slant-lipped mages, in an evil star,
The monstrous archives of a war that ran
Through wasted aeons, and the prophecy
Of wars renewed, that shall commemorate
Some enmity of wivern-headed kings,
Even to the brink of time. I know the blooms
Of bluish fungus, freaked with mercury,
That bloat within the craters of the moon,
And in one still, selenic hour have shrunk
To pools of slime and fetor; and I know
What clammy blossoms, blanched and cavern-grown,

Are proffered in Uranus to their gods
By mole-eyed peoples; and the livid seed
Of some black fruit a king in Saturn ate,
Which, cast upon his tinkling palace-floor,
Took root between the burnished flags, and now
Hath mounted, and become a hellish tree,
Whose lithe and hairy branches, lined with mouths,
Net like a hundred ropes his lurching throne,
And strain at starting pillars. I behold
The slowly-thronging corals, that usurp
Some harbour of a million-masted sea,
And sun them on the league-long wharves of gold—
Bulks of enormous crimson, kraken-limbed
And kraken-headed, lifting up as crowns
The octiremes of perished emperors,
And galleys fraught with royal gems, that sailed
From a sea-deserted haven.

                                    Swifter grow
The visions: Now a mighty city looms,
Hewn from a hill of purest cinnabar,
To domes and turrets like a sunrise thronged
With tier on tier of captive moons, half-drowned
In shifting erubescence. But whose hands
Were sculptors of its doors, and columns wrought
To semblance of prodigious blooms of old,
No eremite hath lingered there to say,
And no man comes to learn: For long ago
A prophet came, warning its timid king
Against the plague of lichens that had crept
Across subverted empires, and the sand
Of wastes that Cyclopean mountains ward;
Which, slow and ineluctable, would come,
To take his fiery bastions and his fanes,

And quench his domes with greenish tetter. Now
I see a host of naked giants, armed
With horns of behemoth and unicorn,
Who wander, blinded by the clinging spells
Of hostile wizardry, and stagger on
To forests where the very leaves have eyes,
And ebonies like wrathful dragons roar
To teaks a-chuckle in the loathly gloom;
Where coiled lianas lean, with serried fangs,
From writhing palms with swollen boles that moan;
Where leeches of a scarlet moss have sucked
The eyes of some dead monster, and have crawled
To bask upon his azure-spotted spine;
Where hydra-throated blossoms hiss and sing,
Or yawn with mouths that drip a sluggish dew,
Whose touch is death and slow corrosion. Then,
I watch a war of pigmies, met by night
With pitter of their drums of parrot's hide,
On plains with no horizon, where a god
Might lose his way for centuries; and there,
In wreathèd light, and fulgors all convolved,
A rout of green, enormous moons ascend,
With rays that like a shivering venom run
On inch-long swords of lizard-fang.

                                        Surveyed
From this my throne, as from a central sun,
The pageantries of worlds and cycles pass;
Forgotten splendours, dream by dream unfold,
Like tapestry, and vanish; violet suns,
Or suns of changeful iridescence, bring
Their rays about me, like the coloured lights
Imploring priests might lift to glorify
The face of some averted god; the songs

Of mystic poets in a purple world,
Ascend to me in music that is made
From unconceivèd perfumes, and the pulse
Of love ineffable; the lute-players
Whose lutes are strung with gold of the utmost moon,
Call forth delicious languors, never know
Save to their golden kings; the sorcerers
Of hooded stars inscrutable to God,
Surrender me their demon-wrested scrolls,
Inscribed with lore of monstrous alchemies,
And awful transformations. *** If I will,
I am at once the vision and the seer,
And mingle with my ever-streaming pomps,
And still abide their suzerain: I am
The neophyte who serves a nameless god,
Within whose fane the fanes of Hecatompylos
Where arks the Titan worshippers might bear,
Or flags to pave the threshold; or I am
The god himself, who calls the fleeing clouds
Into the nave where suns might congregate,
And veils the darkling mountain of his face
With fold on solemn fold; for whom the priests
Amass their monthly hecatomb of gems—
Opals that are a camel-cumbering load,
And monstrous alabraundines, won from war
With realms of hostile serpents; which arise,
Combustible, in vapours many-hued,
And myrrh-excelling perfumes. It is I,
The king, who holds with scepter-dropping hand
The helm of some great barge of chrysolite,
Sailing upon an amethystine sea
To isles of timeless summer; For the snows
Of hyperborean winter, and their winds,
Sleep in his jewel-built capital,

Nor any charm of flame-wrought wizardry,
Nor conjured suns may rout them; so he flees,
With captive kings to urge his serried oars,
Hopeful of dales where amaranthine dawn
Hath never left the faintly sighing lute
And fields of lisping moly. Or I fare,
Impanoplied with azure diamond,
As hero of a quest Achernar lights,
To deserts filled with ever-wandering flames,
That feed upon the sullen marl, and soar
To wrap the slopes of mountains, and to leap,
With tongues intolerably lengthening,
That lick the blenchèd heavens. But there lives
(Secure as in a garden walled from wind)
A lonely flower by a placid well,
Midmost the flaring tumult of the flames,
That roar as roars the storm-possessèd sea,
Implacable forever: And within
That simple grail the blossom lifts, there lies
One drop of an incomparable dew,
Which heals the parchèd weariness of kings,
And cures the wound of wisdom. I am page
To an emperor who reigns ten thousand years,
And through his labyrinthine palace-rooms,
Through courts and colonnades and balconies
Wherein immensity itself is mazed,
I seek the golden gorget he hath lost,
On which the names of his conniving stars
Are writ in little sapphires; and I roam
For centuries, and hear the brazen clocks
Innumerably clang with such a sound
As brazen hammers make, by devils dinned
On tombs of all the dead; and nevermore
I find the gorget, but at length I find

A sealèd room whose nameless prisoner
Moans with a nameless torture, and would turn
To hell's red rack as to a lilied couch
From that whereon they stretched him; and I find,
Prostrate upon a lotus-painted floor,
The loveliest of all beloved slaves
My emperor hath, and from her pulseless side
A serpent rises, whiter than the root
Of some venefic bloom in darkness grown,
And gazes up with green-lit eyes that seem
Like drops of cold, congealing poison.

                                                  Hark!
What word was whispered in a tongue unknown,
In crypts of some impenetrable world?
Whose is the dark, dethroning secrecy
I cannot share, though I am king of suns
And king therewith of strong eternity,
Whose gnomons with their swords of shadow guard
My gates, and slay the intruder? Silence loads
The wind of ether, and the worlds are still
To hear the word that flees me. All my dreams
Fall like a rack of fuming vapours raised
To semblance by a necromant, and leave,
Spirit and sense unthinkably alone,
Above a universe of shrouded stars,
And suns that wander, cowled with sullen gloom,
Like witches to a Sabbath. *** Fear is born
In crypts below the nadir, and hath crawled
Reaching the floor of space and waits for wings
To lift it upward, like a hellish worm
Fain for the flesh of seraphs. Eyes that gleam,
But are not eyes of suns or galaxies,
Gather and throng to the base of darkness; flame

Behind some black, abysmal curtain burns,
Implacable, and fanned to whitest wrath
By raisèd wings that flail the whiffled gloom,
And make a brief and broken wind that moans,
As one who rides a throbbing rack. There is
A Thing that crouches, worlds and years remote,
Whose horns a demon sharpens, rasping forth
A note to shatter the donjon-keeps of time,
And crack the sphere of crystal. *** All is dark
For ages, and my tolling heart suspends
Its clamour, as within the clutch of death,
Tightening with tense, hermetic rigours. Then
In one enormous, million-flashing flame,
The stars unveil, the suns remove their cowls,
And beam to their responding planets; time
Is mine once more, and armies of its dreams
Rally to that insuperable throne,
Firmed on the central zenith.

                          Now I seek
The meads of shining moly I had found
In some remoter vision, by a stream
No cloud hath ever tarnished; where the sun,
A gold Narcissus, loiters evermore
Above his golden image: But I find
A corpse the ebbing water will not keep,
With eyes like sapphires that have lain in hell,
And felt the hissing embers; and the flow'rs
About me turn to hooded serpents, swayed
By flutes of devils in a hellish dance,
Meet for the nod of Satan, when he reigns
Above the raging Sabbath, and is wooed
By sarabands of witches. But I turn
To mountains guarding with their horns of snow

The source of that befoulèd rill, and seek
A pinnacle where none but eagles climb,
And they with failing pennons. But in vain
I flee, for on that pylon of the sky,
Some curse hath turned the unprinted snow to flame—
Red fires that curl and cluster to my tread,
Trying the summit's narrow cirque. And now,
I see a silver python far beneath—
Vast as a river that a fiend hath witched,
And forced to flow remèant in its course
To fountains whence it issued. Rapidly
It winds from slope to crumbling slope, and fills
Ravines and chasmal gorges, till the crags
Totter with coil on coil incumbent. Soon
It hath entwined the pinnacle I keep,
And gapes with a fanged, unfathomable maw,
Wherein great Typhon, and Enceladus,
Were orts of daily glut. But I am gone,
For at my call a hippogriff hath come,
And firm between his thunder-beating wings,
I mount the sheer cerulean walls of noon,
And see the earth, a spurnèd pebble, fall
Lost in the fields of nether stars—and seek
A planet where the outwearied wings of time
Might pause and furl for respite, or the plumes
Of death be stayed, and loiter in reprieve
Above some deathless lily: For therein,
Beauty hath found an avatar of flow'rs—
Blossoms that clothe it as a coloured flame,
From peak to peak, from pole to sullen pole,
And turn the skies to perfume. There I find
A lonely castle, calm and unbeset,
Save by the purple spears of amaranth,
And tender-sworded iris. Walls upbuilt

Of flushèd marble, wonderful with rose,
And domes like golden bubbles, and minarets
That take the clouds as coronal—these are mine,
For voiceless looms the peaceful barbican,
And the heavy-teethed portcullis hangs aloft
As if to smile a welcome. So I leave
My hippogriff to crop the magic meads,
And pass into a court the lilies hold,
And tread them to a fragrance that pursues
To win the portico, whose columns, carved
Of lazuli and amber, mock the palms
Of bright, Aidennic forests—capitalled
With fronds of stone fretted to airy lace,
Enfolding drupes that seem as tawny clusters
Of breasts of unknown houris; and convolved
With vines of shut and shadowy-leavèd flow'rs,
Like the dropt lids of women that endure
Some loin-dissolving rapture. Through a door
Enlaid with lilies twined luxuriously,
I enter, dazed and blinded with the sun,
And hear, in gloom that changing colours cloud,
A chuckle sharp as crepitating ice,
Upheaved and cloven by shoulders of the damned
Who strive in Antenora. When my eyes
Undazzle, and the cloud of colour fades,
I find me in a monster-guarded room,
Where marble apes with wings of griffins crowd
On walls an evil sculptor wrought, and beasts
Wherein the sloth and vampire-bat unite,
Pendulous by their toes of tarnished bronze,
Usurp the shadowy interval of lamps
That hang from ebon arches. Like a ripple,
Borne by the wind from pool to sluggish pool
In fields where wide Cocytus flows his bound,

A crackling smile round that circle runs,
And all the stone-wrought gibbons stare at me
With eyes that turn to glowing coals. A fear
That found no name in Babel, flings me on,
Breathless and faint with horror, to a hall
Within whose weary, self-reverting round,
The languid curtains, heavier than palls,
Unnumerably depict a weary king,
Who fain would cool his jewel-crusted hands
In lakes of emerald evening, or the fields
Of dreamless poppies pure with rain. I flee
Onward, and all the shadowy curtains shake
With tremors of a silken-sighing mirth,
And whispers of the innumerable king,
Breathing a tale of ancient pestilence,
Whose very words are vile contagion. Then
I reach a room where caryatides,
Carved in the form of tall, voluptuous Titan women,
Surround a throne of flowering ebony
Where creeps a vine of crystal. On the throne,
There lolls a wan, enormous Worm, whose bulk,
Tumid with all the rottenness of kings,
O'erflows its arms with fold on creasèd fold
Of fat obscenely bloating. Open-mouthed
He leans, and from his throat a score of tongues,
Depending like to wreaths of torpid vipers,
Drivel with phosphorescent slime, that runs
Down all his length of soft and monstrous folds,
And creeping among the flow'rs of ebony,
Lends them the life of tiny serpents. Now,
Ere the Horror ope those red and lashless slits
Of eyes that draw the gnat and midge, I turn,
And follow down a dusty hall, whose gloom,
Lined by the statues with their mighty limbs,

Ends in a golden-roofed balcony
Sphering the flowered horizon.

                            Ere my heart
Hath hushed the panic tumult of its pulses,
I listen, from beyond the horizon's rim,
A mutter faint as when the far simoon,
Mounting from unknown deserts, opens forth,
Wide as the waste, those wings of torrid night
That fling the doom of cities from their folds,
And musters in its van a thousand winds,
That with disrooted palms for besoms, rise
And sweep the sands to fury. As the storm,
Approaching, mounts and loudens to the ears
Of them that toil in fields of sesame,
So grows the mutter, and a shadow creeps
Above the gold horizon, like a dawn
Of darkness climbing sunward. Now they come,
A Sabbath of abominable shapes,
Led by the fiends and lamiae of worlds
That owned my sway aforetime! Cockatrice,
Python, tragelaphus, leviathan,
Chimera, martichoras, behemoth,
Geryon and sphinx, and hydra, on my ken
Arise as might some Afrite-builded city,
Consummate in the lifting of a lash,
With thundrous domes and sounding obelisks,
And towers of night and fire alternate! Wings
Of white-hot stone along the hissing wind,
Bear up the huge and furnace-hearted beasts
Of hells beyond Rutilicus; and things
Whose lightless length would mete the gyre of moons—
Born from the caverns of a dying sun,
Uncoil to the very zenith, half disclosed

From gulfs below the horizon; octopi
Like blazing moons with countless arms of fire,
Climb from the seas of ever-surging flame
That roll and roar through planets unconsumed,
Beating on coasts of unknown metals; beasts
That range the mighty worlds of Alioth, rise,
Aforesting the heavens with multitudinous horns,
Within whose maze the winds are lost; and borne
On cliff-like brows of plunging scolopendras,
The shell-wrought tow'rs of ocean-witches loom,
And griffin-mounted gods, and demons throned
On sable dragons, and the cockodrills
That bear the spleenful pygmies on their backs;
And blue-faced wizards from the worlds of Saiph,
On whom Titanic scorpions fawn; and armies
That move with fronts reverted from the foe,
And strike athwart their shoulders at the shapes
Their shields reflect in crystal; and eidola
Fashioned within unfathomable caves
By hands of eyeless peoples; and the blind
And worm-shaped monsters of a sunless world,
With krakens from the ultimate abyss,
And Demogorgons of the outer dark,
Arising, shout with multitudinous thunders,
And threatening me with dooms ineffable
In words whereat the heavens leap to flame,
Advance on the magic place! Thrown before,
For league on league, their blasting shadows blight
And eat like fire the amaranthine meads,
Leaving an ashen desert! In the palace,
I hear the apes of marble shriek and howl,
And all the women-shapen columns moan,
Babbling with unknown terror. In my fear,
A monstrous dread unnamed in any hell,
I rise, and flee with the fleeing wind for wings,

And in a trice the magic palace reels,
And spiring to a single tow'r of flame,
Goes out, and leaves nor shard nor ember! Flown
Beyond the world, upon that fleeing wind,
I reach the gulf's irrespirable verge,
Where fails the strongest storm for breath and fall,
Supportless, through the nadir-plungèd gloom,
Beyond the scope and vision of the sun,
To other skies and systems. In a world
Deep-wooded with the multi-coloured fungi,
That soar to semblance of fantastic palms,
I fall as falls the meteor-stone, and break
A score of trunks to powder. All unhurt,
I rise, and through the illimitable woods,
Among the trees of flimsy opal, roam,
And see their tops that clamber, hour by hour,
To touch the suns of iris. Things unseen,
Whose charnel breath informs the tideless air
With spreading pools of fetor, follow me
Elusive past the ever-changing palms;
And pittering moths, with wide and ashen wings,
Flit on before, and insects ember-hued,
Descending, hurtle through the gorgeous gloom,
And quench themselves in crumbling thickets. Heard
Far-off, the gong-like roar of beasts unknown
Resounds at measured intervals of time,
Shaking the riper trees to dust, that falls
In clouds of acrid perfume, stifling me
Beneath a pall of iris.

                              Now the palms
Grow far apart and lessen momently
To shrubs a dwarf might topple. Over them
I see an empty desert, all ablaze
With amethysts and rubies, and the dust

Of garnets or carnelians. On I roam,
Treading the gorgeous grit, that dazzles me
With leaping waves of endless rutilance,
Whereby the air is turned to a crimson gloom,
Through which I wander, blind as any Kobold;
Till underfoot the griding sands give place
To stone or metal, with a massive ring
More welcome to mine ears than golden bells,
Or tinkle of silver fountains. When the gloom
Of crimson lifts, I stand upon the edge
Of a broad black plain of adamant, that reaches,
Level as a windless water, to the verge
Of all the world; and through the sable plain,
A hundred streams of shattered marble run,
And streams of broken steel, and streams of bronze,
Like to the ruin of all the wars of time,
To plunge, with clangour of timeless cataracts,
Adown the gulfs eternal.

                           So I follow,
Between a river of steel and a river of bronze,
With ripples loud and tuneless as the clash
Of a million lutes; and come to the precipice
From which they fall, and make the mighty sound
Of a million swords that meet a million shields,
Or din of spears and armour in the wars
Of all the worlds and aeons: Far beneath,
They fall, through gulfs and cycles of the void,
And vanish like a stream of broken stars,
Into the nether darkness; nor the gods
Of any sun, nor demons of the gulf,
Will dare to know what everlasting sea
Is fed thereby, and mounts forevermore
With mighty tides unebbing.

Lo, what cloud,
Or night of sudden and supreme eclipse,
Is on the suns of opal? At my side,
The rivers run with a wan and ghostly gleam,
Through darkness falling as the night that falls
From mighty spheres extinguished! Turning now,
I see, betwixt the desert and the suns,
The poisèd wings of all the dragon-rout,
Far-flown in black occlusion thousand-fold
Through stars, and deeps, and devastated worlds,
Upon my trail of terror! Griffins, rocs,
And sluggish, dark chimeras, heavy-winged
After the ravin of dispeopled lands,
With harpies, and the vulture-birds of hell—
Hot from abominable feasts and fain
To cool their beaks and talons in my blood—
All, all have gathered, and the wingless rear,
With rank on rank of foul, colossal Worms,
Like pillars of embattled night and flame,
Looms on the wide horizon! From the van,
I hear the shriek of wyverns, loud and shrill
As tempests in a broken fane, and roar
Of sphinxes, like the unrelenting toll
Of bells from tow'rs infernal. Cloud on cloud,
They arch the zenith, and a dreadful wind
Falls from them like the wind before the storm.
And in the wind my cloven garment streams,
And flutters in the face of all the void,
Even as flows a flaffing spirit, lost
On the Pit's undying tempest! Louder grows
The thunder of the streams of stone and bronze—
Redoubled with the roar of torrent wings,
Inseparably mingled. Scarce I keep
My footing, in the gulfward winds of fear,

And mighty thunders, beating to the void
In sea-like waves incessant; and would flee
With them, and prove the nadir-founded night
Where fall the streams of ruin; but when I reach
The verge, and seek through sun-defeating gloom,
To measure with my gaze the dread descent,
I see a tiny star within the depths—
A light that stays me, while the wings of doom
Convene their thickening thousands: For the star
Increases, taking to its hueless orb,
With all the speed of horror-changèd dreams
The light as of a million million moons;
And floating up through gulfs and glooms eclipsed,
It grows and grows, a huge white eyeless Face,
That fills the void and fills the universe,
And bloats against the limits of the world
With lips of flame that open.

NIGHTMARE

As though a thousand vampires, from the day
Fleeing unseen, oppressed that nightly deep,
The straitening and darkened skies of sleep
Closed on the dreamland dale in which I lay.

Eternal tensions numbed the wings of Time,
While through the unending narrow ways I sought
Awakening; up precipitous gloom I thought
To reach the dawn, far-pinnacled sublime.

Rejected at the closen gates of light
I turned, and down new dreams and shadows fled,
Where beetling Shapes of veiled, colossal dread
With Gothic wings enormous arched the night.

OUTLANDERS

By desert-deepened wells and chasmed ways,
And noon-high passes of the crumbling nome
Where the fell sphinx and martichoras roam;
Over black mountains lit by meteor-blaze,
Through darkness ending not in solar days,
Beauty, the centauress, has brought us home
To shores where chaos climbs in starry foam,
And the white horses of Polaris graze.

We gather, upon those gulfward beaches rolled,
Driftage of worlds not shown by any chart;
And pluck the fabled moly from wild scaurs:
Though these are scorned by human wharf and mart—
And scorned alike the red, primeval gold
For which we fight the griffins in strange wars.

NYCTALOPS

Ye that see in darkness
When the moon is drowned
In the coiling fen-mist
Far along the ground—
Ye that see in darkness,
Say, what have ye found?

—We have seen strange atoms
Trysting on the air—
The dust of vanished lovers
Long parted in despair,
And dust of flowers that withered
In worlds of otherwhere.

We have seen the nightmares
Winging down the sky,
Batlike and silent,
To where the sleepers lie;
We have seen the bosoms
Of the succubi.

We have seen the crystal
Of dead Medusa's tears.
We have watched the undines
That wane in stagnant weirs,
And mandrakes madly dancing
By black, blood-swollen meres.

We have seen the satyrs
Their ancient loves renew
With moon-white nymphs of cypress,
Pale dryads of the yew,
In the tall grass of graveyards
Weighed down with evening's dew.

We have seen the darkness
Where charnel things decay,
Where atom moves with atom
In shining swift array,
Like ordered constellations
On some sidereal way.

We have seen fair colours
That dwell not in the light—
Intenser gold and iris
Occult and recondite;
We have seen the black suns
Pouring forth the night.

SHADOWS

Thy shadow falls on the fount,
On the fount with the marble wall . . . .
And in alien time and space
On the towns of a doomèd race
The shadows of glaciers mount;
And patchouli-shadows crawl
On the mottling of boas that bask
In the fire of a moon fantasque;
And the light shades of bamboo
Flutter and ruffle and lift;
In the silver dawn they sift
On the meadows of Xanadu. . . .

They shall fall, till the light be done,
By moon and cresset and sun,
From gnomon and fir-tree and throne,
And the vine-caught monoliths leaning
In the woods of a world far-flown;
They shall pass on the dim star-dials
By the peoples of Pluto wrought;
They shall follow the shifted vials
Of a sorceress of Fomalhaut;
They shall move on the primal plains
In the broken thunder and rains;
They shall haply reel and soar
Where the red volcanoes roar
From the peaks of a blackening sun;
They shall haply float and run
From the tails of the lyre-birds preening
On the palms of a magic mead;
And their mystery none shall read,
And none shall have known their meaning
Ere night and the shadows are one.

THE ENVOYS

None other saw them when they came
Across the many-clangoured mart,
But in mine eyes and in my heart
They passed as might the pillared flame
Of lightning loosened on the tombs,
Or errant suns that wander by
To dawn on the Cimmerii.

Great monarchs, proud and cypress-tall,
With gowns and crowns of argentry,
They were, who proffered royally
Full urns of pulsing gems to all:
The blood-warm gems of lunar wombs,
Pale ores, and opals pavonine,
And beryls like to leopard's eyne.

Their eyes were lit with alien day,
Were filled of alien worlds; their feet
With starry splendours paved the street,
And silver dust of some bright way
Feel from their garments, with perfumes
More strange than breath of vernal gales
From Saturn's moly-cinctured vales.

What embassy were they, from suns
Of Aldebar or Capricorn—
From planets of remoter morn
In flaming fields where Taurus runs—
Or haply come, immediate,
From out a four-dimensioned world
Within the occlusive ether furled?

They strode upon the swooning pave,
They towered by the trembling spires,
Tall as apocalyptic fires
Above the peoples of the grave:
But, sightless and inveterate,
To Mammon vowed, the throng went by,
Charneled beneath an iron sky.

Yes, blinder than the steel and stone,
Men took not from their proffered store
One gift of all the gifts they bore,
But sued for gold to gods foreknown.
I, too, bemused, inebriate,
Amort with splendour, could but stand
And see them pass, with empty hand.

FANTAISIE D'ANTAN

Lost and alien lie the leas,
Purpled all with euphrasies,
Where the lunar unicorn
Breasts an amber-pouring morn
Risen from Hesperian seas
Of a main that has no bourn.
Only things impossible
There in deathless glamour dwell:
Pegasus and sagittary,
Trotting, part the ferns of faery,
Succubi and seraphim
Tryst among the cedars dim;
Where the beaded waters brim,
White limoniads arise,
Interlacing arms and tresses
With the sun-dark satyresses;

There, on Aquilonian skies,
Gryphons, questing to and fro
For the gold of long ago,
Find at eve an aureate star
In the gulf crepuscular;
There the Hyperboreans,
Pale with wisdom more than man's,
Tell the wileful centauresses
Half their holocryptic lore;
There, at noon, the tritonesses,
All bemused with mandragore,
Mate with satyrs of the shore.

Love, could we have only found
The forgotten road that runs
Under all the sunken suns
To that time-estrangèd ground,
Surely, love were proven there
More than long and lone despair;
Holden and felicitous,
Love were fortunate to us;
And we too might ever dwell,
Deathless and impossible,
In those amber-litten leas,
Circled all with euphrasies.

IN THESSALY

When I lay dead in Thessaly,
The land was rife with sorcery:
Fair witches howled to Hecate,
Pouring the blood of rams by night
With many a necromantic rite
To draw me back for their delight. . . .

But I lay dead in Thessaly
With all my lust and wizardry:
Somewhere the Golden Ass went by
To munch the rose, and find again
The shape and manlihead of men:
But in my grave I stirred not then,

And the black lote in Thessaly
Its juices dripped unceasingly
Above the rotting mouth of me;
And worm and mould and graveyard must,
And roots of cypress, darkly thrust,
Transformed the dead to utter dust.

RESURRECTION

Sorceress and sorcerer,
Risen from the sepulchre,
From the deep, unhallowed ground,
We have found and we have bound
Each the other, as before,
With the fatal spells of yore,
With Sabbatic sign, and word
That Thessalian moons have heard.

Sorcerer and Sorceress,
Hold we still our heathenness—
Loving without sin or shame—
As in years of stake and flame.
Share we now the witches' madness,
Wake the Hecatean gladness,
Call the demon named Delight
From his lair of burning night.

Love that was, and love to be,
Dwell within this wizardry:
Lay your arm my head beneath
As upon some nighted heath
Where we slumbered all alone
When the Sabbat's rout was flown;
Let me drink your dulcet breath
As in evenings after death.

Witch beloved from of old,
When upon Atlantis rolled
All the dire and wrathful deep,
You had kissed mine eyes asleep;
On my lids shall fall your lips
In the final sun's eclipse;
And your hand shall take my hand
In the last and utmost land.

TIMEUS GAYLORD (1893-   )

THE OWLS

In shelter of the vaulted yews,
Like alien gods who shun the world,
The flown owls wait with feathers furled;
Darting red eyes, they dream and muse.

In rows unmoving they remain
Till the sad hour that they remember,
When, treading down the sun's last ember,
The towering night resumes its reign.

Their attitude will teach the seer
How wise and needful is the fear
Of movement and of travailment:

For shadow-drunken wanderers bear
On all their ways the chastisement
Of having wished to wend elsewhere.

MARK VAN DOREN (1894-   )

THE ORCHARD GHOST

Strictly at noon the mist was there,
Between two pear trees like a web.
There was no other mist abroad,
There was no other hand to grab
And tackle nothing but the sun,
Beneath the blossoms making fun.

He put it safely out of mind,
And sauntered home; but came again
Upon another shining day,
Upon another whitened noon.
And there it was as thin as dew;
And the sun was coming through;

And there were two rows of ribs
Around a heart that shook and glistened,
Like a poppy that the sun
Within a web of beams had fastened.
And there were elbows; and a face
Smiled transparently in place.

He closed his eyes and struck the thing;
He opened them and it was dancing:
Left and right, a little stiffly.
And it bowed, and with a mincing
Gesture came; but he was gone.
They found him lying on the lawn,

And they say that he will never
Leave the door while there is light.
After sunset on the mountain
He can start; though he must wait
And watch the west a fearful minute
Lest it have a spider in it.

ARTHUR INMAN (1895-   )

WEREWOLF

And I wake in the darkness and find darkness paled to defulgent light;
My body is shed; I am quadruped close to the odorous ground;
I am loosened spirit impulsed to flight, acceptive of night,
Primal spell upon strange lycanthropic errand bound.

Cry in my throat utters no voice of mind, and the wail
Of it rises to stars that are sharper than cosmic stars, and there
Is returned no echo to me of mankind and of man's travail,
Of the human heart, of the weariness of old despair.

The long steppes undulate in the bold moonlight, and my feet scarcely
    stir
The tall tips of the delicate grasses, and no sound trails my flight,
And sensuous lie the still hairs of my smooth and tenebrous fur:
Discarnate motion am I in a fluent and measureless night.

Outstrip the trains of man with their roaring reptilic speed;
Go faster than wings in the sky; be bodied and bodiless;
Know a single lusting call and a solitary greed:
Be creature lasciviously moving toward an end, unmuscled, tireless.

Dogs howl as I pass, and cocks awake to crow, and the presence
Of incorporeal things flows past as I progress,
And I am of all weird life the swift exceptional essence
Unformulated to constrictions or duress.

Swerve I for water, avoid fire, weapons tipped with silver come
Not near; for the rest be free as a beam of cold moonlight thrown
Across distances imperviable: the eerie sum
Of all terror am I, alien to man's world, creature alone.

STEPHEN VINCENT BENÉT (1898-1943)

METROPOLITAN NIGHTMARE

It rained quite a lot, that spring. You woke in the morning
And saw the sky still clouded, the streets still wet,
But nobody noticed so much, except the taxis
And the people who parade. You don't, in a city.
The parks got very green. All the trees were green
Far into July and August, heavy with leaf,
Heavy with leaf and the long roots boring and spreading,
But nobody noticed that but the city gardeners
And they don't talk.
            Oh, on Sundays, perhaps, you'd notice:
Walking through certain blocks, by the shut, proud houses
With the windows boarded, the people gone away,
You'd suddenly see the queerest small shoots of green

Poking through cracks and crevices in the stone
And a bird-sown flower, red on a balcony,
But then you made jokes about grass growing in the streets
And politics and grass-roots—and there were songs
And gags and a musical show called "Hot and Wet."
It all made a good box for the papers. When the flamingo
Flew into a meeting of the Board of Estimate,
The new Mayor acted at once and called the photographers.
When the first green creeper crawled upon Brooklyn Bridge,
They thought it was ornamental. They let it stay.

That was the year the termites came to New York
And they don't do well in cold climates—but listen, Joe,
They're only ants and ants are nothing but insects.
It was funny and yet rather wistful, in a way
(As Heywood Broun pointed out in the *World-Telegram*)
To think of them looking for wood in a steel city.
It made you feel about life. It was too divine.
There were funny pictures by all the smart, funny artists
And Macy's ran a terribly clever ad:
"The Widow's Termite" or something.
                                    There was no
Disturbance. Even the Communists didn't protest
And say they were Morgan hirelings. It was too hot,
Too hot to protest, too hot to get excited,
An even, African heat, lush, fertile and steamy,
That soaked into bone and mind and never once broke.
The warm rain fell in fierce showers and ceased and fell.
Pretty soon you got used to its always being that way.

You got used to the changed rhythm, the altered beat,
To people walking slower, to the whole bright
Fierce pulse of the city slowing, to men in shorts,
To the new sun-helmets from Best's and the cops' white uniforms,

And the long noon-rest in the offices, everywhere.
It wasn't a plan or anything. It just happened.
The fingers tapped the keys slower, the office-boys
Dozed on their benches, the bookkeeper yawned at his desk.
The A. T. & T. was the first to change the shifts
And establish an official siesta-room,
But they were always efficient. Mostly it just
Happened like sleep itself, like a tropic sleep,
Except for a few tourists and one damp cop.
They ran boats to see the big lilies on the North River
But it was only the tourists who really noticed
The flocks of rose-and-green parrots and parrakeets
Nesting in the stone crannies of the Cathedral.
The rest of us had forgotten when they first came.

There wasn't any real change, it was just a heat spell,
A rain spell, a funny summer, a weather-man's joke,
In spite of the geraniums three feet high
In the tin-can gardens of Hester and Desbrosses.
New York was New York. It couldn't turn inside out.
When they got the news from Woods Hole about the Gulf Stream,
The *Times* ran an adequate story.
But nobody reads these stories but science-cranks.

Until, one day, a somnolent city-editor
Gave a new cub the termite yarn to break his teeth on.
The cub was just down from Vermont, so he took the time.
He was serious about it. He went around.
He read all about termites in the Public Library
And it made him sore when they fired him.
                              So, one evening,
Talking with an old watchman, beside the first
Raw girders of the new Planetopolis Building
   (Ten thousand brine-cooled offices, each with shower)

He saw a dark line creeping across the rubble
And turned a flashlight on it.

                     "Say, buddy," he said,
"You better look out for those ants. They eat wood, you know,
They'll have your shack down in no time."

                          The watchman spat.
"Oh, they've quit eating wood," he said, in a casual voice,
"I thought everybody knew that."

                    —and, reaching down,
He pried from the insect jaws the bright crumb of steel.

NIGHTMARE NUMBER THREE

We had expected everything but revolt
And I kind of wonder myself when they started thinking—
But there's no dice in that now.

                 I've heard fellows say
They must have planned it for years and maybe they did.
Looking back, you can find little incidents here and there,
Like the concrete-mixer in Jersey eating the wop
Or the roto press that printed "Fiddle-dee-dee!"
In a three-color process all over Senator Sloop,
Just as he was making a speech. The thing about that
Was, how could it walk upstairs? But it was upstairs,
Clicking and mumbling in the Senate Chamber.
They had to knock out the wall to take it away
And the wrecking-crew said it grinned.

                   It was only the best
Machines, of course, the superhuman machines,
The ones we'd built to be better than flesh and bone,
But the cars were in it, of course . . .

                 and they hunted us
Like rabbits through the cramped streets on that Bloody Monday,
The Madison Avenue busses leading the charge.

The busses were pretty bad—but I'll not forget
The smash of glass when the Duesenberg left the show-room
And pinned three brokers to the Racquet Club steps
Or the long howl of the horns when they saw men run,
When they saw them looking for holes in the solid ground . . .

I guess they were tired of being ridden in
And stopped and started by pygmies for silly ends,
Of wrapping cheap cigarettes and bad chocolate bars
Collecting nickels and waving platinum hair
And letting six million people live in a town.
I guess it was that. I guess they got tired of us
And the whole smell of human hands.

                                        But it was a shock
To climb sixteen flights of stairs to Art Zuckow's office
(Nobody took the elevators twice)
And find him strangled to death in a nest of telephones,
The octopus-tendrils waving over his head,
And a sort of quiet humming filling the air. . . .
Do they eat? . . . There was red . . . But I did not stop to look.
I don't know yet how I got to the roof in time
And it's lonely, here on the roof.

                                        For a while, I thought
That window-cleaner would make it, and keep me company.
But they got him with his own hoist at the sixteenth floor
And dragged him in, with a squeal.
You see, they coöperate. Well, we taught them that
And it's fair enough, I suppose. You see, we built them.
We taught them to think for themselves.
It was bound to come. You can see it was bound to come.
And it won't be so bad, in the country. I hate to think
Of the reapers, running wild in the Kansas fields,
And the transport planes like hawks on a chickenyard,
But the horses might help. We might make a deal with the horses.
At least, you've more chance, out there.

And they need us, too.
They're bound to realize that when they once calm down.
They'll need oil and spare parts and adjustments and tuning up.
Slaves? Well, in a way, you know, we were slaves before.
There won't be so much real difference—honest, there won't.
(I wish I hadn't looked into that beauty-parlor
And seen what was happening there.
But those are female machines and a bit high-strung.)
Oh, we'll settle down. We'll arrange it. We'll compromise.
It won't make sense to wipe out the whole human race.
Why, I bet if I went to my old Plymouth now
(Of course you'd have to do it the tactful way)
And said, "Look here! Who got you the swell French horn?"
He wouldn't turn me over to those police cars;
At least I don't think he would.

Oh, it's going to be jake.
There won't be so much real difference—honest, there won't—
And I'd go down in a minute and take my chance—
I'm a good American and I always liked them—
Except for one small detail that bothers me
And that's the food proposition. Because, you see,
The concrete-mixer may have made a mistake,
And it looks like just high spirits.
But, if it's got so they like the flavor . . . well . . .

FRANK BELKNAP LONG (1903-   )

THE GOBLIN TOWER

The Goblin Tower stood and stood
  And stood for years and years:
And it was haunted splendidly
  By twenty thousand Fears.

The Fears were tall and very old,
  With scars upon their faces;
And there were Greek and Hindoo Fears,
  And Fears of Saxon races.

The Tower's windows looked upon
  A moat of thunderous green;
And red lights shone behind the panes
  Where gallant ghosts had been.

The ghosts were shyer than the rats
  That lived in Roland's hall;
And they reposed upon the chairs
  Or walked upon the wall.

Until the Fears took up the lance
  And chased them screaming hence;
And now they wander in the moat
  Or climb the castle fence.

I dreamed the Goblin Castle fell
  And vanished in the night:
And yet for years and years and years
  It was a gorgeous sight.

IN MAYAN SPLENDOR

In misty dreams and shadowed memories
Of fabled cities I have dwelt apace;
And from strange springs set round with guardian trees
Have slaked my thirst, and scornful of the face
Of harsh reality have stooped to trace
Dark figures on the sands of alien keys:
In Mayan splendour I have spanned the seas
And clothed myself in legendary grace.

In Copan I have dwelt where serpent stones
And skies of dusky violet merge to form
A glimmering gate of wonder whereto bones
Of warrior dead are gathered in a storm
Of whirling clouds and crimson flames that roar
Beneath the sky-vault where great condors soar.

SONNET

The gods are dead. The earth has covered them,
And they are less than shadows in our sight;
Young Helios is banished from delight,
Who once wore flame upon his garment's hem.
The world was young when tall Osiris died,
And it was old when Bacchus ceased to be;
A Light there was that towered deathlessly,
But once again has He been crucified.

The world is lonely now without its gods;
We stand forlorn beneath the stars of heaven,
For unto us no new joy can be given,
And we must always bear the bitter rods
Of heat and frost and harsh necessity:
There are no wonders now on land or sea.

A KNIGHT OF LA MANCHA

"The stars," he said, "are very low,
The sky above them arches so,
And hieroglyphics of the night
Have robbed the moon of touch and sight:
But Sancho, did the lanterns glow
Above La Mancha long ago?

"Why, Sancho, in the narrow streets
Ragged boys sold kites and sweets;

And like San Pedro's cross there flamed
A dozen inns where unashamed
We munched on cheese and fancy meats,
And you were tossed in yellow sheets.

"And then we woke with sudden fear
And saw the mountains disappear
Beyond the road, above the town;
For mountains move, and tumble down!
Sancho, Sancho, do you hear?
Mountains *walk*—with no one near!"

ON READING ARTHUR MACHEN

There is a glory in the autumn wood,
The ancient lanes of England wind and climb
Past wizard oaks and gorse and tangled thyme
To where a fort of mighty empire stood:
There is a glamor in the autumn sky;
The reddened clouds are writhing in the glow
Of some great fire, and there are glints below
Of tawny yellow where the embers die.

I wait, for he will show me, clear and cold,
High-raised in splendor, sharp against the North
The Roman eagles, and through mists of gold
The marching legions as they issue forth:
I wait, for I would share with him again
The ancient wisdom, and the ancient pain.

THE ABOMINABLE SNOW MEN

Blue shadows lay upon the crater's rim,
And far above the town a traveller moved
In circles through the snow; his eyes were dim
From glint of sun on ice in worlds unproved.

A thousand feet below him at an inn
His host smiled wanly, said: "The fool will find
Small prints upon the snow—so small, so thin—
He will not know that they are prints which bind."

"He will not know that they are prints which bind!"
His very words gained substance on a height,
As to his knees the traveler fell, half-blind,
And grovelled in the dimness of his sight.

"They dwell in barrows on a skyward wold
And make no sound; shrill hunger is their goad:
'Tis said they feed on men when men are bold,
When men are scarce on flesh of fowl or toad."

The silence on the heights gave way to shrieks
As to a shattered cairn the traveller clung
And fought a shape with bright and slimy streaks
Of blood upon its fat, protruding tongue.

They came in swarms from out the crater's rim,
The thin snow men, abominable and cold;
They came in swarms, and tore him limb from limb
And strewed his flesh in ribbons on the wold.

THE HORROR ON DAGOTH WOLD

"I have it here," he said and stroked the rust
    Upon his box,—his eyes were twin dark stars—
"Medusa's head that turns desire to dust!
    They buried it a fathom deep on Mars.

"I waited till the stars were right, and then
    I robed myself in ermine flaked with gold,
And with a silver spade, unwatched by men,
    I crept to where it lay in Dagoth Wold.

"I crept to where it lay, and working fast,
 I drew it from its red and sentient tomb;
 From jellied earth that whispered in the gloom,
And mired my feet until I woke at last."
 "You woke?" I stared at him in pained surprize,
 Forgetful of the star-glint in his eyes.

"To futile toil," he said, "our race is bound,
 And to the waking world it must return:
Some vileness in us makes us scorn and wound
 The shapes of flame for which our spirits yearn.

"But men go back again to dreams for things
 They left behind; perchance to fetch a cloak,
Or gather up a batch of stolen rings,
 Or catch a word some sweet, soft woman spoke.

"I have it here," he said, and tapped the lid
 Upon his box,—his eyes were twin dark stars—
"When Perseus died they sought to keep it hid,
 And buried it a fathom deep on Mars."

MERRILL MOORE (1903-   )

JUST THEN THE DOOR

Just then the door decided to close itself.
In walked One, in walked Two, in walked Three.

With the door shut it was impossible for that to be,
You say, but they walked right in through the door.

And One sat down cross-legged on the floor
And the second propped himself against the wall
And Three, chiefly because he was so tall,
Sat down on and let his legs dangle from the shelf.

Then they all spoke, first one, then another,
Every one of them distinctly calling me "brother"

And every one smiling in his ghastly way
As if his eyes contradicted what his mouth would say,

And each one disappeared like whirling smoke
Just about the time the morning broke.

YETZA GILLESPIE (1903-   )

FORGETFUL HOUR

When time wears thin
As the shadows lying,
And the whippoorwills call
For the souls of the dying,

When the bitter moon wears
A star on her horns,
And the heart in your breast
Remembers thorns,

Be wise, and touch iron!
Put salt on your bread,
Lest some of the Ancient
Forget they are dead.

THE SPECTER'S TALE

An awesome thing happened
In a sea coast town,
When the herrings schooled
And the moon hung down.

The men were reaping silver
They never had sown
With a net for a sickle
In a field never mown.

Womenfolk of prudence
Were thankful for a lock,
Knitting by the hearth-fire,
Deaf to a knock.

But, oh! the wind was calling
Through the crack of the door,
And one less was minded
Of the curved white shore.

She never saw the shadow,
Or the boat in the cove,
Till she was treasure added
To the pirates' trove.

A man must be heedful
To handle a boat—
And knives are keen and thirsty
For a Turkoman's throat.

A lass might win the shingle
Who knew the tides well,
And a dead body rolling
With its soul in hell

Is heart-freezing company.
He died with a curse.
Those waiting on shipboard
Were living, but worse.

Water-fear is weaker
Than the pull of the land;
Ravishers less certain
Than a lover's own hand.

Some queer woeful catches
Are lifted at last
From snares under water
That rock held fast.

When a seine is lifted
Oh, it is a bitter thing
To see a gold-haired lassie,
And your own pledged ring!

In time he lost the heart-break
Of the limpet on her cheek;
But his grey hairs remembered
How her hands trailed weak

Fingers in the meshes
Of a herring-net.
What her breastbone cradled
He never could forget.

Long past and gone like driftwood
This sorrow of the sea.
Oh, very well I know it,—
For it happened to me.

THE HAUNTED STAIRS

The staircase narrow as the way
Unto salvation's door,
Leads from a hall as dark as sin
With deep stains on the floor.

Nobody knows who climbed halfway
To where the turn is black,
What clutching fingers waited there,
Who felt the heartstrings crack.

And no one knows what now ascends
The thirteenth step—and stops,
And flutters like a netted bird
Before it moans, and drops. . . .

I'll step into the hall some night
When I forget my prayers,
And to my sorrow, see what stands
Upon the dreadful stairs.

FRANCIS FLAGG (1899-1946)

THE SNAKE

But yesterday I met a snake
All coiled beneath a live-oak tree,
And seven rattles chirred and spake
A chant of hate to man and me.

His sinuous length was blue and gray,
And forked his tongue and green his eyes

As emeralds, and where he lay
   Crouched death the torturer in disguise.

Yet still no bruising stone I threw
   Nor set my heel upon his head,
But only awe and wonder knew
   For something marvelous instead.

Around him like a legion stood
   Mythologies and fables told
By lips long dumb, a phantom brood
   Of legends old as man is old.

In some dim dawn, in some far shade,
   Perhaps beneath a live-oak tree,
Where Tigris' silted waters made
   A paradise of greenery,

The first lean poet sat and sang
   A song of woman and the snake,
A song of sinuous length and fang
   Poised lidless-eyed within the brake,

Or sang a song of all the race
   Held in a serpent-god's embrace
When the great reptile coiled and curled
   And breathed its glamor on the race.

THE DREAMER IN THE DESERT

Near Time's white dawn the cities stood
In fabled grandeur by a flood
That rolled where now the desert lies
Burning beneath its molten skies.

Strange galleons on inland seas
Bore golden freights for monarchies
Ruling from gorgeous peacock thrones
Long mingled with the desert stones.

Green grew the grass and smiled the lake
Where now the lizards and the snake
Lie somnolent, the orchards fair
Are gone the way of dust and air.

Only a wraith of all its glory
The desert mutely tells the story
For dreaming men to muse upon
From crystal dawn to crystal dawn.

Yes, here it was that Arnor lay,
And lads and lasses passed this way
Through smiling field and tangled wood
In search of lovers' solitude.

The Temple priests went chanting here
To bless the harvest of the year,
And troths were pledged beneath the sky
That fruits might blush and corn grow high.

The god-man came on shoulders strong
Of the intoning, reverent throng,
The goddess came with raven hair
And pallid face of carved despair;

The conqueror trod with martial train
Victorious from the wars again,
And judgments rang through silver halls
That only dreaming now recalls.

Ah, vain their pomp and vain their pride,
Their glory scattered far and wide,
Their loot of jasper, jade and gold
One with the unrelenting mold.

Where is the might of Arnor now,
The triple crown on empire's brow?
Question the wind, the sun, the air,
The spider's web, the wildcat's lair,

For ruthless Time has gnawed the face
Of high gods in their holy place,
And only ghostly towers rise
In phantom glory to the skies.

But poets dream and rivers run
With crystal waves beneath the sun,
And deserts bloom and cities grow
As they revive the long ago.

The poet sees the king and slave
That Time has couched in common grave,
The "eternal" nations that could not stand
The might of wind, the strength of sand,

And wakes from dreams—the plains are bare,
With only heat-waves rolling there.

STRANGE

He had been to the far places
And heard the music of distant spheres,
So the home hearth could never hold him
Or other music attract his ears.

He had looked into dark waters
And seen strange tides on a stranger shore
So never could his own beach hold him
Who had been far, who had seen more.

He had kissed strange lips in other places
And known strange loves on his distant way
So the arms that were his could not hold him
Whose spirit was restless and would not stay.

There's no peace for the man who at home abides
When he's known strange places, strange lips and tides.

FOREST GOD

Keep out of the forest
Hearken to advice,
For those whom Pan caresses
Never see him twice.

Those who know Pan's touches
And those who feel Pan's kiss
Know that there is nothing
Ever to equal this.

Those who hear Pan's music
And look into Pan's eyes,
Will always hear his laughter,
Will always be too wise.

Still it's worth the risking
Loneliness and pain
To have the hope to cherish
That Pan might come again.

TREE WOMAN

Deep in the fastness of a Druid wood
She saw no path between the sombre trees;
Leaf-mold and moss were dank, and where she stood
Silence was older than the cypresses.
There crept along her veins a chilly flow
Of something not of flesh; her fingers curled
On emptiness. Ten thousand years ago
This might have been the dawn-dusk of the world.

Strange how her feet were rooted there; she heard
Her lips moan like the wind, her arms, uptossed,
Were long and supple, and a dark-winged bird
Perched on her shoulder. Beautiful and lost,
She felt upon her brow, once white and fair
A crown of leaves that nestled softly there.

THE WOLVES OF EGREMONT

Beware the wolves of Egremont,
The wolves that prowl night after night;
Beware the wolves by any light
But surely when the moon is bright.

Beware the wolves of Egremont,
The wolves that run in deadly pack,
That wait in ambush to attack
And torture surely as the rack.

Beware the wolves of Egremont,
The wolves that run by night and day,
Who, when you hunt, are far away—
The wolves that only blood can stay.

Beware the wolves of Egremont;
The wolf pack numbers more than ten,
But others join them in their den.
These gaunt, gray wolves that once were men
The wolves of Egremont!

ROBERT ERVIN HOWARD (1906-1936)

THE HARP OF ALFRED

I heard the harp of Alfred
 As I went o'er the downs,
When thorn-trees stood at even
Like monks in dusky gowns;
I heard the music Guthrum heard
 Beside the wasted towns;

When Alfred, like a peasant,
 Came harping down the hill,
And the drunken Danes made merry
With the man they sought to kill,
And the Saxon king laughed in their beards
 And bent them to his will.

I heard the harp of Alfred
　　As twilight waned to night;
I heard ghost armies tramping
　　As the dim stars flamed white;
And Guthrum walked at my left hand,
　　And Alfred at my right.

FUTILITY

Golden goats on a hillside black,
　　Silken hose on a wharf-side trull,
Naked girl on a silver rack—
　　What are dreams in a shadowed skull?

I stood at a shrine and Chiron died,
　　A woman laughed from the bawdy roofs,
And he burned and lived and rose in his pride
　　And shattered the tiles with clanging hoofs.

I opened a volume dark and rare,
　　I lit a candle of mystic lore—
Bare feet throbbed on the outer stair
　　And the candle faltered to the floor.

Ships that sail on a windy sea,
　　Lovers that take the world to wife,
What doth the harlot hold for me
　　Who scarce have lifted the veil of Life?

THE SINGER IN THE MIST

At birth a witch laid on me monstrous spells,
　　And I have trod strange highroads all my days,
　　Turning my feet to gray, unholy ways.
I grope for stems of broken asphodels;

High on the rims of bare, fiend-haunted fells,
   I follow cloven tracks that lie ablaze;
   And ghosts have led me through the moonlight's haze
To talk with demons in their granite hells.

Seas crash upon long dragon-guarded shores,
   Bursting in crimson moons of burning spray,
And iron castles ope to me their doors,
   And serpent-women lure with harp and lay.
The misty waves shake now to phantom oars—
   Seek not for me; I sail to meet the day.

ARKHAM

Drowsy and dull with age the houses blink
   On aimless streets the rat-gnawed years forget—
But what inhuman figures leer and slink
   Down the old alleys when the moon has set?

SOLOMON KANE'S HOME-COMING

The white gulls wheeled above the cliffs, the air was slashed with foam,
The long tides moaned along the strand when Solomon Kane came home.
He walked in silence strange and dazed through the little Devon town,
His gaze, like a ghost's come back to life, roamed up the streets and
   down.

The people followed wonderingly to mark his spectral stare,
And in the tavern silently they thronged about him there.
He heard as a man hears in a dream the worn old rafters creak,
And Solomon lifted his drinking-jack and spoke as a ghost might speak:

"There sat Sir Richard Grenville once; in smoke and flame he passed,
"And we were one to fifty-three, but we gave them blast for blast.
"From crimson dawn to crimson dawn, we held the Dons at bay.
"The dead lay littered on our decks, our masts were shot away.

"We beat them back with broken blades, till crimson ran the tide;
"Death thundered in the cannon smoke when Richard Granville died.
"We should have blown her hull apart and sunk beneath the Main."
The people saw upon his wrists the scars of the racks of Spain.

"Where is Bess?" said Solomon Kane. "Woe that I caused her tears."
"In the quiet churchyard by the sea she has slept these seven years."
The sea-wind moaned at the window-pane, and Solomon bowed his
   head.
"Ashes to ashes and dust to dust, and the fairest fade," he said.

His eyes were mystical deep pools that drowned unearthly things,
And Solomon lifted up his head and spoke of his wanderings.
"Mine eyes have looked on sorcery in the dark and naked lands,
"Horror born of the jungle gloom and death on the pathless sands.

"And I have known a deathless queen in a city old as Death,
"Where towering pyramids of skulls her glory witnesseth.
"Her kiss was like an adder's fang, with the sweetness Lilith had,
"And her red-eyed vassals howled for blood in that City of the Mad.

"And I have slain a vampire shape that sucked a black king white,
"And I have roamed through grisly hills where dead men walked at
   night.
"And I have seen heads fall like fruit in the slaver's barracoon,
"And I have seen winged demons fly all naked in the moon.

"My feet are weary of wandering and age comes on apace;
"I fain would dwell in Devon now, forever in my place."
The howling of the ocean pack came whistling down the gale,
And Solomon Kane threw up his head like a hound that snuffs the trail.

A-down the wind like a running pack the hounds of the ocean bayed,
And Solomon Kane rose up again and girt his Spanish blade.

In his strange cold eyes a vagrant gleam grew wayward and blind and
    bright,
And Solomon put the people by and went into the night.

A wild moon rode the wild white clouds, the waves in white crests
    flowed,
When Solomon Kane went forth again and no man knew his road.
They glimpsed him etched against the moon, where clouds on hilltop
    thinned;
They heard an eery echoed call that whistled down the wind.

MOON MOCKERY

I walked in Tara's Wood one summer night,
    And saw, amid the still, star-haunted skies,
    A slender moon in silver mist arise,
And hover on the hill as if in fright.
Burning, I seized her veil and held her tight:
    An instant all her glow was in my eyes;
    Then she was gone, swift as a white bird flies,
And I went down the hill in opal light.

And soon I was aware, as down I came,
    That all was strange and new on every side;
    Strange people went about me to and fro,
And when I spoke with trembling mine own name
    They turned away, but one man said: "He died
    In Tara Wood, a hundred years ago."

THE KING AND THE OAK

Before the shadows slew the sun the kites were soaring free,
And Kull rode down the forest road, his red sword at his knee;
And winds were whispering round the world: "King Kull rides to
    the sea."

The sun died crimson in the sea, the long gray shadows fell;
The moon rose like a silver skull that wrought a demon's spell,
For in its light great trees stood up like specters out of hell.

In spectral light the trees stood up, inhuman monsters dim;
Kull thought each trunk a living shape, each branch a knotted limb,
And strange unmortal evil eyes flamed horribly at him.

The branches writhed like knotted snakes, they beat against the night,
And one great oak with swayings stiff, horrific in his sight,
Tore up its roots and blocked his way, grim in the ghostly light.

They grappled in the forest way, the king and grisly oak;
Its great limbs bent him in their grip, but never a word was spoke;
And futile in his iron hand, the stabbing dagger broke.

And through the tossing, monstrous trees there sang a dim refrain
Fraught deep with twice a million years of evil, hate and pain:
"We were the lords ere man had come and shall be lords again."

Kull sensed an empire strange and old that bowed to man's advance
As kingdoms of the grass-blades bow before the marching ants,
And horror gripped him; in the dawn like someone in a trance

He strove with bloody hands against a still and silent tree;
As from a nightmare dream he woke; a wind blew down the lea,
And Kull of high Atlantis rode silent to the sea.

RECOMPENSE

I have not heard lutes beckon me, nor the brazen bugles call,
But once in the dim of a haunted lea I heard the silence fall.
I have not heard the regal drum, nor seen the flags unfurled,
But I have watched the dragons come, fire-eyed, across the world.

I have not seen the horsemen fall before the hurtling host,
But I have paced a silent hall where each step waked a ghost.
I have not kissed the tiger-feet of a strange-eyed golden god,
But I have walked a city's street where no man else had trod.

I have not raised the canopies that shelter revelling kings,
But I have fled from crimson eyes and black unearthly wings.
I have not knelt outside the door to kiss a pallid queen,
But I have seen a ghostly shore that no man else has seen.

I have not seen the standards sweep from keep and castle wall,
But I have seen a woman leap from a dragon's crimson stall,
And I have heard strange surges boom that no man heard before,
And seen a strange black city loom on a mystic night-black shore.

And I have felt the sudden blow of a nameless wind's cold breath,
And watched the grisly pilgrims go that walk the roads of Death,
And I have seen black valleys gape, abysses in the gloom,
And I have fought the deathless Ape that guards the Doors of Doom.

I have not seen the face of Pan, nor mocked the dryad's haste,
But I have trailed a dark-eyed Man across a windy waste.
I have not died as men may die, nor sinned as men have sinned,
But I have reached a misty sky upon a granite wind.

ALWAYS COMES EVENING

Riding down the road at evening with the stars for steed and shoon
I have heard an old man singing underneath a copper moon;
"God, who gemmed with topaz twilights, opal portals of the day,
"On your amaranthine mountains, why make human souls of clay?

"For I rode the moon-mare's horses in the glory of my youth,
"Wrestled with the hills at sunset—till I met brass-tinctured Truth.
"Till I saw the temples topple, till I saw the idols reel,
"Till my brain had turned to iron, and my heart had turned to steel.

"Satan, Satan, brother Satan, fill my soul with frozen fire;
"Feed with hearts of rose-white women ashes of my dead desire.
"For my road runs out in thistles and my dreams have turned to dust,
"And my pinions fade and falter to the raven-wings of rust.

"Truth has smitten me with arrows and her hand is in my hair—
"Youth, she hides in yonder mountains—go and seek her, if you dare!
"Work your magic, brother Satan, fill my brain with fiery spells.
"Satan, Satan, brother Satan, I have known your fiercest Hells."

Riding down the road at evening when the wind was on the sea,
I have heard an old man singing, and he sang most drearily.
Strange to hear, when dark lakes shimmer to the wailing of the loon,
Amethystine Homer singing under evening's copper moon.

THE GHOST KINGS

The ghost kings are marching; the midnight knows their tread,
From the distant, stealthy planets of the dim, unstable dead;
There are whisperings on the night-winds and the shuddering stars
    have fled.

A ghostly trumpet echoes from a barren mountainhead;
Through the fen the wandering witch-lights gleam like phantom arrows
    sped;
There is silence in the valleys and the moon is rising red.

The ghost kings are marching down the ages' dusty maze;
The unseen feet are tramping through the moonlight's pallid haze,
Down the hollow clanging stairways of a million yesterdays.

The ghost kings are marching, where the vague moon-vapor creeps,
While the night-wind to their coming, like a thund'rous herald sweeps;
They are clad in ancient grandeur, but the world, unheeding, sleeps.

THE LAST HOUR

Hinged in the brooding west a black sun hung,
  And Titan shadows barred the dying world.
  The blind black oceans groped; their tendrils curled
And writhed and fell in feathered spray, and clung,
Climbing the granite ladders, rung by rung,
  Which held them from the tribes whose death-cries skirled.
  Above, unholy fires red wings unfurled—
Gray ashes floated down from where they swung.

A demon crouched, chin propped on brutish fist,
  Gripping a crystal ball between his knees;
    His skull-mouth gaped, and icy shone his eye.
  Down crashed the crystal globe—beneath the seas
The dark lands sank—Ione in a fire-shot mist
    A painted sun hung in a starless sky.

WHICH WILL SCARCELY BE UNDERSTOOD

Small poets sing of little, foolish things,
As more befitting to a shallow brain
That dreams not of the pre-Atlantean kings,
Nor launches on that dark uncharted Main
That holds grim islands and unholy tides,
Where many a black mysterious secret hides.

True rime concerns her not with bursting buds,
The chirping bird, the lifting of the rose—
Save ebon blooms that swell in ghastly woods,
And that grim, voiceless bird that ever broods
Where through black boughs a wind of horror blows.

Oh, little singers, what know you of those
Ungodly, slimy shapes that glide and crawl

Out of unreckoned gulfs when midnights fall,
To haunt the poet's slumbering, and close
Against his eyes thrust up their hissing head,
And mock him with their eyes so serpent-red?

Conceived and bred in blackened pits of hell,
The poems come that set the stars on fire;
Born of black maggots writhing in a shell
Men call a poet's skull—an iron bell
Filled up with burning mist and golden mire.

The royal purple is a moldy shroud;
The laurel crown is cypress fixed with thorns;
The sword of fame, a sickle notched and dull;
The face of beauty is a grinning skull;
And ever in their souls' red caverns loud
The rattle of the cloven hoofs and horns.

The poets know that justice is a lie,
That good and light are baubles filled with dust-
This world's slave-market where swine sell and buy,
This shambles where the howling cattle die,
Has blinded not *their* eyes with lies and lust.

Ring up the demons from the lower Pit,
Since Evil conquers goodness in the end;
Break down the Door and let the fires be lit,
And greet each slavering monster as a friend.

Let obscene shapes of Darkness ride the earth,
Let sacrificial smokes blot out the skies,
Let dying virgins glut the Black Gods' eyes,
And all the world resound with noisome mirth.

Break down the altars, let the streets run red,
Tramp down the race into the crawling slime;
Then where red Chaos lifts her serpent head,
The Fiend be praised, we'll pen the perfect rime.

LINES WRITTEN IN THE REALIZATION THAT I MUST DIE

The Black Door gapes and the Black Wall rises;
  Twilight gasps in the grip of Night.
Paper and dust are the gems man prizes—
  Torches toss in my waning sight.

Drums of glory are lost in the ages,
  Bare feet fail on a broken trail—
Let my name fade from the printed pages;
  Dreams and visions are growing pale.

Twilight gathers and none can save me.
  Well and well, for I would not stay:
Let me speak through the stone you gave me:
  He never could say what he wished to say.

Why should I shrink from the sign of leaving?
  My brain is wrapped in a darkened cloud;
Now in the Night are the Sisters weaving
  For me a shroud.

Towers shake and the stars reel under,
  Skulls are heaped in the Devil's fane;
My feet are wrapped in a rolling thunder,
  Jets of agony lance my brain.

What of the world that I leave for ever?
  Phantom forms in a fading sight—
Carry me out on the ebon river
  Into the Night.

DONALD WANDREI (1908-   )

SONNETS OF THE MIDNIGHT HOURS

After Sleep

It is not blessed sleep. It looms as hateful,
As dreaded as some strange disease's pain,
As fearful as the haunts of the insane.
The days for which the heart should be most grateful
Are sick with memories awesome, eerie, fateful,
Of nights that seemed eternities, of vain
Attempts to flee from depths where hope was slain;
Of secret worlds that have no name or place.

For in the midnight hours, when sleep descends,
I dream through realms where naught begins or ends,
Where all things are, yet are not; time and space
But phantoms; life and death part each of other;
Where far, unhuman beings' dark embrace
Holds me till in unending dooms I smother.

Purple

There where I wandered, purple shadows ran
Along a purple ground to purple cliffs
And back; and purple suns flamed northerly
Across a velvet sky. And when I came,
And when I crossed the imperial weaving span
Of purple leagues, violet hippogriffs
With wings of beating purple flew to me
Through sullen skies empurpled with vast flame.
And so I soared on pinions of the night

Through mightier gulfs where still the purple rule
Held sway, with purple dreamlands all around.
And when my steed permitted me to light,
I seemed to sink in some huge cosmic pool,
And in a sea of purple shadows drowned.

The Hungry Flowers

The fleshly flowers whispered avidly:
This being's face is soft, he shall not pass;
And all the little jeweled blades of grass
Made mutterings that sounded like low glee.
I looked across the great plain warily.
These glittering swords that shone like splintered glass,
Though singly impotent, might be in mass
A savage, indestructible enemy.

So, hesitantly, I put forth my foot
To seek, beneath the flower-heads, a path.
I found my leg become a hellish root,
I saw the hungry flowers toward me crawl
With bright-eyed ecstasy, exultant wrath,
And on my flesh their mouths, devouring, fall.

The Eye

A deep force pulls me toward the window-blind,
Some impulse urges me to raise the shade;
Why is it that I tremble, half afraid,
With formless terrors running through my mind?
What are the dim dread images that bind
My hand? Why is my arm so strongly stayed?
What sense of overhanging doom has made
Me fearful? What the sight that I shall find?

Some warning voice calls out: Go back—go back!
I could not turn though fronted by the rack.
And so I slowly raise the shade to greet
Whatever on the other side should lie,
And stare and stare in horror as I meet
The leering of a huge and sightless eye.

The Torturers

As I remember, there were clanging gongs
That beat the air to frenzy; dirges, knells,
A tolling like a myriad decibels
From metal monsters humming voiceless songs.
As I remember, there were flaming tongs
That flayed my flesh, and I was bound by spells
Of lunar sorcerers; a thousand hells
Were better than their hideous, measured wrongs.

As I remember, in my agony
I begged the gods to save me from such pain.
I heard a sound of cosmic revelry,
Then beating to the chambers of my brain
The answer came, where I in torment lay,
For silence unto silence died away.

The Statues

I knocked upon the portal till with clang
On long, metallic clang, the brazen door
Curled inward, flowerwise. I stood before
Weird, lifeless birds that talked and harshly sang.
Quick to my side two black, sleek leopards sprang
With eyes of golden fury; while a score
Of revelers turned statue, and no more
Their mirthless muttering through the palace rang.

Past them the leopards led me on and on
Where vast, dark marbles stood in endless miles,
And when I saw these titans, thereupon
Their enigmatic laughter filled the aisles;
But when I passed and left them in their gloom,
The vacant halls were quiet as a tomb.

The Old Companions

Amidst great cobwebs hanging everywhere
My old companions waited all around:
Wan hands and heads that showed no trace of wound,
Misshapen creatures peering through the air.
Out of a dusky corner came the stare
Of some white form that made a rattling sound.
Along the walls dwelt living mummies, bound
In swathes of long, still growing, human hair.

What goal, what new companion did I seek?
Was it an hour? Eternity? A week?—
Until I felt that tongue or talon stroke
My neck, and heard that husky, gurgling choke
As of some ancient corpse about to speak. . . .
I could not move though mind and spirit broke.

The Head

The head most strangely seemed like one I knew;
It rolled, and spun, and stopped in front of me,
While its pale eyes kept watching patiently
Till memory slowly came, and knowledge grew.
It was my own; my own face had that hue,
My own the lineaments that seemed to be
Bloodless, the blind eyes of eternity,
The mouth where something dark was trickling through.

It watched me, waiting, while I stared as long
As all the years of Hercules' great labors,
Stared at my own dead eyes unearthly lit.
Oh heart, cease beating; ears, close; sight, be wrong:
The head sprang high; but slashed by unseen sabers
It fell in parts, and I was part of it.

In the Attic

Slowly I climbed the worn old attic stairs
In darkness absolute, and listening hard,
For what, I did not know, yet tense, on guard
As I went onward toward those upper lairs.
Then at the top I stood on magic squares
That glowed with fitful lights, and each one starred
With signs unreadable, on each the shard
Of some imprisoned thing with old despairs.

I watched them till, from out the greater dark,
The swart hand crawled, through mid-air lengthening,
And I drew back; but still the hand with stark,
Tremendous fingers, growing, strengthening,
Pursued and pounced; an arm that had no source
Yet twined around me with inhuman force.

The Cocoon

My loved one made soft cooing sounds, and so
I stroked the glistening webwork on its head,
The strange cocoon, not living yet nor dead
But inbetween; whose phosphorescent glow
And shining eyes bespoke caresses, slow
And languid, warming into life; no dread
Had I, although I knew on what it fed,
The substance of it in the long ago.

But all at once the shell of that cocoon
Burst; mindless, mewing as it tried to speak,
Not woman, man, or child crawled in my lap,
But something from the dark side of the moon
Whose black, scaled body had for head a beak,
A beak that, darting, closed me in its trap.

The Metal God

In that far, future time where I was fleeing
Through mighty chambers, hunted and alone,
I came upon a curious great throne
Where sat an even greater, stranger being,
A king who saw but used no eyes for seeing,
A metal titan shapen like a cone,
Quicksilvery, pulsing with a deep soft tone
That filled all worlds, all space; vibrations freeing
All substances and creatures from the bond
Of aimless life, of aimless death. Long since
The hands that wrought it vanished in its power,
And I, though struggling, in that selfsame hour
Felt flesh dissolve in motes of silver tints
That streamed to join the nothingness beyond.

The Little Creature

Oh little creature, lost in time and space,
You've come again. You keep me company here,
You drift upon the moonlight hovering near
And watch, or seem to watch, me for your face
I can not find, nor do I seem to place
Your limbs, if limbs you have; nor is it clear
What form you have, for always you appear
Changing and new, so hard to know, to trace.

Oh little creature, whether old or young,
Make this your home for I will make it yours;
And though you never talk (do you have tongue?)
I'll talk of future times and alien shores.
Oh little creature, here's a tale of doom. . . .
How strange. How strangely empty is the room.

The Pool

Unto my feet a little trickle crept
Progressing slowly underneath the door
And widening inch by inch along the floor
Until, my shaking limbs grown weak, I stepped
Aside. The flow turned toward me, and it kept
Increasing, spreading more and ever more
As if there never were an end in store.
Now here, now there I fled; still on it swept.

Around me, solid walls of no escape,
Before me, one closed portal, and the flow
Whose source could only be some fearful shape
With blood that had so curious a glow:
The door must open, showing why the hue
Of this fresh pool of thin and brilliant blue.

The Prey

Vast wings were flapping in the night. I heard
Them fill the air with measureless strong beat—
What nameless hunter searching for its meat?
So huge the wings, I wondered what the bird
That clove through midnight where no other stirred,
What sight in later hours would haply greet
The dawn, when those great wings had made retreat:
For in the talons I was fast immured.

Though endlessly we traversed far abysses,
At length all motion ceased, upon a crag,
And when the talons loosened, I could see
The burning harpy eyes, head of a hag,
Before I dropped away, for I was free—
To fall amid colossal precipices.

The Rack

They clamped hot irons on my throbbing head;
They poured fresh acid on my blinding eyes;
They added madness to my frantic cries
By bathing me in streams of molten lead.
They slit me till a hundred raw wounds bled;
They burned me, bound me with deep-knotted ties;
They crushed me, broke me till I could not rise,
Then hurled me, shapeless, on a needle-bed.

Beyond the rack's red searing agony
One thought more torturing usurped my brain,
A thought my tongueless mouth could never speak;
Though they, with cruel joy, had given me
This never ending night of mounting pain,
It merely hinted of the coming week.

Escape

Now was I destined after all to die,
I who had fought so hard to reach my goal?
Would maggots in my starved, gaunt body loll
When I collapsed beneath that burning sky?
The sun stared on me like a blood-red eye,
In all this hideous land the only soul!
Yet, when toward farther desolate wastes I stole,
I thought ironic laughter passed me by.

Though they who tortured me were far behind,
My bloodprints in the dead sands marked my trail.
Each step eternal, on I struggled, trying
To reach the haven I would never find.
I stumbled forward, knowing I must fail,
For they were deathless hunters, I the dying.

Capture

They caught me in the wasteland in the west,
Caught me with safety but a league away.
For my escape I knew what I must pay:
Tortures would mark the finish of my quest.
They drove me back with never pause for rest,
Back through the desert for those fiends to flay,
To burn, to break; their pleasure not to slay
But punish, since their power I dared to test.
The dark walled city slowly came in view,
The magic towers, the skyward thrusting spires,
The windows burning bright with eldritch fires;
And when at last my captors bore me through
The ebony gates, one savage curse I cried,
And I, and all that phantom city, died.

In the Pit

Now they have buried me in this dark pit,
And all around their other victims wait,
Like me uncertain of their final fate
Though they are broken too, and their flesh slit.
There's one small shape that mews upon a spit;
The chewed remains of something used for bait;
Another mass their hungry pet half-ate,
Rejected. Nameless others near me sit.

They gave me back my eyes so I could peer
Around and see the comrades that are mine;
They left me morsels, curious and queer,
To make my sufferings worse if I should dine.
I know that I'll by them be watched for ever
And in recurring deaths escape them never.

The Bell

All night I heard the tolling of a bell;
All night I heard the cadences of doom
Across the boiling seas' own muffled boom;
From sunken cities rose the solemn knell.
The waters mounted in one surge whose swell
Laid bare the mystery of the vast sea-tomb,
And from those giant caverns' lifted gloom
The tolling came like measures for a spell.

Then all the seas united with a roar
Of wave that smote against colossal wave,
Engulfed again the riddles of the ocean;
The bell beneath the seas, beyond the shore,
Grew fainter in the silence of its grave:
I heard alone the surging tides in motion.

The Ultimate Vision

I dreamed the waters of the world had dried,
The ocean beds were open now, and free,
And all strange things once covered by the sea
Showed everywhere, while flopping creatures died.
There lay a bed of shells and bones; I spied
A city of a vast antiquity;
Ten thousand ships and more; shapes great and wee
And weird encrusted forms on every side.

I saw the vales and mountains of the deep,
I saw the dwellers of the ocean night,
The weedy pastures and the drowned, the dead;
And in the fading vision of my sleep
I saw rise up a substance soft and white
That feebly moved its pulpy, eyeless head.

August Derleth (1909-   )

WELDON HOUSE

Sometimes passing late at night,
moonlight glowing bright
from its deserted panes, I think of how old Joshua died,
murdered, how his brother moped and cried
and hanged himself—failures, both, as men,
who could not keep even their acres, only ten.

And going by
under the moonlit sky,
I think the old house now has something more to say,
time-gentled, moon-estranged: as never in the light of day,
something to tell of Josh and Bill,
something that keeps it restless, far from still,
something that hovers over its stones,
and rests secure with Weldon bones.

I. LOIS MALONE

Who could forget her wild black eyes?
Her rose-red mouth and her kisses?

Who could forget how she walked, her cries
of delight, her smile? And who misses
her now?
            Something went out of Lois Malone
when Ted left town; something no one thought
would leave her: the light from her eyes. She walked alone
thereafter, and they whispered Ted had bought
her for a string of pearls, a ring,
some honeyed words. She never told anything,
but went her way, heart full of Ted,
mind full of Ted—so they said—
walked one night out into the sibilant soft snow,
and was gone, was gone, no one knew where,
like a wreath of vapor into the air.

Lois Malone, oh, Lois Malone!
Where did she go? Where did she go?

II. TED BIRKETT

If wind could talk, and the birds,
I would that they hasten, and carry my words
to Lois Malone, wherever she is:
"I love you still, but wait no longer;
the bride I have is far far stronger
even than you, my Lois!"

You knew where I went that night,
for the money Bart owed me,
to get married with, to put things right
between us. It was Bart, it was he
pushed me off the trestle to the water below,
left me to die in the river's swift flow!

Less than two miles away, forever alone,
I lie under sand, yours, yet never yours, Lois Malone.

III. BART HINCH

They called him a hermit, those who walked
sometimes past his lonely cabin in the hills:
a dark man, given to drink, who seldom talked,
companioned by owls and whippoorwills.
But in his last years, he seemed to crave
the company of other men, came over the trestle into town,
seemed superstitious with his "Someone waitin' on my grave!"
and the way he steadily looked down,
avoiding eyes.
What was it he mumbled in his cups one night?
About Ted Birkett and money due, and a fright
he had once on the trestle where
he said, "He's waitin' there."
Whoever it was, he met him one night of blowing snow,
when the through train caught Bart, flung him dead below.

THE SHORES OF NIGHT

The seas' sound and the seas' drifting!

Waking in the night far, far inland,
I heard, I rose, I walked into the dark,
the confines of the house, an island
in the night, near childhood's park
forever and goodbye. Venus lifting
from the eastern rim: the voice of a bird
unknown.

But I heard, I heard!
the seas' sound and the seas' drifting!

(Or was it the wheeling over of the stars?
Was it the restless movement of the spheres?
Was it the turning under of the years?)

Darkness, darkness, darkness all around—
but stars and echo of the wars.
Remembering your breasts,
your arms enclosing, the hot loins, bound
my senses. But I walked here alone; you walk apart
in distant unenvisioned wests
of mind and heart.
                    I am alone
again, with grief of old my own.

And yet, yet—somewhere in this dark,
somewhere on edge of childhood's arc-lit, abandoned park,
I heard on this Midwestern island
the water's stirring beyond the spirit's remote land—

(Or was it the wheeling over of the stars?
Was it the restless movement of the spheres?
Was it the turning under of the years?)

over the voice of that unknown bird,
under the morning star's bright lifting,
I heard, I heard!

the seas' sound and the seas' drifting!

MAN AT THE WINDOW

A man paused at the window to look in,
and I glanced up and caught his eye;
only a moment so
before he turned to go,

but I thought for that moment, Is it I
or another there? Myself without and
   the man within?

Man at the window looking in,
his eyes saying clearly: *We are alone,*
you and I, each with his own—
his coat, his book, his little shell,
each in his heaven or his little hell;
and I could not remember who it was out there in
the dark, and who within.

He was gone but for eyes and smile
half made: a man in the dark peering in
curious to know what it looked like within,
gone in silence from mile to mile.

It could be lonelier under roof
   than under sky. . . .

Who was it there, he or I?

STRANGER IN THE NIGHT

Footfalls, footfalls
coming clear,
coming near—-

I turned at last
to look beneath the lamp just passed,
and saw a stranger there,
his footfalls loud in winter air.

We were alone, we two.
I crossed the street, and he did, too,
a stranger and I, a man I did not know,
seen but once under streetlamp glow.

Fear and passing fear—
footfalls coming near:
the wintered trees gaunt with spectral laughter,
a stranger following after,
quick pulse and step, steadily he came on,
while I kept hoping to find him gone:
footfalls which rang out stark
and loud in January dark.

Footfalls coming clear,
footfalls coming near . . .

His head held down, I could not see
him clearly in the shadow of a tree;
I stepped aside to snow-held grass
to let him pass,
and follow after . . .

Swiftly, swiftly, footfalls coming near,
before, behind,
making a monotone in mind,
before, behind, a stranger there,
his footfalls loud in winter air.

Who was it there?
Who was it passed me by
under the starlit sky?
Footfalls, footfalls
coming clear,
coming near

in the wind's dark laughter.
Who was it there
but I
who was, and I
who am, we two alone under lamplight glow,
alone in a world of snow—

but which went first, and which came after?

MARK OF MAN, MARK OF BEAST

Mark of some puny creature here below:
man track alone in all this space
of winter, man track mote-like in this place
of air and sky, of tree and snow.
Forward and back and angling off, he ran
swiftly as the drifted snow would let a man,
caught here his coat, and here hung
by some cloth:
                    the snow unbroken as the bitter air,
no other mark is there.

No mark before, and none behind,
he ran here as one blind
might run.
What had he done?
Whence came he and where did he go
into what world of drifted snow?

These tracks alone in all vast
snow, mark of a man fleeing his past,
his present time: some man who passed
here after wind and cold

had wrought these embattlements of snow;
his was the first track and the last
to break the white unbroken snow.

Forward and back, ran
under the trees, a man,
through knee-deep snow, forward and back
made his solitary track—
bayed by what spectral hound
whose sound
rang in no other's ear
to fill him too with fear?

No one knows, was he young or old?
Where did he go?
Who would run here in this place
but to make escape from space?

The mark is here, the solitary track:
forward and back, forward and back . . .

ANTHONY BOUCHER (1911-   )

SONNET OF THE UNSLEEPING DEAD

That night when all the clamor of the sea
met with the pelting clatter of the rain
to guard her fresh-dug tomb, despairingly
I thought I could not know despair again.
The widower of beauty, I resolved
to take fair horror to my lonely bed.
Now wise in arcane learning, I had solved
the riddle of the living and the dead.

The last lost words were spoken, and the last
unguents bestowed upon the rigid flesh.
Her chill sojourn beyond the tomb was past;
she moved. And then I saw (this was the knife
which freed my mind from sanity's frail mesh)
her eyes too bright with that which was not life.

BYRON HERBERT REECE (1917-   )

FOX HUNTERS OF HELL

Of all who went to the woods of Hate
With dog, and gun as well,
Only the meekest will relate
How the foxes ran in hell.

Now, only a morn of the finest frost
Would do for the dogs to run in,
And the time came right and the stars were lost
In a cold and frosty morning.

And the fox rose up from the heavy brush
And the dogs were quick to follow;
And the hunters ran in a cloppy rush
Over ridge and hollow.

The day came up before the sun,
And the hills were hidden under
A sheet of fog, and the sound of a gun
Rang in the air like thunder.

The fox he flashed in the rime-bright air
And the dogs were quick behind him;
And a hunter aimed upon him fair,
But a bullet would not find him.

And the fox he ran, and the dogs they ran,
And the hunters headlong after,
And loud they shouted man to man,
Filling the woods with laughter.

And when the sun was on the rim
Of the hills like a staring eye,
With a fierce black hound by the side of him
A man came running by.

And Orey Duval came suddenly
On the man in the autumn wood,
Leaning against a black gum tree
In a black and terrible mood.

And the man said, "Run as the fox has run
In the blue and bitter air!"
And he snatched forth Duval's horn and gun,
And he leaped on Duval's mare.

And Cedric saw, who was close behind,
That a hound as black as night
Was running as swiftly as the wind
For the devil's own delight.

And a strange man rode on Duval's mare,
Making a loud "Hallo,"
And Cedric heard him whoop and swear
How a fox of hell could go!

And Abner, who came riding next,
Saw Cedric fall to the ground
And rise a fox that was sorely vexed
By a swift and midnight hound.

And Abner had no sooner come
Into the strange man's sight
Than another fox went running home
For the devil's own delight.

And Albert who rode last, and fast
Under the boughs of evil,
Swears he rode like a wintry blast
Hunting fox with the devil.

And he came forth from the autumn wood
On a cold and frosty morning
Solitary from solitude,
And he left the foxes running.

And still they say the strange man rides
Hard on his stolen mare,
And the black hound stirs the cold hillsides
With his yelps in the frosty air.

And any man who will go alone
When the day has come to a hush
Can hear the hoofs on the clattering stone,
And the foxes break from the brush!

DUANE W. RIMEL (1915-   )

DREAMS OF YITH

In distant Yith past crested, ragged peaks;
  On far-flung islands lost to worldly eyes,
A shadow from the ancient star-void seeks
  Some being which in caverns shrilly cries
A challenge; and the hairy dweller speaks
  From that deep hole where slimy Sotho lies.
But when those night-winds crept about the place,
They fled—for Sotho had no human face!

Beyond the valleys of the sun which lie
  In misty chaos past the reach of time;
And brood beneath the ice as aeons fly,
  Long waiting for some brighter, warmer clime;
There is a vision, as I vainly try
  To glimpse the madness that must some day climb
From age-old tombs in dim dimensions hid,
And push all angles back—unseal the lid!

Beside the city that once lived there wound
  A stream of putrefaction writhing black;
Reflecting crumbling spires stuck in the ground
  That glow through hov'ring mist whence no stray track
Can lead to those dead gates, where once was found
  The secret that would bring the dwellers back.
And still that pitch-black current eddies by
Those silver gates of Yith to sea-beds dry.

On rounded turrets rising through the visne
  Of cloud-veiled aeons that the Old Ones knew:

On tablets deeply worn and fingered clean
  By tentacles that dreamers seldom view;
In space-hung Yith, on clammy walls obscene
  That writhe and crumble and are built anew;
There is a figure carved; but God! those eyes,
That sway on fungoid stems at leaden skies!

Around the place of ancient, waiting blight;
  On walls of sheerest opal rearing high,
That move as planets beckon in the night
  To faded realms where nothing sane can lie;
A deathless guard tramps by in feeble light
  Emitting to the stars a sobbing cry.
But on that path where footsteps should have led
There rolled an eyeless, huge and bloated head.

Amid dim hills that poison mosses blast,
  Far from the lands and seas of our clean earth,
Dread nightmare shadows dance—obscenely cast
  By twisted talons of archaen birth
On rows of slimy pillars stretching past
  A daemon-fane that echoes with mad mirth.
And in that realm sane eyes may never see—
For black light streams from skies of ebony.

On those queer mountains which hold back the horde
  That lie in waiting in their mouldy graves,
Who groan and mumble to a hidden lord
  Still waiting for the time-worn key that saves;
There dwells a watcher which can ill afford
  To let invaders by those hoary caves.
But some day then may dreamers find the way
That leads down elfin-painted paths of gray.

And past those unclean spires that ever lean
  Above the windings of unpeopled streets;
And far beyond the walls and silver screen
  That veils the secrets of those dim retreats,
A scarlet pathway leads that some have seen
  In wildest visions that no mortal greets.
And down that dimming path in fearful flight
Queer beings squirm and hasten in the night.

High in the ebon skies on scaly wings
  Dread batlike beasts soar past those towers gray
To peer in greedy longing at the things
  Which sprawl in every twisted passageway.
And when their gruesome flight a shadow brings
  The dwellers lift dim eyes above the clay.
But lidded bulbs close heavily once more;
They wait—for Sotho to unlatch the door!

Now, though the veil of troubled visions deep
  Is draped to blind me to the secret ways
Leading through blackness to the realm of sleep
  That haunts me all my jumbled nights and days,
I feel the dim path that will let me keep
  That rendezvous in Yith where Sotho plays.
At last I see a glowing turret shine,
And I am coming, for the key is mine!

NOSTALGIA

There is a clang of gongs within my ears,
    A touch of lotus on my fingertips.
Dark slant-eyes stare behind my candid blue,
    And unknown accents tremble on my lips.

My heart-beats strangely quicken to the sound
    Of weird and whining music without tune.
I sometimes long for watered fields of rice,
    To see familiar corn beneath the moon.

What pagan taint of blood is in our line?
    What long-forgotten sire bequeathed to me
The memory of arched bridges o'er a stream
    Half choked with blossoms from a cherry-tree?

The white man's blood flows ruddy in my veins;
    My Saxon fathers knew this Saxon place . . .
Yet . . . *what is this calm squatting form I see?*
    A wisp of pungent smoke obscures the face . . .

ECHIDNA

Who has seen Echidna
    Where the swamp ooze dries,
Where the swamp things slither
    In the wan moonrise?
Who has seen Echidna's
    Eyes?

Who has heard Echidna,
  In the scaly guise
Of a black swamp serpent,
  Hiss her wind-soft sighs?
Who has heard Echidna
  Flies!

Who has seen Echidna
  With her bright black eyes,
As her serpent body
  In the swamp mud lies?
Who has seen Echidna
  Dies!

LEAH BODINE DRAKE (1914-   )

CHANGELING

I am out on the wind
  In the wild, black night;
On the wings of the owl
  I take my flight,
On the ghostly wings of the great white owl;
And whether the night be fair or foul,
Or the moon be up or the thunder growl,
  Happy I be,
  Happy I be
When the changeling blood runs green in me!

When meek folk sleep
  In their dull, soft beds,
I creep over roots
  That the weasel treads,

Where the squat green lamps of the toadstools glow—
And only the fox knows the ways I go,
And nobody knows the things I know. . . .
  Wise I be,
  Wise I be
When the changeling blood runs green in me!

O Mother, slumber
  And do not wake! . . .
Thin voices called
  From the rain-wet brake,
And the child you cradled against your breast
Is out in the night on the black wind's crest,
For only the wild can give me rest. . . .
  Sad I be,
  Sad I be
When the changeling blood runs green in me.

WOOD WIFE

In a hollow oak-tree
  I live by the wood,
A bit more than human
  And much less than good.

I've queer spells, potent spells,
  That I went to learn
To the goat-hooved and shaggy ones
  Who hide in the fern.

The good-wives, the house-wives,
  They shudder at my sin:
But much they'd give to learn to weave
  Cloth of spiders'-spin!

My pet fox, my russet fox,
　　He ravishes their geese:
Yet none dare call out the hounds
　　If they would know peace!

On a day of falling leaves
　　I met the young Squire.
I gave him a sidelong look
　　That set his face afire.

The bonny young Squire,
　　He dreams in a spell;
But not of golden curlylocks
　　Of Parson Jones' Nell—
But of red hair, and green eyes
　　That have looked on Hell!

Dream, pretty Squire-kin!
　　It's small use to burn!
For when the moon is up
　　The wood-wife will turn

Three times widdershins,
　　And greet where you stood
The shagged-men, the satyr-men
　　Who creep from the wood!

IN THE SHADOWS

As we went up the narrow stair,
　　My candle slim and I,
From the crouching shadows came
　　A little tired sigh.

And there was nothing on the stair
   Or in my garret room,
But cobwebs on the rafters,
   And corners filled with gloom.

And still and silent was the house,
   And dark and still the air. . . .
But where the shadows wavered
   In the candle-flare,
Something small, unearthly, sighed
   Out of some strange despair.

THE PATH THROUGH THE MARSH

There is a path through a marsh
   That I must take to go home. . . .
   Mallows, and thick black loam,
Alder, and bog-grass harsh,

And the marsh-pools glinting with lights
   Of the sunset that stains the sky:
   That is all to the eye,
Yet something is there that affrights.

Something which I never see
   Though I feel its eyes on my back
   As I cross on that narrow track,
Something that watches me.

It is never bittern, who thumps
   At his hidden churn in the reeds.
   It is never heron, who feeds
In the shallows beside old stumps,

Or spotted bull-frog, who eyes
　　Me passing his tiny lake
　　Where the great green bubbles break
And the veils of the bog-mist rise.

But deeper than long-drowned log
　　Something that never sleeps
　　Lies crouched in those oozy deeps,
Something as old as the bog. . . .

They say that there was a time
　　When Indians called this sod
　　"The place of the evil god,"
And prayed to the quivering slime.

They say that a Face would appear
　　In the mists that the night-winds brew,
　　And would ask for its ancient due:
One human heart a year.

All that is a long-closed book. . . .
　　But still, as I pass on that track,
　　I feel something's eyes on my back
And I never dare turn to look,

For fear that the mists should spread
　　And curdle to mouth and eyes
　　Malefic and old and wise,
Demanding Its terrible bread!

THE TENANTS

Among the black trees spider-webbed
　　Against a red and wintry dusk,
I leaned upon the sagging gate
　　And looked up at the evil husk

Of that old house, remote from town
   And haunted, so the farm-folk said,
By brother-ghosts—the victim stabbed,
   The killer hanged 'til he was dead.

"How does it feel," I asked the pair
   Of farmers lounging in the door,
"To live within a haunted house?
   You must have nerves of steel and more!"

A hoot-owl cried within the wood;
   The sky above was red as sin;
The shadows deepened; side by side,
   Each figure eyed me with a grin.

Then one replied, "We have to stay—
   This is our home, the land we tilled—
For I'm the one they hanged," he said,
   "And he's the one I killed."

ALL-SAINTS' EVE

Look! . . .

   There—beyond the window-pane,
Through the withered and rattling vine!
A wee face, spangled with silver rain,
Lovely and wan, stares in at mine!

White as a shell upon the sands
Where the black billows break and pass,
Something is pressing tiny hands
Against the barrier of the glass.

Something eerie and fay and pale
Is peering in from the haunted night,
At our small room snug from the angry gale
Where faces glow in the firelight.

Slant, strange eyes under sea-green hair
Look wistfully in through the window-pane. . . .
Quick! . . .

    Open the casement! . . . What is there
    That cries in the wind and the streaming rain?

It has gone, it has gone—there is nothing there
Blown by the storm to our window-pane. . . .
Only the night and the chill sea-air
And the voice of the sorrowful rain.

THE BALLAD OF THE JABBERWOCK:

*A True Tale of Squankom Town**

My grandmother tells me,
   When the lights are low,
How the Jabberwock appeared
   In Squankom, long ago.

First a frightened farmer,
   Tearing into town,
Told how his wife had seen
   Something big and brown,

* Squankom, which in Indian means *the place of the evil god,* was the early name of the little South Jersey village of Williamstown, one of the places where the mysterious creature variously called the "Jersey Devil" or "Jabberwock" was seen around the turn of the century. *The Ballad of the Jabberwock* won first prize in the 1946 Stephen Vincent Benét Ballad Contest, held annually by the Word Weavers.

Horned like a billy-goat
   And scaled like a dragon,
Perched cross-legged on
   Their brand-new wagon.

It leaped into the barn
   And hid in the hay.
She screeched blue murder
   And fainted away!

The Timmermans saw it,
   Coming from Cross Keys;
It crept through Corkray's Wood
   And peered 'round the trees.

Footprints were found in fields
   Clawed like a bird's;
It clumped over Marsh's roof,
   Gibbering words.

Then folks began to see It
   Here and everywhere,
Clinging to the steeple,
   Winging through the air

With vans of a mighty bat;
   Or walking in a pasture
Upright as any man,
   And cocky as a master!

Squankom locked all its doors,
   And bright lamps were lit
In chilly front parlors
   Where folks seldom sit

Except for a funeral,
  Or the minister's call.
But what lurks in darkness?
  They lighted up all.

Some few were skeptical
  And would only smile;
But the path to the barn at night
  Seemed like a mile!

Reverend Walsey preached of sin,
  And most folks agreed
That It was a warning
  They had better heed.

They named It *The Jabberwock*
  For want of another;
But some shook their heads: "It's
  The Devil's own brother!"

The people came to church
  Who'd never been yet.
Some patched up a quarrel,
  And some paid a debt.

Cousin Jo and Cousin Kate
  Forgot they didn't speak;
And Old Man Jones stayed sober
  For one amazing week.

Wives left off nagging,
  And husbands kissed their wives.
The Claybrook brothers went to work
  For once in their lives.

No one watered any milk
  Or cut the measures down;
And Tillie got religion
  And all her girls left town!

Then one day the town awoke
  To find It had fled;
No one saw It squatting
  On his barn or shed.

No one saw those footprints
  Huge upon his lawn . . .
Suddenly, as it had come,
  The Jabberwock had gone.

The church held a meeting
  And great thanks were given
That Satan had done his worst
  And left them scared but shriven.

Satan had romped about
  Like a roaring lion;
But Squankom held firm, and now
  Was a little Zion.

They were the wonder-town
  Of the countryside!
They had driven Evil out!
  They let good abide

For almost a fortnight . . .
  Then someone stole a sack
Of flour out of Barker's store,
  And Tillie's girls came back.

HEARD ON THE ROOF AT MIDNIGHT

As I sat by my fire one night
Witches I heard on the roof alight.
I heard their broomsticks whinny and neigh,
And then I heard one beldame say:

"Well met in darkness, Tess, my lass!
Have you seen our coven comrades pass?"
"Aye, Lib! The Kelpie from her tarn,
And half the cats from the miller's barn
Tore through the air with fiery eyes,
Each one grown to twice his size!
Then hen-wife passed in a weasel's habit—
Oh, the coven gathers for the Sabbat!"

Then my blood ran cold, and hot again,
As I heard the witches (heard them plain),
Cry, "You who doze by the dullard hearth,
Open your soul to the ancient mirth!
Chain no longer your secret self;
Take down the besom from its shelf!
The owl's cried twice, the night wind moans,
The moon grins over the Sarsen Stones,
Fling wide the casement, mount and ride,—
Walpurgis Night is all outside!"

Then I barred the window, I said a prayer;
(To listen longer I didn't dare!)
I clasped the Book and I closed my eyes . . .
I heard them rush through the midnight skies!
So I looked out the window: all was bare,
Roof and ridgepole and milky air,
And only two bats, who vanished soon,
Were winging their way across the moon.

HARVEY WAGNER FLINK (1902-   )

WAYFARERS

We heard the dead leaves rustle
As we walked down the path;
And you would go to Endor,
But I was bound for Gath.

We lingered where the roads forked,
Then parted at the last;
For you would know the future,
And I would drown the past.

TWO HUNTERS

We hunted that day in the forest; I started an antlered buck
And came home in the thinning sunlight, proud of my hunter's luck.

No brother returned as evening gathered, no brother returned at
dawn . . .
But he stood like a ghost in the doorway, when the seventh year had
gone.

His blighted face was a wrinkled fungus; his form was shrunken and
bent;
And he blinked at me like a man just freed from dark imprisonment.

"I saw an enchanted cavern," he cried, "huge chests heaped with gold.
I drank from a magic flagon—and I shall never grow old!"

I started up—my brother uttered a cry . . .
And there was no one under the starlit sky.

COLEMAN ROSENBERGER (1915-   )

STAR GAZER

The round eye-socket holds all space, pulling
The spiral nebula and ringed saturn to the synapses,
Pressing on the retina the whirling dog star.

From Syria to this suburb, filament on filament
The eye has turned, taking the angle of the Pleiades
Plotting the epicycles with Ptolemy, aiming a glass with Kepler
To focus on the brain the incomprehensible.

Can you see, O star gazer, the isles of the blest?
Or find past Andromeda a happy land?

DEATH AT SEA

Under and over forever
Under and over
Twists the taut lover.

Closer than love was
Is sea in the skull hollow
In ribs the sea rhythm
Closer than bone's marrow.

Under and over
Twists the bright bone:
The skeleton
Arched to the sea.

THE GOATS OF JUAN FERNANDEZ: A Note on Survival

The fern grows in the volcanic dust, the green
Frond, surviving a thousand spores, turning
From the water to this island in the water,
The fossil's heir, extending its stipe and blade;

The sea elephants swim, sporting and mating
Keeping the cunning contours for survival;
And the fur seals, gregarious in the rookeries,
Gathering the harems, mating and surviving;

Concealed by its color and foliage is
The green bird guarding the fertilized egg,
Its mate, above, poised over the pinnacles,
Is supported by what generations of wings?

Here Juan Fernandez, the Devil's sailor,
Sea sorcerer, rider of trade winds,
Piloted goats to anchorage and the island.
The goats survived.